1 qa ⌐

ROBERT LOWELL / COLLECTED PROSE

ROBERT LOWELL

COLLECTED

PROSE

Edited and introduced by

ROBERT GIROUX

Farrar / Straus / Giroux

New York

Copyright © 1987 by Caroline Lowell,
Harriet Lowell, and Sheridan Lowell
Introduction copyright © 1987 by Robert Giroux
All rights reserved
First printing, 1987
Printed in the United States of America
Published simultaneously in Canada by
Collins Publishers, Toronto
Designed by Cynthia Krupat
Library of Congress Cataloging-in-Publication Data
Lowell, Robert, 1917–1977.
Collected prose.
Bibliography: p. 375
1. Giroux, Robert.   II. Title.
PS3523.089A6   1987   809.1   86–29098

For Harriet and Sheridan

Contents

Three

Introduction
by Robert Giroux

During his lifetime Robert Lowell embarked on two extended works of prose which for quite different reasons he did not complete. The first was his autobiography, for which he asked me to send him a publishing contract, signing it promptly in April 1955. This was so uncharacteristic of him—he sometimes forgot to sign contracts altogether, or misplaced and lost them, but never before had he *proposed* one—that I concluded he wanted the legal document to serve as a goad to writing. It was impossible not to connect his sudden interest in writing his autobiography with the shock of his mother's death in Rapallo the previous year. If the contract was meant to guarantee the book's completion, it didn't. Though he wrote around two hundred pages during the next two years, he reached an impasse and more or less abandoned it. Yet this foray into his past had a happy result: it led to the composition of most of the poems he published as *Life Studies* (1959), generally considered his best book. He also used "91 Revere Street," a section taken from the autobiography, as a prose interlude in the American edition of the poems.

The other uncompleted prose work which he was preparing during his last years was a collection of essays for which he already had a tentative title, *A Moment in American Poetry*. The theme he had in mind, as I understood it, was outlined in his acceptance speech on the occasion of receiving the National Book Award for *Life Studies*:

> Something earth-shaking was started about fifty years ago by the generation of Eliot, Frost, and William Carlos Williams. We have had a run of poetry as inspired, and perhaps as important and sadly brief, as that of Baudelaire and his early successors, or that of the dying [Roman] Republic and early Empire.

Yet when we went over his proposed contents, I pointed out something he was well aware of: many of the essays seemed to be at cross-purposes with his title. For example, his book opened with Ford Madox Ford (as does this book), and had pieces on Homer, Vergil, Ovid, Hopkins, Ivor Richards, and others who were not American, as well as Cotton Mather, Lincoln, Hawthorne, and others who were not poets. He promised to find a more suitable title (or revise the contents to justify it) but never did, and intended to write a preface but death intervened. At the time of his death he was also working on the long essay "New England and Further," which appears here in unfinished form. After his death I found that he had left behind other excellent prose in addition to the essays he had earmarked for *A Moment in American Poetry*.

Discovery can afford one of the greatest pleasures of editing, as I learned when I read through Elizabeth Bishop's posthumous papers for her *Collected Prose* (1984), finding seven pieces—especially her marvelous memoir of Marianne Moore—which Elizabeth, in her perfectionist fashion, had withheld from publication. Similarly, among Lowell's papers I discovered five prose pieces in various stages of completion, some of which rank with his best. The first, in order of appearance in this book, is "Two Controversial Questions," written at the time of T. S. Eliot's death in 1965. I have placed it after his review of *Four Quartets*, written in 1943. The difference in tone between the rather stiff formality and religiosity of Lowell the critic at twenty-six and his relaxed personal approach and sharp insights after twenty-two years is striking.

The second piece, "Art and Evil"—apparently prepared as a lecture, though I've not been able to find a record of its public delivery—was fortuitously rescued from oblivion. The first two-thirds of this essay, which Elizabeth Hardwick located, were so fascinating that I thought of including it even though incomplete. Happily, the last third was then discovered in the Houghton Library at Harvard—minus a line or two, but the last paragraph starts with the word "Finally," which clearly indicates he was almost at the end. (One would still like to know exactly what he meant by "that old practical joke" played on Iago, whom he describes as having gone so far in evil as to doom himself along with Othello. Lowell calls this "the joke of the torturer boiled . . . ," at which point the manuscript breaks off.) Even with this lacuna, "Art and Evil" belongs with his collected prose and appears here for the first time.

The third discovery is "Poets and the Theater," whose theme is the paradoxical and apparently simultaneous "fascination and fury" poets entertain about the theater. The opening sentence of this essay itself almost convinced me it belonged in this book: "The English stage's most terrible affliction is not Milton, its enemy, but Shakespeare, its friend." Perhaps he put this essay aside because he was misled or misdirected by his working title, "Shakespeare in New York." His theme is much larger in scope than that; references to New York occur infrequently and he is dealing with three universal elements—plays as literature, the English-speaking theater, and (from his own experience) poets as playwrights.

The other prose pieces that have never been published in their entirety—although Ian Hamilton quoted from them in *Robert Lowell: A Biography* (1982)—are two self-contained and finished sections of his autobiography, which bear the chapter titles he gave them. "Antebellum Boston," which deliberately echoes the opening lines of *The Education of Henry Adams*, is an account of the years preceding the First World War and his birth, and his reconstruction of his parents' engagement and marriage. The other, "Near the Unbalanced Aquarium," is an extraordinary record of his hospitalization and treatment for what he calls "an attack of pathological enthusiasm." It is interwoven with memories of his childhood, and the deaths and burials of his parents. I have placed it at the end of this book. Rarely has the experience of mental illness been set forth in such excellent prose by the sufferer himself.

In listing these "discoveries," I do not mean to imply that all the other essays have been easily accessible in print. The sources and notes on page 375 record the bibliographical facts. For instance, "On the Gettysburg Address," which he had included in the contents of A *Moment in American Poetry*, was read at the Library of Congress only a few sad weeks after President Kennedy's assassination. Though Lowell refers to Lincoln and Jefferson as perhaps the "only Presidents who could genuinely use words," he added a note on his manuscript: "This sentence was written before I had read President Kennedy's undelivered address." (I quote from this little-known text in the notes.) The brevity of his remarks on Lincoln's speech convinces me he was consciously trying not to exceed the 270 words of the original. Finally, one of the few political statements in this book—aside from his letters to Presidents Roosevelt and Johnson in the appendix—occurs in his introduction of the Russian poet Andrei Voznesensky at a poetry reading in 1967; it appears here for the first time.

Robert Lowell never really set up as a critic in the way that his contemporaries Randall Jarrell and John Berryman did in *Poetry and the Age, The Freedom of the Poet*, and other writings. "You yourself have written very little criticism," Frederick Seidel reminded Lowell in the course of his 1961 interview for *Paris Review* (see page 235), and the only criticism Seidel cites for that period is the essay on Hopkins and the review of Richards's poems. Lowell's modest response to this comment is that he was "anxious in criticism *not* to do the standard analytical essay" and preferred to be "much sloppier and more intuitive." His instinct was right, of course, and this book demonstrates that he exercised his own brand of literary appreciation with the freedom of a highly individual poet. Though he could be just as learned as the specialists, he was never academic or pedantic. His prose pieces are almost always inspired by occasions, such as the tributes he was moved to write on the deaths of Robert Frost, John Crowe Ransom, William Carlos Williams, Berryman, and Jarrell, and the reviews with which he greeted the appearance of such new books as *Four Quartets* or *Paterson,* or Elizabeth Bishop's first book, *North & South;* or a new translation of Ovid's *Metamorphoses,* or John Thompson's scholarly treatise on *The Founding of English Metre,* and so on.

Our friendship covered thirty-six years, and Cal was a warm and lovable friend. I first met him in 1941, when he was married to Jean Stafford, and introduced him to Eliot in 1947, the year following the publication of his first trade book, *Lord Weary's Castle* (his earlier book, *Land of Unlikeness,* had been privately printed). The first book to bear the new imprint of Farrar, Straus and Giroux was *For the Union Dead* (1963), which he inscribed in the beaten way of friendship as "this book with both our names, with affection and gratitude." Often while working on the present book I have thought of his fellow poet and friend Derek Walcott's moving elegy: "In life we looked at that large head, heard his soft jokes, watched his circling hands, knowing that he would become one of the great dead. . . . The head was square and noble, but it was also an ordinary American head, and it was this unrelenting ordinariness that denied itself any sort of halo. He was a man of enormous pride and fanatical humility." I also like the tribute of poet Frank Bidart, who worked so closely with Cal in his last years. "Valéry's words about Mallarmé come irresistibly to mind: 'Near him while he was still alive, I thought of his destiny as already realized.' "

Of all our conversations, I remember most vividly Cal's words about the new drug, lithium carbonate, which had such good results and gave him reason to believe he was cured: "It's terrible, Bob, to think that all I've suffered, and all the suffering I've caused, might have arisen from the lack of a little salt in my brain." The dedication he prepared for A *Moment in American Poetry* has of course been retained here—to his son and daughter.

I wish to express my thanks to the Lowell Estate and its executor, Robert Silvers, for asking me to edit this book. For help in locating manuscripts and dating them as accurately as possible, I am indebted to Rodney Dennis, Curator of Manuscripts; James Lewis, Curator of the Reading Room; and the members of the staff of the Houghton Library, Harvard. For editorial advice and the editing of "New England and Further" I wish to thank Elizabeth Hardwick. I have been helped at various stages by Frank Bidart, Caroline Blackwood, Jane Bobko, Blair Clark, Evgenia Citkowicz, Michael di Capua, Yvette Eastman, Carmen Gomezplata, Ian Hamilton, Eliza Knowlton, Cynthia Krupat, Kathleen McKenna, Jacqueline Onassis, Frank Parker, Frederick Seidel, Peter Taylor, John Thompson, and Derek Walcott, to all of whom my thanks.

One

Ford Madox Ford

I first met Ford in 1937, a year after the publication of his collection of poems, *Buckshee*, and two years before his death. Reading these poems once again in 1966* is like stepping back in time to Ford in his right setting, France, to a moment when both he and Europe between the wars were, imperceptibly, miraculously, a little younger, hopeful, and almost at a pause in the onrush. When I knew Ford in America, he was out of cash, out of fashion, and half out of inspiration, a half-German, half-English exile in love with the French, and able to sell his books only in the United States. Propped by his young wife, he was plodding from writers' conference to writers' conference, finally ending up as writer-in-residence at Olivet College in Michigan.

He seemed to travel with the leisure and full dress of the last hectic Edwardian giants—Hudson, James, and Hardy. He cried out, as if wounded, against the eminence, pomp, and private lives of Tennyson, Carlyle, and Ruskin, the false gods, so he thought, of his fathers. He was trailed by a legend of personal heroism and slump, times of great writing, times of space-filling past triumph and past humiliation, Grub Street drudgery, and aristocratic indolence. He was the friend of all good writers, and seemed to carry a concealed pistol to protect them and him-

* See *Notes and Sources*, page 375.

self against the shoving noncreative powers of editors, publishers, businessmen, politicians, college presidents, literary agents—his cronies, his vultures.

Always writers and writing! He was then at work on his last book, *The March of Literature*, and rereading the classics in their original tongues. At each college stop he picked up arm-loads of Loeb Classics, and reams of unpublished manuscript. Writers walked through his mind and his life—young ones to be discovered, instructed, and entertained; contemporaries to be assembled, telegraphed, and celebrated; the dead friend to be resurrected in anecdote; the long, long dead to be freshly assaulted or defended. Ford was large, unwieldy, wheezy, un-well, and looked somehow like a British version of the Re-publican elephant. His conversation, at least as finished as his written reminiscences, came out in ordered, subtly circuitous paragraphs. His marvelous, altering stories about the famous and colorful were often truer than fact. His voice, always sotto voce, and sometimes a muffled Yorkshire gasp, made him a man for small gatherings. Once I watched an audience of hundreds walk out on him,* as he exquisitely, ludicrously, and inaudibly imitated the elaborate periphrastic style of Henry James. They could neither hear nor sympathize.

Largeness is the key word for Ford. He liked to say that genius is memory. His own was like an elephant's. No one ad-mired more of his elders, or discovered more of his juniors, and so went on admiring and discovering till the end. He seemed to like nothing that was mediocre, and miss nothing that was good. His humility was edged with a mumbling insolence. His fanatical life-and-death dedication to the arts was messy, British, and amused. As if his heart were physically too large for his body, his stamina, imperfection, and generosity were extreme.

Ford's glory and mastery are in two or three of his novels. He also never stopped writing and speaking prose. He had a religious fascination with the possibilities of sentence structure

* This was in 1937 at the University of Colorado Writers' Conference.

and fictional techniques. About poetry, he was ambivalent. He had a flair for quoting beautiful unknown or forgotten lines, yet he called poetry something like "the less civilized medium," one whose crudity and barbarism were decked out with stiff measures and coarse sonorities. Like Boris Pasternak, he preferred Shakespeare's prose to his blank verse, and thought no poetry could equal the novels of Flaubert.

He himself wrote poetry with his left hand—casually and even contemptuously. He gives sound and intense advice to a beginning poet: "Forget about *Piers Plowman*, forget about Shakespeare, Keats, Yeats, Morris, the English Bible, and remember only that you live in our terrific, untidy, indifferent empirical age, where not a single problem is solved and not a single Accepted Idea from the poet has any more magic." Yet he himself as a poet was incurably of the nineteenth century he detested, and to the end had an incurable love for some of its most irritating and overpoetic conventions. His guides were always "Christabel," the Browning of "My Last Duchess," the Rossettis, Morris, and their successors, the decadents. He is Pre-Raphaelite to the heart. Their pretty eloquence, their passionate simplicities, their quaint neo-Gothic, their vocabulary of love and romance, their keyed-up Christianity, their troubadour heresies, and their terribly overeffective rhythms are always peeping through Ford's railway stations and straggling free verse.

For Ford and his ablest contemporaries—Hardy, Hopkins, Housman, Yeats, De la Mare, Kipling, and Pound—the influence and even the inspiration of the Pre-Raphaelites were unavoidable. Each, in his way, imitated, innovated, modified, and revolted. Ford's early imitations have a true Pre-Raphaelite brio, but he is too relaxed and perhaps too interested in life to have their finest delicacy, conviction, and intensity. His revolt is brave and resourceful, but the soul of the old dead style remains to hamper him. Even in prose, except for *The Good Soldier* and *Parade's End*, he had difficulty in striking the main artery; in poetry, he almost never struck it. His good phrases and rhythms grow limp or hopped up with impatient diffidence, and seldom reach their

destination. The doggerel bounce and hackneyed prettiness of
lines like

> *The poor saint on his fountain*
> *On top of his column*
> *Gazes up sad and solemn*

(to choose a bad example) keep breaking in on passages that are
picturesque and lovely. His shorter poems are brisk; his longer,
diffuse.

Pound's famous command that *poetry be at least as well
written as prose* must have been inspired by Ford, though I
doubt if Ford believed this a possibility, or really had much
fondness for a poetry that wasn't simple, poetic, and pastoral.
I heard someone ask him about Pound's influence on Yeats's
later style. "Oh," Ford said, "I used to tell Ezra that he mustn't
write illiterate poetic jargon. Then he'd go to Yeats and say the
same thing." This was tossed off with such flippant finality that
I was sure it was nonsense. Years later, however, Pound told me
the same story. He said, too, that Ford actually lived the heroic
artistic life that Yeats talked about. There must be something
more to the story.

Ford had no gift like Yeats for combining a conversational
prose idiom with the grand style. I think he must often have felt
the mortification of seeing the shining abundance of his novels
dwindle away in his poetry to something tame, absentminded,
and cautious. He must have found it hard to get rid of his
jingling, hard to charge his lines, hard to find true subjects, and
harder still to stick to them when found. Even such an original
and personal poem as "On Heaven" is forever being beguiled
from the road. Yet a magnificence and an Albigensian brightness
hover over these rambling steps: Ford and Pound were companions on the great road from twelfth-century Toulouse to
twentieth-century London.

Buckshee is Ford, the poet, at his best. It, too, is uneven
and rambling—uneven, rambling, intimate, and wonderful.
Gardening in Provence, or hearing a night bell strike two in

Paris, Ford ruminates with weary devotion on his long labors, and celebrates his new young marriage—O minutes out of time, when time was short, and the air stiff with Nazi steel and propaganda! In his last years, Ford's political emotions were to the left, but his memory, pace, and tastes were conservative. He didn't like a place without history, a patina of dust, "Richelieu's Villa Latina with its unvarying *statu quo ante.*" Above all, he hated a world ruled by the "maniacal monotone of execration." I remember how he expressed his despair of the America he was part of, and humorously advised me to give up eating corn lest I inherit the narrow fierceness of the Red Indian.

In "Coda," the last, supreme poem in this sequence, he is back in Paris, his great threatened love and symbol for civilization. In his dark apartment, he watches the lights of a taxi illuminate two objects, the "pale square" of his wife's painting, "Spring in Luxembourg," and the galleys of his manuscript, momentarily lit up like Michelangelo's scroll of the Fates. Then he says to his wife, the painter:

> *I know you don't like Michelangelo*
> *But the universe is very large having room*
> *Within it for infinities of gods.*

"Buckshee" coughs and blunders a bit in getting off, but in "Champêtre," "Temps de Sécheresse," and "Coda" Ford finds the unpredictable waver of his true inspiration. In these reveries, he has at last managed to work his speaking voice, and something more than his speaking voice, into poems—the inner voice of the tireless old man, the old master still in harness, confiding, tolerant, bohemian, newly married, and in France.

[1966]

Robert Frost

After Frost's wife died in the thirties, he stepped up the pace of his public readings. He must have gotten consolation from being Robert Frost, from being the image of himself that he had perfected with such genius. I have heard him say mockingly that hell was a half-filled auditorium. This was a hell he never had to suffer. Year after year after year, he was as great a drawing card as Dylan Thomas was in his brief prime. Yet there was a strain; never in his life was he able to eat before a reading. A mutual friend of ours once said with pity, "It's sad to see Frost storming about the country when he might have been an honest schoolteacher."

Frost had an insatiable yearning for crowds, circles of listeners, single listeners—and even for solitude. Can we believe him when he says he "took the road less travelled by"? He ran, I think, in no tracks except the ones he made for himself. The thinker and poet that most influenced him was Emerson. Both had something of the same highly urbane yet homemade finish and something of the same knack for verbal discovery. Both went about talking. Both leaned on and defied the colleges. A few of their poems are almost interchangeable. "In May when sea winds pierced our solitudes / I found the fresh Rhodora in the woods." Part of Frost was wary of Emerson. "Great is the art / Great shall be the manners of the bard." He knew better than anyone that his neighbors would find this manner boring and insufferable. He tried to make himself a man of many ruses, subtle surprises, and weathered agility. He was almost a farmer. Yet under the camouflage there was always the Brahma crouching, a Whitman, a great-mannered bard. If God had stood in his sunlight, he would have elbowed God away with a thrust or a joke.

He wasn't quite a farmer even in his early, isolated years. He didn't quite make a living; he got up at noon. He said the cows got used to his hours more easily than his neighbors. There was nothing very heroic or out of the ordinary here, yet these fifteen years or so of farming were as valuable to him as Melville's whaling or Faulkner's Mississippi. Without exactly knowing it, and probably not intending it, Frost found he was different from other men of letters. He used to tell a story about a Florida train trip he took with Wallace Stevens. The two poets were nervous with each other. Stevens, however, was more in the vacationer's mood. He made witty remarks, and finally said, "The trouble with your poetry, Frost, is that it has subjects." I don't want to spoil the weird, whimsical rightness of Stevens's taunt. Frost had an unfashionable hold on subjects. What were they?

I suppose what I liked about Frost's poems when I read them thirty years ago was their description of the New England country, a world I knew mostly from summer and weekend dips into it. It was a boy's world, fresher, grainier, tougher, and freer than the city where I had to live. "Back out of all this now too much for us," "Over back there where they speak of life as staying," "the dory filled to the gunnels with flowers," "the tar-banded ancient cherry trees"; one man saying, "Weren't you relieved to find he wasn't dead?" and the other answering, "No! and yet I don't know—it's hard to say / I went about to kill him fair enough." I used to wonder if I knew anything about the country that wasn't in Frost. I always had the pleasure either of having my own knowledge confirmed or of learning something new that completed it. I hardly cared which.

The arts do not progress but move along by surges and sags.

Frost, born in 1875, was our last poet who could honestly ignore the new techniques that were to shatter the crust. He understood the use of tools, often wonderful tools, that five or ten years later would be forever obsolete. He was a continuer and completer and not a copyist. When he began to write, the American cultural scene was unimaginably different from anything we know now. There were no celebrated masters to meet, no one to imitate. Poetry was the great English Romantics and Victorians and their famous, official American offshoots. Through their practice, criticism, and translations, the known past had been reborn in their image.

Frost had a hundred years' tradition he could accept without question, yet he had to teach himself everything. Excellence had left the old poetry. Like the New England countryside, it had run through its soil and had been dead a long time. Frost rebuilt both the soil and the poetry: by edging deeper and deeper into the country and its people, he found he was possessed by the old style. He became the best strictly metered poet in our history, and our best local observer, at least in meter. The high wind of inspiration blew through his long, packed, isolated rustication. By the time he was forty and had finished his second book, *North of Boston*, he had arrived. Step by step, he had tested his observation of places and people until his best poems had the human and seen richness of great novels. No one had helped him to learn, and now no one could, because no one wrote better.

Randall Jarrell has a fine phrase about Frost's "matter-of-fact magnificence." He writes that the poems' subjects are isolation, extinction, and the learning of human limitation. These three themes combine, I think, in a single main theme, that of a man moving through the formless, the lawless, and the free, of moving into snow, air, ocean, waste, despair, death, and madness. When the limits are reached, and sometimes almost passed, the man returns.

This is what I remember about Frost. There was music in his voice, in the way he made his quotations ring, in the spin on his language, in the strange, intuitive waywardness of his toleration. He was less of the specialized literary man than other poets and more curious personally.

Last November I walked by his house on Brewster Street in Cambridge. Its narrow gray wood was a town cousin of the farmhouses he wrote about, and stood on some middle ground between luxury and poverty. It was a traveler from the last century that had inconspicuously drifted over the customs border of time. Here one night he was talking about the suicide of a young friend, and said that sometimes, when he was excited and full of himself, he came back by thinking how little good his health could do those who were close to him.

The lights were out that night; they are out for good now, but I can easily imagine the barish rooms, the miscellaneous gold-lettered old classics, the Georgian poets, the Catullus by his bedside, the iron stove where he sometimes did his cooking, and the stool drawn up to his visitor's chair so that he could ramble and listen.

[1963]

Wallace Stevens

Wallace Stevens is one of the best poets of the past half
century. If he has never had the popularity of Robert Frost, or
the international reputation of T. S. Eliot or Ezra Pound, he has
nevertheless been fortunate in the criticism that he has received.
R. P. Blackmur's essay in *The Double Agent* is a masterpiece of
imaginative elucidation. Ivor Winters's essay in *The Anatomy
of Nonsense* is less brilliant, and its dismissal of Stevens's later
work appears to me to be overdone. But Winters's evaluation is
a corrective to Blackmur's appreciation; and by combining the
two essays one can come to a calmer and more objective understanding of Stevens than is, perhaps, possible with any other
contemporary American writer.

A few poems in *Transport to Summer* (1947) are better
than anything that Stevens has written since *Harmonium*, but
the earlier book is far more exciting and successful as a whole.
Before I praise what is wonderful in Stevens, I shall try to describe briefly what I think are his principal themes, his faults in
general, and the ways in which he has developed or deteriorated.

The subject throughout Stevens's poems is the imagination,
and its search for forms, myths, or metaphors that will make the
real and the experienced coherent without distortion or sim-
plification.

You must become an ignorant man again
And see the sun again with an ignorant eye
And see it clearly in the idea of it.

This is a threefold process: the stripping away of dead forms, the observation of naked reality, and the construction of new and more adequate forms. In his later poems Stevens often uses an elaborate machinery of abstractions, but what he is saying has changed very little. His world is an impartial, hedonistic, speculative world—he is closer to Plato than to Socrates, and closer to the philosophy and temperament of George Santayana than to Plato. Directly or indirectly, much of his thought is derived from the dialectic idealism of Hegel.

The detachment and flexibility of a poet who can say in one place that Christianity is too nebulous, in another that it is too rigid, and in another that "the death of Satan was a tragedy / For the imagination" are disarming. But perhaps Stevens is too much the leisured man of taste. As with Santayana, one feels that the tolerance and serenity are a little too blandly appropriated, that a man is able to be an imagination and the imagination able to be disinterested and urbane only because it is supported by industrial slaves. Perhaps if there are to be Platonists, there must always be slaves. In any case, Stevens has little of the hard ugliness and virtue of Socrates. His places are places visited on a vacation, his people are essences, and his passions are impressions. Many of his poems are written in a manner that is excessively playful, suave, careless, and monotonous. And their rhetoric, with its Tennysonian sound effects, its harmonious alliteration, and its exotic vocabulary, is sometimes no more than an enchanting inflection of the voice.

The later poems are more philosophical, and consider many things in this world of darkness ("Lenin on a bench beside a lake disturbed / The swans. He was not the man for swans") which the Stevens of *Harmonium* would have excluded as unpoetic. His language is simpler and more mature. But structural differences make all that has been gained precarious. Nothing like the dense, large-scale organization of his "Sunday Morning," or even the small perfection of his "Peter Quince at the Clavier," is attempted. The philosophy is not exhaustive and marshaled as in Lucretius; and it is seldom human and dramatic as in Donne. When one first reads this poetry that juggles its terminology with such lightness and subtlety, one is delighted; but as one rereads, it too often appears muddled, thin, and repetitious. How willingly one would exchange much of it for the concrete, gaudy wit of *Harmonium*.

The points that I have been making are probably overstated, and they are necessarily simplified. But few poets of Stevens's stature have tossed off so many half-finished improvisations. Underneath their intellectual obscurity and whimsy, their loose structures, their rhetorical and imagistic mannerisms, and their tenuous subject matter, there seems to be something in the poet that protects itself by asserting that it is not making too much of an effort.

The best poems in *Transport to Summer* are as good as any now being written in English. "Notes Toward a Supreme Fiction," the longest poem in the book, is a sequence in three parts entitled *It Must Be Abstract, It Must Change*, and *It Must Give Pleasure*. Each part has ten sections consisting of twenty-one blank-verse lines arranged in groups of three. In spite of a few beautiful sections—particularly *Begin, ephebe, by perceiving; The first idea was not our own; Not to be realized; It feels good as it is; The great statue*; and *A lasting visage*—and many fine moments, the whole seems to me to be unsuccessful. Its structure is sloppy, idiosyncratic, and repetitious. It rambles and rambles without gathering volume, and many of the sections are padded to fill out their twenty-one lines. Much of the rhetoric is extremely mannered. Certain details, such as Canon Aspirin, and Nanzia Nunzio Confronting Ozymandias, seem written for Stevens's private amusement. Of the shorter poems, I think the best is "No Possum, No Sop, No Taters." It is objective and subtle in its rhythms and perceptions, and is certainly one of Stevens's most magical and perfect slighter pieces. Other small poems in *Transport to Summer* approach it in excellence but are imperfect, or have much less to them. "Dutch Graves in Bucks

County" is much grander and more ambitious. The past and the present are opposed dramatically:

> *Angry men and furious machines*
> *Swarm from the little blue of the horizon*
> *To the great blue of the middle height.*
> *Men scatter throughout the clouds.*
> *The wheels are too large for any noise . . .*
>
> *And you, my semblables, in gaffer-green,*
> *Know that the past is not part of the present.*

It is written with tremendous feeling, pathos, and power. I think that no living poet would be able to match the magnificence of its rhetoric and resonance. A few lines are slightly mannered, and there is something a little long, formless, and vague about its development. But it is a very large undertaking wonderfully executed.

Esthétique du Mal is a sequence in fifteen blank-verse sections. It is almost as good and important as T. S. Eliot's *Four Quartets* or *Ash Wednesday*. Its subject is: How shall the imagination act when confronted with pain and evil? The structure is not very tight, two or three sections are not particularly good, and several others have a great number of bad or overwritten lines. The good parts can be detached, but they lose some of their momentum. *Esthétique du Mal* is more in the grand manner than any poetry since Yeats's; and it reminds one of parts of *Cymbeline* and *The Winter's Tale*—slow and rapid, joining the gorgeous with the very simple, wise, elaborate, open, tolerant without apathy, understanding with the understanding of having lived long.

> *The death of Satan was a tragedy*
> *For the imagination. A capital*
> *Negation destroyed him in his tenement*
> *And, with him, many blue phenomena.*

It was not the end he had foreseen. He knew
That his revenge created filial
Revenges. And negation was eccentric.
It had nothing of the Julian thundercloud:
The assassin flash and rumble . . . He was denied.
Phantoms, what have you left? What underground?
What place in which to be is not enough
To be? You go, poor phantoms, without place
Like silver in the sheathing of the sight,
As the eye closes . . .

[1947]

John Crowe Ransom

I / Mr. Ransom's Conversation

Virgin, whose image bent to the small grass
I keep against this tide of wayfaring,
O hear the maiden pageant ever sing
Of that far away time of gentleness.

Robert Frost, Wallace Stevens, William Carlos Williams, Ezra Pound, Marianne Moore, T. S. Eliot, and John Crowe Ransom were all born between 1875 and 1888. Never before or since have there been so many good poets in America; nor in England—unless we go back more than two hundred and fifty years. Who outranks whom will be disputed; but one would hesitate to call the least of these seven small, and it is perhaps no longer doubtful that the good poems of all must last as long as the language.

Ransom's production is small—his selected poems take up only seventy-five pages; to which one would like to add about twenty more that he rejected. It is the work of a lifetime. When I reread it, I marveled at its weight—few English poets have written so many lyrics that one wants to read over and over. If the pathetic, incompetent, and shoving people who usually compile our anthologies (who else can make money or reputation on anthologies?) have any sense, Ransom will always be read and remembered in some quantity.

Why should be easy to say—the poems are definite and substantial enough. Yet I find it hard to put it all clearly. First there is the language; it's a curious mixture of elaboration and bluntness; courtesy and rudeness. It has its analogies to the language of Henry James—particularly in two characteristics: extreme urbanity and (what you wouldn't expect) a force that discovers itself in a certain puffing and sweating: the pushing of utterance to the limits of one's abilities—and beyond. Ransom's language is the language of his prose and of his conversation; it could only have come out of his personality and culture.

I want to take up Ransom's teaching for a paragraph. No other American English teacher has had as many talented students. In the last thirty years Allen Tate, Andrew Lytle, Robert Penn Warren, Cleanth Brooks, Randall Jarrell, and Peter Taylor have studied under him. Among them are several of the country's best teachers; several of its best writers. That many, or any, writers should come from the Thracian Athens of Vanderbilt University and the *declension* of Tennessee was surprising; but perhaps their being with Ransom was an irrelevant accident. And yet I think the teacher may have made the difference—a hard one to put one's finger on. It was not the classes but the conversations that mattered. We used to endlessly memorize and repeat and mimic Ransom sentences. We learned something from that. Somehow one left him with something inside us moving toward articulation, logic, directness, and complexity— one's intuitions were more adroit and tougher after one had contemplated the stamina and wit that his writings had required of him. So much for imitation. Imitation of Ransom was not like that of another great teacher, Yvor Winters. Fortunately, it was not possible to become a replica. One took what one could, and went on, God willing, as one's self.

This has its bearings on the language used in Ransom's poems. How few modern poems—however obscure, fierce, sonorous, pretentious, million-dollar-worded—have the distinction of good conversation. I do not mean mannered conversation, the humor the English are said to inherit or get in their schools; but a distinction that a man must have in him, for he can never fake it or buy it. Literary people as a rule have less of their own to say and consequently use words with less subtlety and precision than a Maine farmer. But this is not what is in question. To appreciate the language of Ransom's poems, you must realize that it is the language of one of the best talkers that has ever lived in the United States:

> *Autumn days in our section*
> *Are the most used-up thing on earth*
> *(Or in the waters under the earth)*
> *Having no more color nor predilection*
> *Than cornstalks too wet for the fire . . .*

Of course language is only one quality, perhaps not the most important, that makes the poems. Someday I hope that I shall be able to say with the proper wisdom and elaboration what they are. But in passing: the style in itself fascinates, but it is such as to cause the separate poems to blur together. There is the unusual structural clarity, the rightness of tone and rhythm, the brisk and effective ingenuity, the rhetorical fireworks of exposition, description, and dialogue; but even more: the sticking to concrete human subjects—the hardest; and a balance, temperament. All these qualities were necessary for him to write, as few poets in the world have done, of the death of a child, a child's hen, or a childish coquette, without cynicism, sentimentality, or trifling. These are the hardest of poems; their admirers must have something of the sensibility of Alexander Pope. And they were necessary for Ransom to compress into thirty-six lines of his poem "Painted Head" all that he has stated in several closely worked volumes of critical theory and aesthetics—to say it all, and more, and better. His fifteen or so best poems (one would have trouble naming just which they are) have the magic which

Matthew Arnold esteemed and called *Celtic*, and which, whatever it is, art must never lack, if it desires to delight.

> *All day the clock will metronome*
> *Your gallant fear; the needles clicking,*
> *The heels detonating the stair's cavern.*

> *Freshening the water in the blue bowls*
> *For the buckberries with not all your love,*
> *You shall be listening to the low wind,*
> *The warning sibilance of pines.*

[1948]

II / John Crowe Ransom
1888–1974

Twenty-six years ago, I wrote a short festschrift piece
on Ransom's conversation. I thought his poetry was conversation
as much as his criticism and talk. Since then, his image hasn't
changed except for half a dozen elegiac essays on other poets and
eight poems curiously and dubiously revised. I have nothing new
to express but my wonder. My lasting, almost daily, picture of
Ransom is slightly too symbolic, and such as he couldn't have
been. I was nineteen or twenty then, loud-humored, dirty, and
frayed—I almost needed to be persuaded to comb my hair, tie
my shoes, and say goodbye when leaving a house. I knew more
about Dryden and Milton than most students but had never read
a word by a philosopher or logician. I could not decode John's
(none of us dared call him this till three years after graduation)
metaphysical terms, ontology, catharsis, etc., with their homely
Greek derivations and abstract, accurate English meaning so
unlike language.

Ransom detested laurels and the Byronic pose, but his
poetic calling showed in the fine fiber of his phrases, and in a

shyness. His recreations were games, all brisk and precise ones, golf, croquet, crossword puzzles, bridge, charades, the Game. For someone so gracious, he was surprisingly put out by violations. An enemy charade team once divided *Churchill* into *church* and *hill* instead of *church* and *ill*. This brought out sustained aesthetic scoldings from him; so did moving his croquet ball. He could live without cheating within the rules of a game. His rather repelling and unwayward rows of flowers seemed laid out by tape measure and color chart. "I would fill rows of separate plots with flowers to my liking; and very congenial would be the well-clipped horizontal turfs between adjacent plot to walk upon. But I would replace the end flowers of the upper and lower two central plots with ten plants of Burpee's Climax Marigold, which bear blazing orange flowers; and the end flowers of the upper and lower plots with Wayside Gardens' Aster Frikarti, whose blossoms are bright lavender . . . Think how the farmer and the visitors would be intrigued by the displacements of the sloping front border, which do not subtract a foot from its lawful length." His parlors in three successive houses were the same room, bleak, comfortably barren, just-moved-into-looking; no games or students sipping a beer on the rug could injure or alter it. Most of Ransom's original paintings were loaned him by the Kenyon arts professor. They were coarse-textured and large, an affront to the artist-wife of the co-editor of the *Kenyon Review*. Ransom would say, "Mr. Mercer, like William Turner, is better at the sea than farmland."

Ransom's mouth was large and always in slow perceptive motion, quivering with tedium, or tighter-drawn to repel ignorant rudeness, giving an encouraging grimace, or relaxed, though busy in mediation. It was a mouth more expressive than the small, beautiful mouths of girls in his poems. He liked to be a poet, but not to be seen as one; he preferred the manner of a provincial minister or classics professor—someone of his father's generation. He roughened his musical voice almost with a fine gravel, just as he worked to roughen his meters. Once we were watching one of my classmates lope in an apricot corduroy suit across the Kenyon campus. "I guess Nerber is our only Kenyon man whose trousers match his coat." Poor Nerber, nothing else in his whole life matched. Ransom could report a faculty meeting and make it interesting. He could make a sad comic masterpiece of a happening under our noses. My classics professor was a close friend of his and mine, and had been a child prodigy who entered Harvard at thirteen, and later married another child prodigy in classics— remarkable people but fated for divorce and tragedy. They were plain and ironic, yet their divorce was marked with violence and absurdity: a sheet wetted to cause pneumonia, a carving knife left threateningly at a stairhead, a daughter held incommunicado from both parents, insomnia, proofs, floods of persuasive, contradictory, and retold debate. On the much adjourned day of the trial, the presiding judge, a master of sarcasm, was kicked and incapacitated by a mule. Ransom told this story for a season as if possessed, and in an honest rococo style that left listening moralists pale and embarrassed. It was his version of the Southern tall story, and one of the strangest and most fascinating, though true. Ransom's natural conversation was abstract and pithy . . . soft-spoken, as if he were leading a slow actor.

There were moments in Ransom's ironic courtesies that reduced even Allen Tate to white-faced finger-twitching, so far had the conversation seemed to fall from reckless sublimity. In a letter just written to me, Tate rightly boasts of being Ransom's oldest living student. But the relationship could never have been this, they were so near in genius, close in age, and different in character. Ransom affected a fear lest Tate, though matchless, prove too strong for himself, he was so close to the danger areas, France, Rimbaud, Hart Crane, *The Waste Land*; he was too eloquent, obscure, and menacingly gallant. Ransom liked to stand behind, and later off from, the agrarian charge, as if he were an anti-slavery Southern commander with liberal friends in the East.

I suppose I don't need to explain the decentralist provincial hopes of the Tennessee agrarians and traditionalists, a cause as impractical and permanent as socialism, though for now fallen away from the sunlight.

Ransom spent his last thirty-five years, over a third of his whole life, in Ohio. His affections warmed slightly for the avant-garde; his politics grew less cutting and heroic. His Southern first-love leveled or dimmed into an unoptimistic Northern liberalism. The powerful Midwestern farm never became his soil, or his to harvest; it was not even a spot to sightsee. Who knows what are right choices? Did leaving Tennessee strengthen health by draining his inspiration? Health the nurse of function?

Randall Jarrell said the gods who took away the poet's audience gave him students. No student was more brilliant than Jarrell, but Ransom had dozens—Allen Tate, Robert Penn Warren, Andrew Lytle, Peter Taylor, John Thompson, Robie Macauley, James Wright. We carried our academic brand, but we were diverse, unsortable, ungroupable. Ransom's neatness fathered the haphazard. He is known throughout the English departments of America; in Southern universities, he is a cult, everyone has studied under him or knows someone who has, any student can repeat scraps of Ransom dialogue, epigram, and dogma, or laugh at his legendary defeat of some notable or boor. His classes were usually for a dozen or more students; they were homemade, methodical, and humdrum. For five years, he grimly taught *The Faerie Queen*; though he found Spenser's allegory without intellectual meat, it amused him like a crossword puzzle or a blueprint for his garden. More brilliance and flair often came out in casual gossip. Sometimes a class would crackle. Most often it was in aesthetics. "I must transpose Hegel's Triad to more accurate terminology. When a teacher says that, he means his own." He had a fairly rich though sketchy acquaintance with classical-romantic music. Once in aesthetics, we were taken to hear a record of Beethoven's Thirteenth or Fifteenth Quartet. It upset Ransom's grudge against the nineteenth century; he discovered Shelleys everywhere in that unmetaphysical darkness. "Beethoven is a romantic . . . he's too good."

Ransom's Prose. He thought philosophy more intellectually stimulating than literary criticism; criticism more masculine than scholarship; scholarship more solid than criticism; poetry more intuitive than philosophy, though a florid and slipshod thinker.

Technique was a skeleton without intuition, but intuition was flabby. "The minds of man and woman grow apart; and how shall we express their differentiation? In this way, I think: man at his best is an intellectualized woman." Or, "The philosopher is apt to see a lot of wood and no trees, his theory is very general and his acquaintance with particulars is not persistent or intimate, especially his acquaintance with technical effects." In the world of the sentiments and art's inexhaustible particularity, child, woman, poetry, and creature are perfect, though they mostly fail before the verifier—bodies without heads. All Ransom's thoughts are dialectical, games of pieces in opposition. No piece can be expelled, or moved without bumping. I hope I haven't suggested that everything is equal to everything in Ransom's aesthetic, a criticism where college course jars against college course and has no umpire or outcome. He was able to suffer breakage and bloodshed, he was a tough and untiring constructor. Ransom received a low but passing grade for writing his final Oxford classics exam in the Latin of Tacitus. No other Latin style seemed close and dense enough. He viewed romantics with fear and pity, and never confused entravagance with sublimity. He himself was a romantic, with the underdog courage of someone smaller, quicker, and brighter than others. He was happier too, though more easily injured.

My friend Jarrell was romantic in another style than Tate or Ransom. He was educated in the preoccupations of the thirties, Marx, Auden, Empson, Kafka, plane design, anthropology since Fraser, and news of the day. He knew everything, except Ransom's closed, provincial world of Greek, Latin, Aristotle, and Oxford. His idiom was boyish and his clothes collegiate. Our college president, Dr. Gordon Chalmers, was a thoughtless disciple of the great American humanists Paul Elmer More and Irving Babbitt. Unlike Ransom, he believed in his anti-romanticism, and forever dried out barbarously for measure, order, and the inner check. For him, the old sages were the new humanist professors. He saw Randall going down a ski crest in his unconventional, unlovely clothes, crying, "I feel just like an *angel.*" Ransom thought Randall had shocked Dr. Chalmers's

belief. The Aristotelian schoolmen had known no such enthusiastic and inordinate angel. "That boy needs a more generous vocabulary." Of course, Randall had already *swallowed the
dictionary*, as they say.

When Ransom wasn't playing games, golfing, or taking us
on hikers' discussions, or gardening in systematic solitude, he was
in his den. It was a compact, unwomanly room, the reproduction of another last-year-moved-out-of den, fresh and secure,
though seasoned with pipe smoke, Greek, Latin, English, an
infirm volume or two in French or German bought at college,
a fine density of philosophy, criticism, a volume or two of Jane
Austen, four of Faulkner, a fair selection of modern poetry,
though adulterated by signed copies from friends. He talked
metaphysics if he could, and poetry if he had to, and gossip if he
could. The strands were indistinguishable; one of Ransom's
critical terms was *nostalgia*. Unlike the poets, he could write
of women, the fresh things of the world.

When Ransom changed his poetry for criticism, everyone
asked why he had stopped writing. They discussed this behind
his back, or stared at him silently with a pained, consolatory eye.
Perhaps the reverse question had only been put to Ransom by
himself. Why make pretty rhymes instead of an honest essay?
Critics condescend to poets and often like to abase their own
medium to poetry. Even Ransom—but he was lucky to find
criticism in his unoccupied hour, a more flexible and controlled
sentence, and stricter sequences. No need to tinsel out syllogism
and sorites with meter; no passion to be puffed like a balloon.
Through criticism, Ransom discovered his *Review*, a correspondence with the other first New Critics; he assembled critics
annually each summer to teach at his School of Criticism. *O bel
eta del oro*, when criticism had an air of winning! When
Ransom's classical pessimism renounced its half warning, "They
won't be content until the old work is done over." Somehow in
the next generation the great analytical and philosophic project
turned to wood, the formidable inertia of the pedagogue, the
follow-up man.

Ransom's poems, if anything, think more clearly than his

prose. Yet the essays have much the same language, and much the same point. His charming, biting Edna Millay piece is like another of his poems to Southern ladies. It has wit and flirtation and avoids poetry. In his criticism, Aristotle, Santayana, and Sir Arthur Quiller-Couch breathe, though introduced as intellectual presences, not portraits. His unruffled rhetoric and arguments against blur and enthusiasm that once seemed perverse now seem like a medicine.

Ransom wanted to go back to poetry. Someone found an envelope he had scribbled with bizarre and comical off-rhymes. No subject or other words. After the war, he published his first *Selected Poems*, with minor and magical revisions. Long after, he spent years rewriting and trying to perfect his old, almost perfect poems in a disastrously new style. I leave this insolence as I wrote it. Not all of Ransom's changes are disastrous, some improve, almost all show surprising ways in which passages can be varied. One has a thousand opportunities to misrevise. A little ground is gained for the more that is lost. One new quatrain in "Prelude to an Evening" has lines like a Shakespeare tragedy. Ransom's prose *defenses* of his new versions are autobiographical and critical; they sometimes change his story. "My third stanza, where *chill* replaces *fever*, is almost unutterably painful; but I was most intent upon it, and managed to the best of my ability. Lines two and three are the saddest perhaps in all my poems." Ah, but I hope the saddest lines were in their first version, because Ransom's revisions have almost certainly ruined them.

Ransom's *Selected* is no longer than most single volumes by other poets; all hip poems would be no longer than two such volumes. He made one or two debatable inclusions, and three or four omissions; these were missed and later restored. What he wrote could have come from knowing Hardy, E. A. Robinson, early Graves, Shakespeare, Milton, Mother Goose, ballads, Plato, and Aristotle. His poems stick apart; and refuse to melt into their neighbors. They seem few until one tries to discover as many in some favorite, more voluminous author. Ransom's essays, even the most dazzling and strong, are like didactic poems (some of

Auden's perhaps), a little monotonous and ill-jointed. The charm of his poems seems to be first in their colors, their people, the beautiful, observant imagery, the grace of rhyme and speed —his undefinable voice. They are short.

Ransom is able to write of women, the young, find them delightful, irritating, not quite human, though mortal. His women cannot be spoiled by abstraction, or impressed into careers. The women are supporting figures, his man stands at the center, almost one unchangeable man whenever he appears— troubled, gaunt, scrupulous-conscienced, philosophizing to no end, Quixotic, Prufrockish, too serious to see his own children . . . apparently not like Ransom in life. The men and women court, quarrel, and whirl into disequilibrium, not tragic but in pain. Nowhere a thoughtless happiness, a mature innocence, a place to "hear the maiden pageant ever sing / of that faraway time of gentleness." Man goes creased and sometimes finds a puzzling joy.

In his art, too, Ransom found pain, or a harmony of dis-equilibrium. He knows why we do not come back to a photo-graph for aesthetic pleasure, no matter how colorful and dramatic, not even if it is of a person loved. We cannot feel, as in paintings, the artist's mothering work of hand and mind. I once asked the master photographer Walker Evans how Ver-meer's *View of Delft* (that perhaps first trompe l'oeil of land-scape verisimilitude) differed from a photograph. He paused, staring, as if his eye could not give the answer. His answer was Ransom's—art demands the intelligent pain or care behind each speck of brick, each spot of paint.

Ransom made no claims for poetry's onomatopeia, superior eeriness, and passionate intensity. He liked his language to be elegant and unpainted, a poetry not far removed, except in its close texture, from written or spoken prose. He wished poetry to show its seams, and show the uncouthness caused by rhyming, compressing, finding right syntax. Only out of pain is the art that can hide art. The poetic in the old sense was all to Ransom. He told me his poems came out of brief, unevoked daydreams, a wisp of imagery, or better—a new fable. Many dreams, few poems. When the daydreams stopped or became inappropriate, so did his muse.

I see Ransom on his hill, as a student must see his loved master. Kenyon had a hill celebrated in student songs. I have left out my friend's personal life, his charming, healthy household, where with Jarrell I spent my second and key college year. I leave out too his wife, Robb Reavil, whose humor and particularity held him back from the small air of metaphysics.

[1974]

William Carlos Williams

I / *Paterson I*

In a review that I imagine will become famous as an example of "the shock of recognition," Randall Jarrell has said about all that can be said in a short space of the construction of *Paterson*. I feel no embarrassment, however, for repeating, poorly but in different words, what has already been written. *Paterson* has made no stir either in the little magazines or in the commercial press; and yet I can think of no book published in 1946 that is as important, or of any living English or American poet who has written anything better or more ambitious.

When it is completed, *Paterson* will run to over a hundred pages, and be in four parts. As only Book One has been published, the critic is faced with many uncertainties, and forced to make many conjectures.* William Carlos Williams's own rather breathless and incoherent introductory note will, perhaps, be of little help. "A man in himself is a city, beginning, seeking, achieving and concluding his life in the ways which the various aspects of the city may embody—if imaginatively conceived—any city, all the details of which may be made to voice his most intimate convictions." The poet begins with a slightly different statement of this purpose: "Rigor of beauty is the quest. But

---

* As the poem stands, it has many insufficiently related odds and ends. It is a defect perhaps that human beings exist almost entirely in the prose passages. R.L.

how will you find beauty when it is locked in the mind past all remonstrance?" The answer is: "To make a start out of particulars . . . no ideas but in things." This may appear crude and vague, but Williams has nothing in common with the coarse, oratorical sentimentalists, most favorably represented by Carl Sandburg, who have written about cities and the people. More than any of his contemporaries, he resembles Wordsworth in his aims and values; and in its maturity, experience, and sympathy, *Paterson* appears to me to be comparable to *The Prelude* and the opening of *Excursion*.

I am not sure that I can say very clearly why, or even how it is that Williams's methods are successful. By personifying Paterson, and by "Patersonizing" himself, he is in possession of all the materials that he can use. First the city is his: all its aspects, its past, its present, its natural features, its population, and its activities are available for him to interrelate and make dramatic. But also he can use his whole life in the city—every detail is an experience, a memory, or a symbol. Taken together, Paterson is Williams's life, and Williams is what makes Paterson alive.

For Williams, a man is what he experiences, and in his shorter lyrics he has perfected a technique of observation and of empathy. He can move from man outward: "The year plunges into night / and the heart plunges / lower than night / to an empty, windswept place / without sun, stars or moon / but a peculiar light as of thought / that spins a dark fire . . ." Or the observed is personified: "Lifeless in appearance, sluggish / dazed spring approaches— / They enter the new world naked, / cold, uncertain of all / save that they enter." Which end he starts from matters little. Williams triumphs in his sense of motion, his ability to observe, and to fit his observations to the right rhythms.

But if the short poems show Williams as an excellent stylist, there is nothing in them to indicate that their thematic structure could be extended to a long poem. How this has been done and how *Paterson*'s various themes are stated, developed, repeated, opposed, broken, and mingled, has been demonstrated at some length by Jarrell in *Partisan Review*. Here I shall confine

myself to quoting passages in which the principal themes are
expressed and to pointing out a few of their more important
connections and meanings. The theme on which all the others
depend is threefold: a city—Paterson, New Jersey—a mountain,
and a river that flows from the mountain into Paterson—a man,
a woman, and the man's thought. First the city:

> *Paterson lies in the valley under the Passaic Falls*
> *its spent waters forming the outline of his back. He*
> *lies on his right side, head near the thunder*
> *of the waters filling his dreams! Eternally asleep*
> *his dreams walk about the city where he persists*
> *incognito. Butterflies settle on his stone ear.*
> *Immortal he neither moves nor rouses and is seldom*
> *seen, though he breathes and the subtleties of his*
> *   machinations*
> *drawing their substance from the noise of the pouring river*
> *animate a thousand automatons.*

The mountain is introduced in a parallel passage:

> *And there, against him, stretches the low mountain.*
> *The Park's her head, carved above the Falls, by the quiet*
> *river; colored crystals the secret of those rocks;*
> *farms and ponds, laurel, and the temperate wild cactus,*
> *yellow flowered . . . facing him, his*
> *arm supporting her, by the* Valley of the Rocks, *asleep.*
> *Pearls at her ankles, her monstrous hair*
> *spangled with apple-blossoms is scattered about into*
> *the back country, waking their dreams—where the deer run*
> *and the wood-duck nests protecting his gallant plumage.*

The passage introducing the river is too long to quote in full.

> *Jostled as are the waters approaching*
> *the brink, his thoughts*
> *interlace, repel and cut under,*

rise rock-thwarted and turn aside
but forever strain forward—or strike
an eddy and whirl, marked by a
leaf or curdy spume, seeming
to forget . . .

The Man-City and the Woman-Mountain are easier to understand than the river which symbolizes thought. It is the ele-
mental thought that lacks a language, the source of life and
motion. It is described again and again, always with such powerful precision that one is in no doubt of its grimness and strength.
It is intercourse between Paterson and the mountain, and above
all, it is Paterson's thoughts, his population—the primal vitality
behind their lives and speech. The two lovers later meet under
its falls, and in the prose records that are interspersed with the
poetry, one reads of the men and women who were drowned in
it, and the pearls and fish that were taken out of it. This threefold main theme is repeated in smaller themes, such as the
African chief with his seven wives on a log, and "the lightnings
that stab at the mystery of a man from both ends." It is broken
up in the two divorces: the university, "a bud forever green, /
tight-curled, upon the pavement, perfect / in juice and substance
but divorced, divorced / from its fellows, fallen low—"; and the
"girls from / families that have decayed and / taken to the
hills . . . Life is sweet / they say: the language! / —the language / is divorced from their minds." "In ignorance a certain
knowledge and knowledge, undispersed, its own undoing."

This is the tragedy of Paterson, what the poem is really
about. It is the divorce of modern life, of intellect and sensibility, spirit and matter, and of the other stock categories that
come to mind. His "quest for beauty" is a search for the whole
man, whose faculties are harmonious, and whose language corre-
sponds with the particulars and mystery of reality. Williams is
liberal, anti-orthodox, and a descendant of Emerson and Whitman. But if a man is intense and honest enough, the half-truth
of any extreme position will in time absorb much of its opposite.
Williams has much in common with Catholic, aristocratic, and

agrarian writers. For all his sympathy with his people, he makes one feel that the sword of Damocles hangs over Paterson, the modern city, and the world. As with Yeats, "things fall apart." The educated lack connection, and the ignorant are filled with speechless passion.

Williams has had much to say about Ezra Pound, one whom he may have envied for being able to "run off toward the peripheries to find loveliness and authority in the world—a sort of springtime toward which his mind aspired." Some of his pronouncements seemed unfair and hysterical, but in *Paterson* his position has paid off, when compared with Pound's. It is a sort of anti-Cantos rooted in America, in one city, and in what Williams has known long and seen often. Not only are its details enriched and verified by experience, but the whole has a unity that is analogous to the dramatic unities of time, place, and action.

Paterson resembles *The Bridge*; but Hart Crane's poem, for all its splendor in its best moments, will not stand up to the comparison. It seems relatively inexperienced, chaotic, and verbal. Even as a rhetorician Williams is much superior. It would be fruitless to compare *Paterson* with the best writing of Eliot, Stevens, Tate, or Auden, for the ways of writing very well are various; but for experience and observation, it has, along with a few poems of Frost's, a richness that makes almost all other contemporary poetry looks a little secondhand. If Parts II, III, and IV are as good as Part I, *Paterson* will be the most successful really long poem since *The Prelude*.

[1947]

II / *Paterson II*

*P*aterson, Book Two, is an interior monologue. A man spends Sunday in the park at Paterson, New Jersey. He thinks and looks about him; his mind contemplates, describes, comments, associates, stops, stutters, and shifts like a firefly, bound only by its milieu. The man is Williams, anyone living in Paterson, the American, the masculine principle—a sort of Everyman. His monologue is interrupted by chunks of prose: paragraphs from old newspapers, textbooks, and the letters of a lacerated and lacerating poetess. This material is merely selected by the author. That the poetry is able to digest it in the raw is a measure of power and daring—the daring of simplicity; for only a taut style with worlds of experience behind it could so resign, and give way to the anthologist. The didactic chapters in *Moby Dick* have a similar function, and are the rock that supports the struggles of Captain Ahab.

The park is Everywoman, any woman, the feminine principle, America. The water roaring down the falls from the park to Paterson is the principle of life. The rock is death, negation, the *nul*; carved and given form, it stands for the imagination, "like a red basalt grasshopper, boot-long with window-eyes." The symbols are not allegorical, but loose, intuitive, and Protean.

Paterson, like Hart Crane's "Marriage of Faustus and Helen," is about marriage. "Rigor of beauty is the quest." Everything in the poem is masculine or feminine, everything strains toward marriage, but the marriages never come off, except in the imagination, and there, attenuated, fragmentary, and uncertain. "Divorce is the sign of knowledge in our time." The people "reflect no beauty but gross . . . unless it is beauty to be, anywhere, so flagrant in desire." "The ugly legs of the young girls, pistons without delicacy"; "not undignified"; "among the working classes *some* sort of breakdown has occurred." The preacher in the second section, attended by the "iron smiles" of his three middle-aged disciples, by "benches on which a few children have been propped by the others against their running off," "bends at the knees and straightens himself up violently with the force of his emphasis—like Beethoven getting a crescendo out of an orchestra"—ineffective, pathetic, and a little phony. He has given up, or says he has given up, a fortune for the infinite riches of our Lord Jesus Christ. Interspersed through his sermon, as an ironic counter-theme, is Alexander Hamilton, whose fertile imagination devised the national debt and envisioned Paterson as a great manufacturing center. Nobody wins. "The church spires still spend their wits against the sky." "The rock-table is scratched by the picnickers' boot-nails, more than by the glacier." The great industrialists are "those guilty bastards . . . trying to undermine us." The legislators are "under the garbage, uninstructed, incapable of self-instruction." "An orchestral dullness overlays their world." "The language, tongue-tied . . . words without style!"

This is the harsh view. Against it is the humorous, the dogs, the children; lovely fragments of natural description; the author's sense of the human and sympathetic in his people.

Williams is noted as an imagist, a photographic eye; in Book One he has written "no ideas but in the facts." This is misleading. His symbolic man and woman are Hegel's *thesis* and *antithesis*. They struggle toward *synthesis*—marriage. But fullness, if it exists at all, only exists in simple things, trees and animals; so Williams, like other Platonists, is thrown back on the "idea." "And no whiteness (lost) is so white as the memory of whiteness." "The stone lives, the flesh dies." The idea, Beauty, must be realized by the poet where he lives, in Paterson. "Be reconciled, Poet, with your world, it is the only truth," though "love" for it "is no comforter, rather a nail in the skull."

Paterson is an attempt to write the American Poem. It depends on the American myth, a myth that is seldom absent from our literature—part of our power, and part of our hubris and deformity. At its grossest the myth is propaganda, puffing and grimacing: Size, Strength, Vitality, the Common Man, the New World, Vital Speech, the Machine; the hideous neo-Roman personae: Democracy, Freedom, Liberty, the Corn, the Land. How hollow, windy, and inert this would have seemed to an imaginative man of another culture! But the myth is a serious matter. It is assumed by Emerson, Whitman, and Hart Crane; by Henry Adams and Henry James. For good or for evil, America *is* something immense, crass, and Roman. We must unavoidably place ourselves in our geography, history, civilization, institutions, and future.

The subjects of great poetry have usually been characters

and the passions, a moral struggle that calls a man's whole person into play. One thinks of the wrath of Achilles, Macbeth and his conscience, Aeneas debating whether he will leave Dido, whether he will kill Turnus. But in the best long American poems—*Leaves of Grass, The Cantos, The Waste Land, Four Quartets, The Bridge,* and *Paterson*—no characters take on sufficient form to arrive at a crisis. The people melt into voices. In a recent essay Eliot has given his reasons why a writer should, perhaps, read Milton; Williams has answered with an essay that gives reasons why a writer should *not* read Milton—Eliot and Williams might learn something from *Paradise Lost* and *Samson Agonistes,* how Milton populated his desert.

Until Books III and IV are published, it is safer to compare *Paterson* with poems that resemble it; not with *The Bridge,* that wonderful monster, so unequal, so inexperienced—dazzling in its rhetoric at times in the way that Keats is dazzling; but with a book in which its admirers profess to find everything, *Leaves of Grass.* Whitman is a considerable poet, and a considerable myth. I can never quite disentangle the one from the other. I would say that Whitman's language has less variety, sureness, and nerve than Williams's; that his imagination is relatively soft, formless, monotonous, and vague. Both poets are strong on compassion and enthusiasm, but these qualities in Whitman are *simpliste* and blurred.

Paterson is Whitman's America, grown pathetic and tragic, brutalized by inequality, disorganized by industrial chaos, and faced with annihilation. No poet has written of it with such a combination of brilliance, sympathy, and experience, with such alertness and energy. Because he has tried to understand rather than excoriate, and because in his maturity he has been occupied with the "raw" and the universal, his *Paterson* is not the tragedy of the outcast but the tragedy of our civilization. It is a book in which the best readers, as well as the simple reader, are likely to find *everything.*

[1948]

III / Dr. Williams

Dr. Williams and his work are part of me, yet I come on them as a critical intruder. I fear I shall spoil what I have to say, just as I somehow got off on the wrong note about Williams with Ford Madox Ford twenty-five years ago. Ford was wearing a stained robin's-egg-blue pajama top, reading Theocritus in Greek, and guying me about my "butterfly existence," so removed from the labors of a professional writer. I was saying something awkward, green, and intense in praise of Williams, and, while agreeing, Ford managed to make me feel that I was far too provincial, genteel, and puritanical to understand what I was saying. And why not? Wasn't I, as Ford assumed, the grandson or something of James Russell Lowell and the cousin of Lawrence Lowell, a young man doomed to trifle with poetry and end up as president of Harvard or ambassador to England?

I have stepped over these pitfalls. I have conquered my hereditary disadvantages. Except for writing, nothing I've touched has shone. When I think about writing on Dr. Williams, I feel a chaos of thoughts and images, images cracking open to admit a thought, thoughts dragging their roots for the soil of an image. When I woke up this morning, something unusual for this summer was going on!—pinpricks of rain were falling in a reliable, comforting simmer. Our town was blanketed in the rain of rot and the rain of renewal. New life was muscling in, everything growing moved on its one-way trip to the ground. I could feel this, yet believe our universal misfortune was bearable and even welcome. An image held my mind during these moments and kept returning—an old-fashioned New England cottage freshly painted white. I saw a shaggy, triangular shade on the house, trees, a hedge, or their shadows, the blotch of decay. The house might have been the house I was now living in, but it wasn't; it came from the time when I was a child, still unable to read, and living in the small town of Barnstable on

Cape Cod. Inside the house was a bird book with an old stiff and steely engraving of a sharp-shinned hawk. The hawk's legs had a reddish-brown buffalo fuzz on them; behind was the blue sky, bare and abstracted from the world. In the present, pinpricks of rain were falling on everything I could see, and even on the white house in my mind, but the hawk's picture, being indoors I suppose, was more or less spared. Since I saw the picture of the hawk, the pinpricks of rain have gone on, half the people I once knew are dead, half the people I now know were then unborn, and I have learned to read.

An image of a white house with a blotch on it—this is perhaps the start of a Williams poem. If I held this image closely and honestly enough, the stabbing detail might come and with it the universal that belonged to this detail and nowhere else. Much wrapping would have to be cut away, and many elegiac cadences with their worn eloquence and loftiness. This is how I would like to write about Dr. Williams. I would collect impressions, stare them into rightness, and let my mind-work and judgments come as they might naturally.

When I was a freshman at Harvard, nothing hit me so hard as the Norton Lectures given by Robert Frost. Frost's revolutionary power, however, was not in his followers, nor in the student literary magazine, the *Advocate*, whose editor had just written a piece on speech rhythms in the "Hired Man," a much less up-to-date thing to do then than now. Our only strong and avant-garde man was James Laughlin. He was much taller and older than we were. He knew Henry Miller, and exotic young American poetesses in Paris, spent summers at Rapallo with Ezra Pound, and was getting out the first number of his experimental annual, *New Directions*. He knew the great, and he himself wrote deliberately flat descriptive and anecdotal poems. We were sarcastic about them, but they made us feel secretly that we didn't know what was up in poetry. They used no punctuation or capitals, and their only rule was that each line should be eleven or fifteen typewriter spaces long. The author explained that this metric was "as rational as any other" and was based on the practice of W. C. Williams, a poet and pediatrician living in Rutherford, New Jersey. About this time, Laughlin published a review somewhere, perhaps even in *The Harvard Advocate*, of Williams's last small volume. In it, he pushed the metric of typewriter spaces, and quoted from a poem, "The Catholic Bells," to show us Williams's "mature style at fifty"! This was a memorable phrase, and one that made maturity seem possible, but a long way off. I more or less memorized "The Catholic Bells," and spent months trying to console myself by detecting immaturities in whatever Williams had written before he was fifty.

THE CATHOLIC BELLS

Tho' I'm no Catholic
I listen hard when the bells
in the yellow-brick tower
of their new church

ring down the leaves
ring in the frost upon them
and the death of the flowers
ring out the grackle

toward the south, the sky
darkened by them, ring in
the new baby of Mr. and Mrs.
Krantz which cannot

for the fat of its cheeks
open well its eyes . . .

What I liked about "The Catholic Bells" were the irrelevant associations I hung on the words *frost* and *Catholic*, and still more its misleading similarity to the "Ring out wild bells" section of *In Memoriam*. Other things upset and fascinated me and made me feel I was in a world I would never quite understand. Was the spelling "Tho' " strange in a realistic writer, and

the iambic rhythm of the first seven words part of some inevitable sound pattern? I had dipped into Edith Sitwell's
criticism and was full of inevitable sound patterns. I was sure
that somewhere hidden was a key that would make this poem as
regular as the regular meters of Tennyson. There had to be
something outside the poem I could hang on to because what was
inside dizzied me: the shocking scramble of the august and the
crass in making the Catholic church "new" and "yellow-brick,"
the cherubic ugliness of the baby, belonging rather horribly to
"Mr. and Mrs. / Krantz," and seen by the experienced, mature
pediatrician as unable to see "for the fat of its cheeks"—this last
a cunning shift into anapests. I was surprised that Williams used
commas, and that my three or four methods of adjusting his
lines to uniform typewriter spaces failed. I supposed he had gone
on to some bolder and still more mature system.

To explain the full punishment I felt on first reading
Williams, I should say a little about what I was studying at the
time. A year or so before, I had read some introductory books
on the enjoyment of poetry, and was knocked over by the
examples in the free-verse sections. When I arrived at college, independent, fearful of advice, and with all the world
before me, I began to rummage through the Cambridge book-
shops. I found books that must have been looking for a buyer
since the student days of Trumbull Stickney: soiled metrical
treatises written by obscure English professors in the eighteen-
nineties. They were full of glorious things: rising rhythm, falling
rhythm, feet with Greek names, stanzas from Longfellow's
"Psalm of Life," John Drinkwater, and Swinburne. Nothing
seemed simpler than meter. I began experiments with an exotic
foot, short, long, two shorts, then fell back on iambics. My
material now took twice as many words, and I rolled out Spen-
serian stanzas on Job and Jonah surrounded by recently seen
Nantucket scenery. Everything I did was grand, ungrammatical,
and had a timeless, hackneyed quality. All this was ended by
reading Williams. It was as though some homemade ship, part
Spanish galleon, part paddle-wheels, kitchen pots, and elastic
bands and worked by hand, had anchored to a filling station.

In "The Catholic Bells," the joining of religion and non-religion, of piety and a hard, nervous secular knowingness are typical of Williams. Further along in this poem, there is a piece of mere description that has always stuck in my mind.

> *(the*
> *grapes still hanging to*
> *the vines along the nearby*
> *Concordia Halle like broken*
> *teeth in the head of an*
> *old man)*

Take out the Concordia Halle and the grapevines crackle in the wind with a sour, impoverished dryness; take out the vines and the Concordia Halle has lost its world. Williams has pages and pages of description that are as good as this. It is his equivalent of, say, the Miltonic sentence, the dazzling staple and excellence which he can always produce. Williams has said that he uses the forms he does for quick changes of tone, atmosphere, and speed. This makes him dangerous and difficult to imitate, because most poets have little change of tone, atmosphere, and speed in them.

I have emphasized Williams's simplicity and nakedness and have no doubt been misleading. His idiom comes from many sources, from speech and reading, both of various kinds; the blend, which is his own invention, is generous and even exotic. Few poets can come near to his wide clarity and dashing rightness with words, his dignity and almost Alexandrian modulations of voice. His short lines often speed up and simplify hugely drawn out and ornate sentence structures. I once typed out his direct but densely observed poem, "The Semblables," in a single prose paragraph. Not a word or its placing had been changed, but the poem has changed into a piece of smothering, magnificent rhetoric, much more like Faulkner than the original Williams.

The difficulties I found in Williams twenty-five years ago are still difficulties for me. Williams enters me, but I cannot

enter him. Of course, one cannot catch any good writer's voice
or breathe his air. But there's something more. It's as if no poet
except Williams had really seen America or heard its language.
Or rather, he sees and hears what we all see and hear and what
is the most obvious, but no one else has found this a help or an
inspiration. This may come naturally to Dr. Williams from his
character, surroundings, and occupation. I can see him rushing
from his practice to his typewriter, happy that so much of the
world has rubbed off on him, maddened by its hurry. Perhaps
he had no choice. Anyway, what other poets have spent lifetimes in building up personal styles to gather what has been
snatched up on the run by Dr. Williams? When I say that I
cannot enter him, I am almost saying that I cannot enter
America. This troubles me. I am not satisfied to let it be. Like
others, I have picked up things here and there from Williams,
but this only makes me marvel all the more at his unique and
searing journey. It is a Dantesque journey, for he loves America
excessively, as if it were *the* truth and *the* subject; his exasperation is also excessive, as if there were no other hell. His flowers
rustle by the superhighways and pick up all our voices.

A seemingly unending war has been going on for as long as
I can remember between Williams and his disciples and the
principals and disciples of another school of modern poetry. The
Beats are on one side, the university poets are on the other.
Lately [in the sixties] the gunfire has been hot. With such unlikely Williams recruits as Karl Shapiro blasting away, it has
become unpleasant to stand in the middle in a position of
impartiality.

The war is an old one for me. In the late thirties, I was at
Kenyon College to study under John Crowe Ransom. The times
hummed with catastrophe and ideological violence, both political
and aesthetical. The English departments were clogged with
worthy but outworn and backward-looking scholars whose tastes
in the moderns were most often superficial, random, and vulgar.
Students who wanted to write got little practical help from their
professors. They studied the classics as monsters that were slowly

losing their fur and feathers and leaking a little sawdust. What one did oneself was all chance and shallowness, and no profession seemed wispier and less needed than that of the poet. My own group, that of Tate and Ransom, was all for the high discipline, for putting on the full armor of the past, for making poetry something that would take a man's full weight and that would bear his complete intelligence, passion, and subtlety. Almost anything, the Greek and Roman classics, Elizabethan dramatic poetry, seventeenth-century metaphysical verse, old and modern critics, aestheticians and philosophers, could be suppled up and again made necessary. The struggle perhaps centered on making the old metrical forms usable again to express the depths of one's experience.

For us, Williams was of course part of the revolution that had renewed poetry, but he was a byline. Opinions varied on his work. It was something fresh, secondary, and minor, or it was the best that free verse could do. He was the one writer with the substance, daring, and staying power to make the short free-verse poem something considerable. One was shaken when the radical conservative critic Yvor Winters spoke of Williams's "By the road to the contagious hospital" as a finer, more lasting piece of craftsmanship than "Gerontion."

Well, nothing will do for everyone. It's hard for me to see how I and the younger poets I was close to could at that time have learned much from Williams. It was all we could do to keep alive and follow our own heavy program. That time is gone, and now young poets are perhaps more conscious of the burden and the hardening of this old formalism. Too many poems have been written to rule. They show off their authors' efforts and mind, but little more. Often the culture seems to have passed them by. And, once more, Dr. Williams is a model and a liberator. What will come, I don't know. Williams, unlike, say, Marianne Moore, seems to be one of those poets who can be imitated anonymously. His style is almost a common style and even what he claims for it—*the American style.* Somehow, written without his speed and genius, the results are usually dull, a poem at best well-made but without breath.

Williams is part of the great breath of our literature. *Paterson* is our *Leaves of Grass*. The times have changed. A drastic experimental art is now expected and demanded. The scene is dense with the dirt and power of industrial society. Williams looks on it with exasperation, terror, and a kind of love. His short poems are singularly perfect thrusts, maybe the best that will ever be written of their kind, because neither the man nor the pressure will be found again. When I think of his last, longish autobiographical poems, I remember his last reading I heard. It was at Wellesley. I think about three thousand students attended. It couldn't have been more crowded in the wide-galleried hall and I had to sit in the aisle. The poet appeared, one whole side partly paralyzed, his voice just audible, and here and there a word misread. No one stirred. In the silence he read his great poem "Of Asphrodel, That Greeny Flower," a triumph of simple confession—somehow he delivered to us what was impossible, something that was both poetry and beyond poetry.

I think of going with Dr. Williams and his son to visit his mother, very old, almost a hundred, and unknowing, her black eyes boring through. And Williams saying to her, "Which would you rather see, us or three beautiful blonds?" As we left, he said, "The old bitch will live on but I may die tomorrow!" You could not feel shocked. Few men had felt and respected anyone more than Williams had his old mother. And in seeing him out strolling on a Sunday after a heart attack: the town seemed to know him and love him and take him in its stride, as we will do with his great pouring of books, his part in the air we breathe and will breathe.

[1962]

T. S. Eliot

I / *Four Quartets*

Four Quartets is a quasi-autobiographical testimony of the experience of *union with God*, or rather, its imperfect approximations in this life. At first glance, the poems appear to be a ragbag stuffed with mythical theology and practice, essays in aesthetics and English history, natural description, the war, and denunciations of secularism. However, everything is pointed toward one end; every line is symbolic. For instance, in Eliot's wrestling with language, artistic craft is analogous to contemplative discipline, aesthetic experience is analogous to ecstasy. The other symbols work in roughly the same way. Eliot frequently uses the strict and paradoxical terminology of St. John of the Cross, which gives his experiences an air of the occult; actually, they are universal and fairly common. Similar experiences are specifically described by innumerable Christian mystics, and close parallels, with crucial differences, can be found in the writings of the Buddha and Islam. My own feeling is that *union with God* is somewhere in sight in all poetry, though it is usually rudimentary and misunderstood. *Four Quartets* is a composite of the symbolic, the didactic, and the confessional. It is probably the most powerful religious poem of the twentieth century, and certainly the most remarkable and ambitious expression of Catholic mysticism in English.

I suppose no poem has come into the world with so many critics to attend it. Both its ideas and their expression are difficult; and the reader who wants to understand them should examine the thorough explanations of Leonard Unger, J. J. Sweeney, F. O. Matthiessen, and Philip Wheelwright. Here I shall limit myself to a little description and a few random suggestions. But I fear that no evaluation that skirts detailed criticism will seem very plausible.

The metrics are casual and formal. Each Quartet is laid to a single pattern. The nearest parallel I can think of is the *canzone*, in which the poet makes a long stanza of any number of lines he pleases and rhymed in any way he pleases and then repeats it. Spenser's *Prothalamium* is the famous example. The *Quartets*, however, are stanzas two hundred lines long and are divided into five parts. Each has two formal lyrics and for the rest is written in loose unrhymed iambics varying from two to seven feet. The various symbols and comments are developed thematically and in this are similar to *The Waste Land*, Pound's *Cantos*, and any number of modern poems. But the repetition of a strict metrical pattern gives the thematic poem the appearance of extreme formality.

Eliot has been censured by a number of critics, most brilliantly by John Crowe Ransom and Yvor Winters, for his loose logic and loose meters. There is no denying that the *Four Quartets* tends to be fragmentary, repetitious, and obscure. Only intuition could have determined when and why it was complete. It is significant that Pound blue-penciled *The Waste Land* down to two-thirds its original length. Here the reasons why one passage should follow another are even less apparent. In Eliot's words, "each venture is a new beginning." What is true of the whole is also true of the parts. Each individual passage seems to dissipate its concentration and drive by the very suppleness of its rhythms. The author's extreme use of adapted and parodied phrases carries this tendency to a point where his objects and situations all but disintegrate under the pressure of their allusions.

Such objections are valid but not altogether to the point because they fail to take into account what is intended. Form is nothing else but unity and integration. The structure of the *Quartets* achieves both these ends as well as one has a right to ask. Each part is written as a reflection or modification of the preceding parts. Taken together, the four poems are immensely more complete and impressive than separately. The last poem, "Little Gidding," carries the weight of all that goes before, but expresses with some finality a deeper penetration into the mystical experience. Probably the contemplative's life, as distinguished from his separate acts, can only be dramatized by a circular and thematic structure. His actions, unlike the tragic hero's, have no beginning, middle, or end: their external unity is a pawn to their unity of intention. His discipline is repetitive and his moments of ecstasy disconnected. Eliot has this one theme in all his writings and its nature in part explains the excellence of the longer poems and the relative failure of the plays.

Given such a structure, irregular meters are appropriate. The job is not to concentrate the parts in themselves but rather to prevent their becoming so water-tight that they are unable to coalesce. The purpose of the formal lyrics is partly to accentuate the pattern and partly to effect variation and shock. By this stratagem, the reader concedes that the prosaic sections are meant to be prosaic.

The quotations have other functions besides the capture of a richer and more inspired texture than the poet could sustain on his own. They vary the tone, argue for the continuity of artistic tradition, and make for a semblance of anonymity, so that even the most confessional passages appear impersonal. *Four Quartets* is something of a community product.

It is probably Eliot's best poem. Although nothing in it is as massive as "Gerontion" or the opening of "A Game of Chess" in *The Waste Land*, the thought is more patient and profound, the language, less quotable, is solider under its surface. The brilliant but sometimes overstating and reckless satirist has all but vanished; when he appears, he speaks with authority. Occasionally the symbols are paradoxically too personal and too general either to exist in themselves or to carry sufficient symbolic meaning:

> ... in the nursery bedroom,
> In the rank ailanthus of the April dooryard,
> In the smell of grapes on the autumn table
> In the evening circle by the winter gaslight.

Fortunately, such writing is rare. If I were to pick purple passages, they would be part one of "Dry Salvages," the unrhymed terza rima section in "Little Gidding," the lyrics *The wounded surgeon plies the steel* and *The dove descending breaks the air,* and possibly *Time and the bell have buried the day.* Even these are more moving in their context. The experience in these poems is dramatic and brutally genuine. It is one of the very few great poems in which craftsmanship and religious depth are equal.

[1943]

II /

Two Controversial Questions

I wept when T. S. Eliot died, and yet I keep putting off writing about him. We are fed up with Eliot elucidations, summations, tributes. They are all "armed visions," expert of their kind, and the critics have said just about all they can. There will be little more, I think, until new masterpieces different from *The Waste Land* have been written and until the world has changed. Eliot now seems like the fatal first example of "the writer of works to be written about." He didn't deserve this; he was alive. I may have nothing fresh to say, and yet I will name a few things that strike me as singular and marvelous.

His influence is everywhere inescapable, and nowhere readily usable. He started with the air of an American dressed up as a Frenchman, preaching to the English. He hit British writing rather than American, wearing a Laforguean mask. As time went on Laforgue grew dimmer, but in the end it is hard to say whether Eliot is American, British, or French. His air of a slightly square *poète maudit* missionary suited no one else, though there are traces of it in Stevens and the Pound of *Mauberly*. Nor did Eliot's mixture of meter and irregularity really suit anyone else. His style of writing religious poetry was too weighty for the religious and anathema to the faithless. Eliot is seldom, if ever, as highly charged as the later Yeats, but his best poems are much longer. His best works are very long short poems, or very short long poems. All the poems have one hero, the Laforguean Prufrock, and depict one journey, from frivolity and hell to somewhere in purgatory, with one man walking, one figure drawn with heavy black lines, slightly narrow, slightly caricatured, always in motion. A destination is reached, whether it is the one intended or not. Certainly no drying up, no waste land except perhaps in the plays.

I want now to touch on two controversial questions, *The Waste Land* and Eliot's religion, and end with a brief personal impression.

What concerns me here is not the meaning of *The Waste Land*, the legitimacy of its technical method, or even primarily its importance in English poetry. Perhaps one should claim it to be no more than an inspired *cri du coeur*, and even allow with Randall Jarrell that it is a personal and idiosyncratic, though heartfelt, cry. I want rather to puzzle over the unanswerable question of whether it is really a picture of the age. It is meaningless to ask whether the picture is true, just as it would be meaningless to ask whether Shakespeare considered life to be as hideous as he showed it to be in *Lear* and *Macbeth*. Shakespeare's tragedies are his deepest thrust. They are about sterility, cruelty, and sex gone haywire, like *The Waste Land* and perhaps all literary tragedy. Of course *The Waste Land* seems in its emblematic, allegorical, New England way to be asserting more than just *a* truth. It's a symbolic key. One could easily say that *The Waste Land* was written in the wake of the horror of the First World War, while the reality that has followed surpasses any nightmare.

Yet I feel the perversity of trying to prove anything, particularly that life is any worse than it is. With all his shortcomings, Eliot in this poem has stabbed very deeply and cruelly. This wound, along with many another, is now part of our history, and it cannot be refuted like a debater's thesis. Each new writer and poet can only remember and forget, and make his own gentler or worse and inevitably different try.

I want to use a comparison to get at Eliot's religion. In my lifetime probably the greatest American writer has been William Faulkner. When Faulkner is set against his equals—I am thinking of Mann and Pasternak—he sometimes strikes us as provincial, somewhat incoherent, and blind in some universal sense, whereas Mann and Pasternak seemed to be at the center, using the great riches of history, their age, and their nations. I don't suppose Faulkner is quite the equal of the very greatest writers. Yet now we know that his bypath, Mississippi, was no bypath but a universe. He struck obliquely and landed in the thick of things. Eliot's Christianity may, in the same way, also seem off the track, a detour and a bypath. Christianity for ages has had a spindly, undistinguished record, increasingly weak and irrelevant in fact, intelligence, and imagination.

Eliot's faith seems almost willfully crooked, dry, narrow, and hard in comparison with what I would like to describe as the toleration, hope, and intuition of Matthew Arnold's tragic liberalism. That silver age seems irrevocably gone. If Christianity seems like a bypath to most of us, Eliot's kind of Christianity seems almost worse, a bypath off a bypath. We remember his slippery wisecrack: "The spirit killeth and the letter giveth life." In his poems Eliot seems surprisingly detached from the letter or the literal, from orthodoxy. *His* letter is the agnostic's "accuracy of the written word." Christ and the Virgin are present, but only as rather icy Congregational anatomies. Yet death and rebirth are at the heart of his poems, in a rather universalist and symbolic guise that perhaps ignores any creed. Eliot has hit on one of the very few things that are still alive in religion: I don't see how man will ever quite be able to get rid of purification, contemplation, and rebirth. Our orthodox sciences—sociology, social reform, psychiatry—and our orthodox prophets—Freud and Marx—still leave this loophole; alas, they must.

As a man, Eliot was lovable. He did the usual good works of little and great attentions, standing up for his values, reading manuscripts, giving piercing and modest guidance, giving endless hours. He had a way of his own of knowing his limits. People have named the time he lived in after him and called him the leader. A strange leader, one who gave thousands of speechless hours to listening to brilliant monologuists. He took a crooked pleasure in this martyrdom, and he was perhaps too intolerant of egotistical exuberance, which is after all one of the glories of life. Yet how dangerous. In America almost all our gods coarsen into giants or shrivel into hollow men. Eliot did neither. His fierceness was restrained, his dullness was never more than the possum's feigned death.

I have never met anyone more brilliant, or anyone who tried so hard to use his brilliance modestly and honestly. One could go on for a long time recalling his gentle, unobtrusive acts of kindness. I would like rather to recall two harsh companionable moments of honesty.

Sometimes Eliot's list of wearying great men seemed all-inclusive. One, by no means the most trying, was Robert Frost. For long years Frost enjoyed taking lecture-hall swipes at Eliot, the "great British poet from St. Louis," etc. Later Frost eased up and toward the end of both their lives rather set his heart on having Eliot to dinner in Cambridge, Mass. Eliot whittled the dinner down to tea or cocktails. After it was over, I asked him how it went. I can see and hear him very well now: a sidelong smirk, then a slow, deep, weary "Oh, you know." Then Eliot's eyes glistened with delight and joy: "You have to watch yourself with the old man, he is very *wicked*."

Eliot never condescended to young people he liked, or made them feel like hayseeds or just numbers. When I was about twenty-five, I met him for the second time. Behind us, Harvard's Memorial Hall with its wasteful, irreplaceable Victorian architecture and scrolls of the Civil War dead. Before us, the rush-hour traffic. As we got stuck on the sidewalk, looking for an opening, Eliot out of a blue sky said, "Don't you loathe being compared with your relatives?" Pause, as I put the question to myself, groping for what I really felt, for what I should decently feel and what I should indecently feel. Eliot: "I do." Pause again, then the changed lifting voice of delight. "I was reading Poe's reviews the other day. He took up two of my family and wiped the floor with them." Pause. "I was delighted."

[1965]

I. A. Richards

On the back cover of his new poems, *Goodbye Earth*,
there is a startling photograph of Richards—heavy socks, climber's knickerbockers, sleeves rolled up, shirt open at the throat. He
is at some halfway point in the Swiss Alps, leaning on his up-
ended pick, which is, like a prisoner's ball-and-chain, penitentially
attached to his belt. In the mountains one feels free, yes, but a
mountain climber is also enslaved. Even now, taking his breather,
and resting before his Byronic scenery as if it were a landscape
he had painted, he knows he should be moving on. The next lap,
the middle foreground's attractively gullied and evergreen rise, is
not a picture—it is a problem. Beyond and above, and really, as
in the photograph, just an arm's swing away, the absolute ma-
lignly beckons. Bald, treeless peaks, lifeless as the mountains on
a relief map, spread the sail-like mirage of their deadness. Malign,
too, and seepingly present, though unrepresented here, is the
other busy, lower world of routine, duties, books, interviews, and
chairs. In this "sporting" photograph, the narrowed eyes and
cheek shadows of the climber's face have a down-dragging gravity. The obstinate chin, the toughness, the knowledge, the
muscle—goodbye earth at last! Nearly a lifetime it took. Richards's first book of poetry is also the first of its kind.

"How difficult and delicate a task even the mere mechanism

of verse is, may be conjectured from the failure of those who have attempted to write verse late in life." Coleridge wrote this sentence, fortunately forced to "conjecture," for the pains and ineptitudes of the late beginner were among the few he never experienced. Compared with these, Coleridge's anguish for his decaying inspiration was commonplace and tolerable. *Goodbye Earth* was begun when Richards was nearly sixty. It bristles with the difficulties of "mere mechanism," and is unique in not providing another exhibit of failure.

The theorist shifting from observation to practice is always on show and likely to become a spectacle. Poetry is almost more encumbered than furthered by the critical mind filled with sustained, subtle reasoning, high, hampering criteria, fierce crotchets, and the sublime whir of favorite quotations. What makes the small sporadic spouts of first-rate poetry written by the great critics peculiarly resilient is the intelligence's creased, gratuitous labors as it struggles with serpentine hesitations.

Richards writing poetry is not much like the usual good critic. He doesn't wave a heavy baton, castigate the indulgences of the age, or try to build classical and exemplary models of rightness. He doesn't steel himself, entrench, and give an impression of unbelievable toils met. He is willing to be conventional, casual, and innocent, if he can be ingenious and himself. Though worlds apart from the slovenly, egotistical sprawl of the bohemian, he glories in ingenuity.

On Richards's front cover, the black-and-white, abstract, yet protozoa-like disc of the yin and yang stares starkly outward, like some device for testing astigmatism. His preface drops a phrase about recent "improved techniques for the exposition of structure," teasingly twits Poe for his failure to give his promised "step-by-step" description of how a "composition attained its ultimate point of completion," then the question is breezily tossed aside. Poems are prefaced by long, deep, and curious quotations; in the appendix, notes explain alternate meanings of words, and give more long, deep, and curious quotations. The poems themselves are loaded with steep reasoning, archaic words, technical terms, slang, special knowledge, and cunningly exploded echoes from other literature. Often teacher, sage, idealist, and humorist huddle in one line—all elbowing and gouging for dominance. Fascinated by a poem's moments, one often has no idea of what it means.

> *In perpetuity*
> *Be here their prayer*:
> > *May* may *become*
> > *While* would *would waft*
> > *Or let* let *be*
> *Our sum   our raft   our quay.*

On one level, these lines are the joyful light fingerwork of a puzzle; on another, they ache with the growing pains of apprenticeship. An almost impossibly forbidding fancy for a poem to make a prayer out of is given an almost impossibly difficult metrical hurdle. The repetitions bang, the three rhyme words in the last line have a blasé disjunctiveness, *waft* is coyly archaic, *let* seems to split into two contradictory and emotionally annihilating meanings. Even here, however, I feel an airy assurance and the amused didactic modesty of authentic style.

About half of Richards's poems are very hard. He has a Welsh streak that loves to jangle words in the manner of Dylan Thomas and to give simple passions a dazzling crackle. Beyond this his mind, brimming with semantics, philosophy, physics, and strange bits of information, is miraculously quick and subtle. He is perhaps the only poet since Empson who deserves to be difficult intellectually and is even forced to be. His harder poems are too jerky, twisted, and abstract to quite come off. They are pioneering drives, grappling with new intractable material—now getting in a sure, devastating thrust, now rocking apart. Perhaps success and failure are irrelevant. What remains and matters is the gallantry and doggedness of the mind refusing to desert its customary tools and targets, its promise to stay standing in the arena of the impossible.

The weight of this battle with abstraction seems to give greater force and delicacy to the many poems and parts of poems where Richards is passionate and direct.

HARVARD YARD IN APRIL: APRIL IN HARVARD YARD

To and fro
Across the fretted snow
Figures, footprints, shadows go.
Their python boughs a-sway
The fountain elms cascade
In swinging lattices of shade
Where this or that or the other thought
Might perch and rest.
       And rest they ought
For poise or reach.
Not all is timely. See, the beech,
In frosty elephantine skin
Still winter-sealed, will not begin
Though silt the alleys hour on hour
Debris of the fallen flower,
And other flowery allure
Lounge sunlit on the Steps and there
Degrees of loneliness confer.

Lest, lest . . . away!
You may
  Be lost by May.

This flashes and zigzags like a hummingbird. The high points of poise are in the form, stiff, firm, yet improvisatory, the slyness in hiding the college girls under "flowery allure," the strange, glistening description, airy yet meticulous, the marvelous shaded pause of "And rest they ought," etc. As Richards darts with his own unrivaled *élan* from the momentary to the absolute, his wavering, intricate, modern mind is joined to an old, joyful simplicity.

He can put speculation, cosmic and grand enough for Lucretius, in a stanza that some late, rather Alexandrian troubadour might have invented as a problem of metrical acrobatics.

> *Balanced up somehow on a ball*
>   *That spins*
>   *And spirals*
>   *As it plummets*
> *Newton walked to Stourbridge Fair*
>   *And bought his prism*
> *That was to fell the founding wall*
>   *Undo the*
>   *All*
>   *Renew the*
>   *Fall*
>   *Bound through all limits*
> *And far and here declare*
>   *The mere abysm.*

No other form could have encompassed this reasoning and given it the right tone of litheness and lightness and spellbinding daring and flat amusement. It is like attending a scientific experiment, one that can be performed only once.

[1960]

Visiting the Tates

April 1937—I was wearing the last summer's mothballish, already soiled white linens, and moccasins, knotted so that they never had to be tied or untied. What I missed along the road from Nashville to Clarksville was the Eastern seaboard's thin fields chopped by stone walls and useless wilderness of scrub. Instead, plains of treeless farmland, and an unnatural, unseasonable heat. Gushers of it seemed to spout over the bumpy, sectioned concrete highway, and bombard the horizon. Midway, a set of Orientally shapely and conical hills. It was like watching a Western and waiting for a wayside steer's skull and the bleaching ribs of a covered wagon.

My head was full of Miltonic, vaguely piratical ambitions. My only anchor was a suitcase, heavy with bad poetry. I was brought to earth by my bumper mashing the Tates' frail agrarian mailbox post. Getting out to disguise the damage, I turned my back on their peeling, pillared house. I had crashed the civilization of the South.

The Tates were stately yet bohemian, leisurely yet dedicated. A schoolboy's loaded .22 rifle hung under the Confederate flag over their fireplace. A reproduced sketch of Leonardo's *Virgin of the Rocks* balanced an engraving of Stonewall Jackson. Below us, the deadwood-bordered Cumberland River was the color of wet concrete, and Mr. Norman, the token tenant, looked like slabs of his unpainted shack padded in workclothes. After an easy hour or two of regional anecdotes, Greenwich Village reminiscences, polemics on personalities, I began to discover what I had never known. I, too, was part of a legend. I was Northern, disembodied, a Platonist, a puritan, an abolitionist. Tate handed me a hand-printed, defiantly gingersnap-thin edition of his *The Mediterranean and Other Poems.* He quoted a stanza from Holmes's "Chambered Nautilus"—"rather beyond the flight of your renowned Uncle." I realized that the old deadweight of poor J. R. Lowell was now an asset. Here, like the battered Confederacy, he still lived and was history.

All the English classics, and some of the Greeks and Latins, were at Tate's elbow. He maneuvered through them, coolly blasting, rehabilitating, now and then reciting key lines in an austere, vibrant voice. Turning to the moderns, he slaughtered whole Chicago droves of slipshod Untermeyer anthology experimentalists. He felt that all the culture and tradition of the East, the South, and Europe stood behind Eliot, Emily Dickinson, Yeats, and Rimbaud. I found myself despising the rootless appetites of middle-class meliorism.

Tate said two things this afternoon that at once struck me as all but contradictory and yet self-evident. He said that he always believed each poem he finished would be his last. His second pronouncement was that a good poem had nothing to do with exalted feelings or being moved by the spirit. It was simply a piece of craftsmanship, an intelligible or *cognitive* object. As examples of cognitive objects, Tate brought forward Mr. Norman, the hand-printed edition of *The Mediterranean,* and finally a tar-black cabinet with huge earlobe-like handles. It was his own workmanship. I had supposed that crafts were repeatable skills and belonged to the pedestrian boredom of manual-training classes. However, something warped, fissured, strained, and terrific about this cabinet suggested that it would be Tate's last.

I came to the Tates' a second time. Ford Madox Ford, the object of my original visit, was now installed with his wife and secretary. Already, their trustful city habits had exhausted the only cistern. On the lawn, almost igniting with the heat, was a tangle of barked twigs in a washtub. This was Ford's Provençal dew pond. The household groaned with the fatigued valor of Southern hospitality. Ida, the colored day-help, had grown squint-eyed, balky, and aboriginal from the confusion of labors, the clash of cultures. Instantly, and with keen, idealistic, adolescent heedlessness, I offered myself as a guest. The Tates' way of refusing was to say there was no room for me unless I pitched a tent on the lawn. A few days later, I returned from Nashville with an olive Sears, Roebuck umbrella tent. I stayed three months. Every other day, I turned out grimly unromantic poems —organized, hard, and classical as a cabinet. They were very flimsy. Indoors, life was Olympian and somehow crackling. Outside, Uncle Andrew, the calf, sagged against my tent sides. I sweated enough to fill the cistern, and breathlessly, I ached for the conviction that each finished poem would be my last.

Like a torn cat, I was taken in when I needed help, and in a sense I have never left. Tate still seems as jaunty and magisterial as he did twenty years ago. His poems, all of them, even the slightest, are terribly personal. Out of splutter and shambling comes a killing eloquence. Perhaps this is the resonance of desperation, or rather the formal resonance of desperation. I say "formal" because no one has so given us the impression that poetry must be burly, must be courteous, must be tinkered with and recast until one's eyes pop out of one's head. How often something smashes through the tortured joy of composition to strike the impossible bull's-eye! The pre-Armageddon twenties and thirties with all their peculiar fears and enthusiasms throb in Tate's poetry; imitated ad infinitum, it has never been reproduced by another hand.

[1959]

Yvor Winters

Walter Bagehot begins a review of Lord Macaulay's *History of England* with this sentence, "This is a marvelous book."

I want to scrap all my impressions, pro and con, of Yvor Winters's critical theories, insights, and prejudices, and say that his *Collected Poems** is a "marvelous book." The best poems have compassion and are made of iron. In their inspiration and largeness, they surpass the works of his best disciples, Baker, Cunningham, and Bowers, they themselves excellent and honest poets. He has a Malherbes-like integrity. Ben Jonson might have written of him:

> *... he*
> *Who casts to write a living line, must sweat*
> *(Such as thine are) and strike the second heat*
> *Upon the Muses' anvil: turn the same,*
> *(And himself with it) that he thinks to frame;*
> *Or for the laurel he may gain a scorn,*
> *For a good* Poet's *made as well as born.*

---

* *Collected Poems* by Yvor Winters. Iowa: Alan Swallow, 1961.

I have been reading Winters continually since 1937. I remember a boiling day in Clarksville, Tennessee, when I came on his "Gawain and the Green Knight" in either *The Nation* or *The New Republic*. Later, I treasured his "To a Military Rifle 1942." When I was the poetry consultant at the Library of Congress in 1947 and 1948, I had the luck to listen frequently to records of Winters reading a dozen or more of his best poems: "Time and the Garden," "John Sutter," "The Marriage," "Heracles," and others. His voice and measures still ring in my ears. They pass Housman's test for true poetry—if I remembered them while shaving, I would cut myself.

Winters likes to declare himself a classicist. Dimwits have called him a conservative. He was the kind of conservative who was so original and radical that his poems were never reprinted in the anthologies for almost twenty years. Neither the avant-garde nor the vulgar had an eye for him. He was a poet so solitary that he was praised adequately only by his pupils and by Allen Tate. Yet Winters is a writer of great passion, one of the most steady rhetoricians in the language, and a stylist whose diction and metric exemplify two hundred years of American culture.

No literary critic has a greater flair than Winters for making the right quotation. I am not myself a practiced critic, and have no gift for the authoritative and lucid comment that somehow makes a quotation sail. However, my desire here is not to write a piece of reasoned analysis but to offer my admiration. I will quote a few of the passages that have most amazed me and gone to my heart.

Here is Heracles in his apotheosis and now a demigod of the Zodiac, as he ends the poem entitled "Heracles":

> *This was my grief, that out of grief I grew—*
> *Translated as I was from earth at last*
> *From the sad pain that Deianira knew.*
> *Transmuted slowly in the fiery blast,*

Perfect, and moving perfectly, I raid
Eternal silence to eternal ends:
And Deianira, an imperfect shade,
Retreats in silence as my arc descends.

A critic of Winters's friend J. V. Cunningham has called him (Cunningham) something like "the greatest modern master of the comma." The same grammarian and fan might say that Winters is the greatest modern master of the anaphora. Here are the last three stanzas of his tragic lyric on the patriarch John Sutter, who was destroyed in the mania of the California gold rush:

With knives they dug the metal out of stone;
Turned rivers back, for gold through ages piled,
Drove knives to hearts, and faced the gold alone;
Valley and river ruined and reviled;

Reviled and ruined me, my servant slew,
Strangled him from the figtree by my door.
When they had done what fury bade them do,
I was a cursing beggar, stripped and sore.

What end impersonal, what breathless age,
Incontinent of quiet and of years,
What calm catastrophe will yet assuage
This final drouth of penitential tears?

Here is part of his lovely poem "The Marriage":

We fed our minds on every mortal thing,
The lacy fronds of carrots in the spring,
Their flesh sweet on the tongue, the salty wine
From bitter grapes, which gathered through the vine

The mineral drouth of autumn concentrate . . .
All this to pass, not to return again.
And when I found your flesh did not resist,
It was the living spirit that I kissed,
It was the spirit's change in which I lay:
Thus, mind in mind we waited for the day.
When flesh shall fall away, and falling, stand
Wrinkling with shadow over face and hand,
Still I shall meet you on the verge of dust
And know you as a faithful vestige must.
And, in commemoration of our lust,
May our heirs seal us in a single urn,
A single spirit never to return.

Finally, I want to quote "A Dream Vision," Winters's last poem
and his most personal, a magnificently defiant and meek confession of his life and practice:

What was all the talk about?
This was something to decide.
It was not that I had died.
Though my plans were new, no doubt,
There was nothing to deride.

I had grown away from youth,
Shedding error where I could;
I was now essential wood,
Concentrating into truth;
What I did was small but good.

Orchard tree beside the road,
Bare to core, but living still!
Moving little was my skill.
I could hear the farting toad
Shifting to observe the kill,

Spotted sparrow, spawn of dung,
Mumbling on a horse's turd,
Bullfinch, wren or mockingbird
Screaming with a pointed tongue
Objurgation without word.

Surely, Yvor Winters is an immortal poet, a poet of great kindness and stamina.

[1961]

Robert Penn Warren's
Brother to Dragons

In spite of its Plutarchan decor, *Brother to Dragons* is a brutal, perverse melodrama that makes the flesh crawl. On a chopping block in a meat house in West Kentucky, "on the night of December 15, 1811—the night when the New Madrid earthquake first struck the Mississippi Valley—" Lilburn and Isham Lewis, nephews of Thomas Jefferson, in the presence of their Negroes, "butchered a slave named George, whose offense had been to break a pitcher prized by their dead mother, Lucy Lewis." Coming upon this preface, the reader is warned that he will not find Monticello and Jefferson with his letters from John Adams, his barometers and portable music stands, but Lizzie Borden braining the family portraits with her ax. This incongruity, which dislocates nearly everyone's sense of Jeffersonian possibility, was fully appreciated by Thomas Jefferson himself, who, so far as we know, never permitted his nephews' accomplishment to be mentioned in conversation. Yet the Lewis brothers are as much in the Southern tradition as their uncle, rather more in the literary tradition which has developed, and so it is workaday that their furies should pursue them with homicidal chivalry, the pomp of Vestal Virgins—and the murk of Warren's four novels. Indeed, these monstrous heroes are so extremely *literary* that their actual lives seem to have been imagined by anti-romantic Southern moderns, and we are tempted to suppose that only gratuitous caprice caused Warren to blame their bestiality on the Deist idealism of their detached relative, Thomas, the first Democratic President. Portentous in their living characters, when Lilburn and Isham Lewis reach in 1953 their first artistic existence, they draw upon a long line of conventions established by their imaginary counterparts: it is as true inheritors that they speak a mixture of Faulkner's iron courtesies, country dialect, and Booth's *sic semper*. Like their ancestor Cain, these latecomers were prior to their poetic fulfillment. The disharmony between the brothers' high connections and their low conduct, however, is less astonishing than Warren's ability to make all his characters speak in unfaltering, unstilted blank verse. (I trust it is this Jeffersonian and noble technical feat, and not the lurid prose melodrama, which has three times caused me to read *Brother to Dragons* from cover to cover without stopping.)

The generals' war between the specialized arts and the specialized sciences is over. We have accepted our traumatically self-conscious and expert modern poetry, just as we have accepted our other perilous technological methods. Eternal providence has warned us that our world lies all before us and nowhere else. Only the fissured atoms which destroyed Hiroshima and Nagasaki can build our New Atlantis. This is what Paul Valéry meant when he wrote with cruel optimism that poetry before Mallarmé was as arithmetic to algebra. Valéry's education was more diversified than ours, and he wrote in a time when men still remembered the old Newtonian universe. We cannot be certain that we even understand the terms of his equation, but as poets and pragmatists we approve. Back in the palmy imperialist days of Victoria, Napoleon's nephew, and Baudelaire, a kind of literary concordant was reached: the ephemeral was ceded to prose. Since then the new poetry has been so scrupulous and electrical, its authors seem seldom to have regretted this Mary-and-Martha division of labor. Poetry became all that was not prose. Under this dying-to-the-world discipline, the stiffest and most matter-of-fact items were repoeticized—quotations from John of the Cross, usury, statistics, conversations, and newspaper clippings. These amazing new poems could absorb everything—everything, that is, except plot and characters, just those things long poems usually relied upon. When modern poets have tried to write dramatic and narrative works, neither genius, shrewdness, nor the most defiant goodwill have prevented most of the attempts from being puffy, paralyzed, and pretentious. Outside of Browning, what nineteenth-century story poems do we still read? What poetic dramas since Dryden and Milton? Are Eliot's three plays, Auden's *Age of Anxiety*, Robinson's narratives, or Hardy's *Dynasts* much better? Yeats's later plays and Frost's monologues are short. Shorter still and more fragmentary are the moments of action and dialogue in *The Waste Land* and Pound's *Cantos*. Here stubborn parsimony is life-preserving tact. But *Brother to Dragons*, though tactless and voluminous, is also alive. That Warren, one of the bosses of the New Criticism, is the author is as though Professor Babbitt had begotten Rousseau or a black Minerva dancing in Congo masks. Warren has written his best book, a big book; he has crossed the Alps and, like Napoleon's shoeless army, entered the fat, populated river bottom of the novel.

Brother to Dragons is the fourth remarkable long poem to have been published in the last ten or twelve years. *Four Quartets*, *Paterson*, and the *Pisan Cantos* are originals and probably the masterpieces of their authors. Warren's poem is slighter, lighter, and less in earnest. This judgment, however, is ungrateful and misleading. *Brother to Dragons* is a model and an opportunity. It can be imitated without plagiarism, and one hopes its matter and its method will become common property. In a sense they are already, and anyone who has read Elizabethan drama and Browning will quickly have opinions on what he likes and dislikes in this new work.

There *are* faults in this work. Warren writes in his preface: "I have tried to make my poem make, in a thematic way, historical sense along with whatever other kind of sense it may be happy enough to make." And more emphatically: "A poem dealing with history is no more at liberty to violate what the writer takes to be the spirit of his history than it is at liberty to violate what the writer takes to be the nature of the human heart." Obviously, the kind of historical sense claimed here is something more serious and subtle than the mere documentary accuracy required for a tableau of Waterloo or a romance set in 1812. The incidents in *Brother to Dragons* are so ferocious and subnormal they make *Macbeth* or Racine's *Britannicus* seem informal interludes in Castiglione's *Courtier*. Warren's tale is fact, but it is too good melodramatically to be true. To make sense out of such material he uses an arrangement of actors and commentators, a method he perhaps derived from Delmore Schwartz's *Coriolanus*, in which Freud, Aristotle, and, I believe, Marx sit and discuss a performance of Shakespeare's play. Warren's spirit of history has a rough time: occasionally it maunders in a void, sometimes it sounds like the spirit of Seneca's rhetoric, again it just enjoys the show. The difficulties are great, yet the commentary often increases one's feelings of pathetic sympathy.

As for the characters, nothing limits the length of their speeches except the not very importunate necessity of eventually completing the story. Warren improves immensely upon that grotesque inspiration which compels Browning to tell the plot of the *Ring* twelve times and each time in sections longer than *Macbeth*. Structurally, however, Browning's characters have the queer compositional advantage of *knowing* they are outrageously called to sustain set pieces of a given length.

A few small points: Warren's bawdy lines—I sometimes think these are pious gestures, a sort of fraternity initiation, demanded, given, to establish the writer firmly outside the genteel tradition. Secondly, the word *definition* is used some fifty times. This appears to be a neo-Calvinist pun, meaning defined, finite, and perhaps definitive and final, or "know thyself for thou art but dust." Warren used this word in his short poems and fiction and in an obsessive way I'm not quite able to follow. Time and History: the poet addresses these ogres with ritualistic regularity, reminding us a bit of a Roman proconsul imposing the Greek gods on the provinces, those gods which have already renounced the world in Eliot's *Four Quartets*.

Some stylistic matters: The hollow bell-sound repetition of

> *I think of another bluff and another river.*
> *I think of another year and another winter.*
> *I think of snow on the brown leaves, and below*
> *That other bluff, how cold and far was light on that northern*
> *river.*
> *I think of how her mouth and mine together*
> *Were cold on the first kiss. Sparsely, snow*
> *Descended among the black trees. We kissed in the cold*
> *Logic of hope and need.*

Passages of stage-direction blank verse, not bad in themselves (squeamishness in absorbing prose would have been crippling) but sometimes "sinking," like a suddenly audible command from the prompter's pit:

> *From an undifferentiated impulse I leaned*
> *Above the ruin in my hand picked up*
> *Some two or three pig-nuts, with the husk yet on.*
> *I put them in my pocket. I went down.*

And these Thersites screams which modern writing channels on its readers like televised wrestlers:

> *and in that simultaneous outrage*
> *The sunlight screamed, while urine splattered the parched*
> *soil.*

Brother to Dragons triumphs through its characters, most of all through two women. Lucy and Laetitia Lewis, Lilburn's mother and wife, charm and overwhelm. They are as lovingly and subtly drawn as some women in Browning. Laetitia, the more baffled and pathetic, uses homely frontier expressions, and her speeches beautifully counterpoint those of the intelligent and merciful Lucy. Unlike the heroines in Warren's novels, those schizophrenic creatures more unflattering to womankind than anything in Pope, Lucy Lewis is both wise and good and proves Warren's point that neither quality can flourish without the other. Both women speak simple and straightforward blank verse, which is wonderfully emphasized by the messy rhetorical violence of the other speakers. As for Lilburn and Isham Lewis, Warren takes them as he finds them: ruins. Lilburn, the villain-protagonist, is a lobotomized Coriolanus, or rather, that hollow, diabolic, Byron–Cain character who is so familiar to us from Warren's novels. He speaks few lines and is seen through the other speakers, because he is almost pure evil and therefore unreal. He sheds a sinister, absorbing glitter, which is probably all he was intended to do. Neither Ahab nor Satan, Lilburn is simply Lilburn—a histrionic void. Isham, Lilburn's younger brother and the subordinate villain, is a cowed imbecile. He is a sturdy, evil, stupefied Laetitia. Unlike Lilburn, he is pure Kentucky and has no Virginian memories. (In *Brother to Dragons*, when the characters pass from Virginia to Kentucky they experience an immense social decline, as if this latter state were a "bad address." The Kentuckians are Elizabethan rustics, all a bit clownish and amazed to be speaking in meter.) Isham is drawn with amusement and horror, although as a key witness he needs a great deal of help from Warren's superior understanding of his own actions. The minor characters are quickly summarized: Dr. Lewis, the father, is shadowy; Aunt Cat is a mask; Laetitia's brother is a mildly amusing "humor," the sort of appendage who stands about, scratching his head and saying, "I'm a simple country fellow." Meriwether Lewis seems altogether out of place in the work.

Jefferson! An original—mean, pale, sour, spoon-riverish! Hardy's Sinister Spirit. In the end, this Robespierre in a tub is converted by Lucy to a higher idealism, to "definition." (The Democrats are out of office, and so perhaps Warren will not suffer public assault because of this black apotheosis.)

Finally there is R.P.W., the author, who speaks at greater

length than any of the other characters and with greater imagination, power, and intelligence. He is Pilgrim, Everyman, Chorus, and Warren, the real person, who like everyone has his own birthplace, parents, personal memories, taste, etc. It is his problem to face, understand, and even to justify a world which includes moronic violence. As with Hugo at the beginning of *Le Fin de Satan,* the crucial catastrophic act is not the eating of the apple but the murder of Abel. Warren suggests that the pursuit of knowledge leads to a split in body and spirit, and consequently to "idealism," and consequently to an inability to face or control the whole of life, and consequently to murder. He is concerned with evil and with the finiteness of man. I'm not sure of Warren's position but it is often close to neo-Humanism and neo-Thomism, and so deliberately close that he frequently suffers from hardness. Yet sometimes you feel he is taking the opposite position and is merely a commonsense, secular observer. The character R.P.W., as we see him in the poem, is himself split between a love for abstractions and an insatiable appetite for sordid detail, as though Allen Tate were rewriting Stavrogin's "Confession." R.P.W. has his own troubles with "definition." The two halves embarrass each other: the character is at once unreal and again irresistibly energetic. I quote a passage—for its power rather than as an expression of character:

> *Well, standing there, I'd felt, I guess, the first*
> *Faint tremor of that natural chill, but then*
> *In some black aperture among the stones*
> *I saw the eyes, their glitter in that dark,*
> *And suddenly the head thrust forth, and the fat, black*
> *Body molten flowed, as though those stones*
> *Bled forth earth's inner darkness to the day,*
> *As though the bung had broke on that intolerable*
>   *inwardness.*
> *And now divulged, thus focused and compacted,*
> *What haunts beneath earth's primal, soldered sill,*
> *And in its slow and merciless ease, sleepless, lolls*
> *Below that threshold where the prime waters sleep.*

Thus it flowed forth, and the scaled belly of abomination
Rustled on stone, rose up
And reared in regal indolence and swag.
I saw it rise, saw the soiled white of the belly bulge,
And in that muscular distention I saw the black side scales
Show their faint flange and tracery of white.
And so it rose and climbed the paralysed light.
On those heaped stones it was taller than I, taller
Than any man, and the swollen head hung
Haloed and high in light; when in that splendid
Nimb the hog-snout parted, and with girlish
Fastidiousness the faint tongue flicked to finick in the sun.

Of course Warren is a remarkable novelist, yet I cannot help feeling that this strange metrical novel is his true medium. It has kept the unique readability of fiction, a charm which is almost always absent from long poems. In this at least, *Brother to Dragons* is superior to any of the larger works of Browning. And yet Warren almost *is* Browning. What this may mean is suggested by an observation by Gide: "Browning and Dostoevsky seem to me to bring the monologue straightaway to perfection, in all the diversity and subtlety to which this literary form lends itself. Perhaps I shock the literary sense of some of my audience by coupling these two names, but I can do no other, nor help being struck by the profound resemblance, not merely in form, but in substance." After reading *Brother to Dragons*, I feel not only that Warren has written a successful poem but that in this work he most truly seems to approach the power of those writers one has always felt hovering about him, those poetic geniuses of prose, Melville and Faulkner. In Warren's case, it is the prose genius in verse which is so startling.

[1953]

Auden at Sixty

Auden's work and career are like no one else's, and have helped us all. He has been very responsible and ambitious in his poetry and criticism, constantly writing deeply on the big subjects, and yet keeping something wayward, eccentric, idiosyncratic, charming, and his own. Much hard, ingenious, correct toil has gone into inconspicuous things: introductions, anthologies, and translations. When one looks at them closely, one is astonished at how well they have been done.

In his twenties, he was already one of our best and most original poets. For long years, he has lived with that genius, never betraying it, or exploiting it, but always adding and varying, a discoverer and a sustainer. His inspiration seems almost as versatile as his styles and his metrical forms, yet I am most grateful for three or four supreme things: the sad Anglo-Saxon alliteration of his beginnings, his prophecies that seemed the closest voice to our disaster, then the marvelous crackle of his light verse and broadside forms, small fires made into great in his hands, and finally for a kind of formal poem that combines a breezy baroque grandeur with a sophisticated Horatian simplicity.

Last winter, John Crowe Ransom said to me that we had made an even exchange when we lost Eliot to England and later gained Auden. Both poets have been kind to the lands of their exile, and brought gifts the natives could never have conceived of.

[1967]

Elizabeth Bishop's
North & South

Nothing more unlike what I have been reviewing [Dylan Thomas's poems] could be imagined than the unrhetorical, cool, and beautifully thought-out poems of Elizabeth Bishop in *North & South*. To some readers, and to all readers at first, their inspiration will appear comparatively modest. Her admirers are not likely to hail her as a giant among the moderns, or to compare anything that she will ever write with Shakespeare or Donne. Nevertheless, the splendor and minuteness of her descriptions soon seem wonderful. Later one realizes that her large, controlled, and elaborate common sense is always or almost always absorbed in its subjects, and that she is one of the best craftsmen alive.

On the surface, her poems are observations—surpassingly accurate, witty, and well arranged, but nothing more. Sometimes she writes of a place where she has lived on the Atlantic Coast; at others, of a dream, a picture, or some fantastic object. One is reminded of Kafka and certain abstract paintings, and is left rather at sea about the actual subjects of the poems. I think that at least nine-tenths of them fall into a single symbolic pattern. Characterizing it is an elusive business.

There are two opposing factors. The first is something in motion, weary but persisting, almost always failing and on the

point of disintegrating, and yet, for the most part, stoically maintained. This is morality, memory, the weed that grows to divide,
and the dawn that advances, illuminates, and calls to work, the
monument "that wants to be a monument," the waves rolling in
on the shore, breaking, and being replaced, the echo of the
hermit's voice saying, "Love must be put in action"; it is the
stolid little mechanical horse that carries a dancer, and all those
things of memory that "cannot forget us half so easily as they can
forget themselves." The second factor is a terminus: rest, sleep,
fulfillment, or death. This is the imaginary iceberg, the moon
which the Man-moth thinks is a small clean hole through which
he must thrust his head; it is sleeping on the top of a mast, and
the peaceful ceiling: "But oh, that we could sleep up there."

The motion-process is usually accepted as necessary and,
therefore, good; yet it is dreary and exhausting. But the formula
is mysterious and gently varies with its objects. The terminus is
sometimes pathetically or humorously desired as a letting-go or
annihilation; sometimes it is fulfillment and the complete harmonious exercise of one's faculties. The rainbow of spiritual
peace seen as the author decides to let a fish go, is both like and
unlike the moon which the Man-moth mistakes for an opening.
In "A Large Bad Picture," ships are at anchor in a northern bay,
and the author reflects, "It would be hard to say what brought
them there/Commerce or contemplation."

The structure of a Bishop poem is simple and effective. It
will usually start as description or descriptive narrative, then
either the poet or one of her characters or objects reflects. The
tone of these reflections is pathetic, witty, fantastic, or shrewd.
Frequently, it is all these things at once. Its purpose is to heighten
and dramatize the description and, at the same time, to unify
and universalize it. In this, and in her marvelous command of
shifting speech tones, Bishop resembles Robert Frost.

In her bare objective language, she also reminds one at times
of William Carlos Williams; but it is obvious that her most important model is Marianne Moore. Her dependence should not
be defined as imitation, but as one of development and transformation. It is not the dependence of her many facile contempo-

raries on Auden, but the dependence of Herrick on Jonson, the Herberts on Donne, or of Pope and Johnson on Dryden. Although Bishop would be unimaginable without Moore, her poems add something to the original, and are quite as genuine. Both poets use an elaborate descriptive technique, love exotic objects, are moral, genteel, witty, and withdrawn. There are metrical similarities, and a few of Bishop's poems are done in Moore's manner. But the differences in method and personality are great. Bishop is usually present in her poems; they happen to her, she speaks, and often centers them on herself. Others are dramatic and have human actors. She uses dreams and allegories. (Like Kafka's, her treatment of the absurd is humorous, matter-of-fact, and logical.) She hardly ever quotes from other writers. Most of her meters are accentual-syllabic. Compared with Moore, she is softer, dreamier, more human, and more personal; she is less idiosyncratic, and less magnificent. She is probably slighter; of course, being much younger, she does not yet have nearly so many extraordinarily good poems.

Bishop's faults leave her best poems uninjured, and I do not need to examine them at length. A few of the shorter poems seem to me quite trivial. On rereading them, one is struck by something a little pert, banal, and overpointed—it is as though they had been simplified for a child. Occasionally the action seems blurred and foggy, especially when she is being most subjective, as in "Anaphora." In others, such as "The Map," "Casabianca," and "The Gentleman from Shallot," she is self-indulgent, and strings a whimsical commentary on an almost nonexistent subject.

Few books of lyrics are as little repetitious as North & South. It can be read straight through with excitement. About ten of its thirty poems are failures. Another ten are either unsatisfactory as wholes, or very slight. This leaves "Roosters" and "The Fish," large and perfect, and, outside of Marianne Moore, the best poems that I know of written by a woman in this century. The first of her "Songs for a Colored Singer" is serious light verse; it is of the same quality as MacNeice's "Bagpipe Music" and

Auden's wonderful "Refugee Blues." In roughly descending order, "The Monument," "The Man-Moth," "The Weed," "Cirque d'Hiver," "A Large Bad Picture," "Sleeping on the Ceiling," the second "Song for a Colored Singer," "Jeronimo's House," "Florida," "Seascape," and "Quai d'Orléans" are all wonderfully successful and good. Bishop's poems are so carefully fitted together, her descriptions give such body to her reflections, and her reflections so heighten her description that it is hard to indicate her stature and solidity by quotation. I will give a few stanzas from a poem published since her book. Faustina is a black servant, and her mistress is dying:

> *Tended by Faustina*
> *yes in a crazy house*
> *upon a crazy bed,*
> *frail, of chipped enamel,*
> *blooming above her head*
> *into four vaguely rose-like*
> *flower-formations,*
>
> *the white woman whispers to*
> *herself. The floor-boards sag*
> *this way and that. The crooked*
> *towel-covered table*
> *bears a can of talcum*
> *and five pasteboard boxes*
> *of little pills,*
>
> *most half-crystallized.*

Then as Faustina bends her "sinister kind face" over the white woman, the poet reflects:

> *Oh, is it*
>
> *freedom at last, a lifelong*
> *dream of time and silence,*

dream of protection and rest?
Or is it the very worst,
the unimaginable nightmare
that never before dared last
        more than a second?

[1947]

Stanley Kunitz's "Father and Son"

I suppose the fashion of looking very, very closely at poems began with *The Waste Land*. This poem was widely attacked as immoral non-sense. Many who liked it found it complex yet unintelligible. The author's footnotes had a breezy, pedantic dash to them that was in itself a warning. They assumed more knowledge than most readers had, yet everywhere in their inadequacy pointed to more work to be done: myths to be pondered, symbols to be harmonized, books to be read. Soon there was a crackling controversy among the admirers of *The Waste Land*, as to whether it was religious, anti-religious, or without beliefs. Long analytical essays began to appear; soon this kind of writing spread, and everything, ancient and modern, was being explained.

Eliot seemed to gaze on this new industry from the background, a friendly god, silent and brooding. But when he broke silence, his remarks were far from helpful. The footnotes, faithfully reprinted according to the author's wishes in each new anthologizing of *The Waste Land*, turned out to be a publisher's afterthought, a trick to make a book out of a poem that was too short to be one. Far from being a devotee of analysis, it seemed that Eliot read it, if at all, with weary, incredulous amazement. Commenting on a book of close critical studies of "the poem," he had many doubts and ended by saying that such writings certainly didn't make for very interesting reading.

Analysis doesn't make for interesting reading. Few of us, I imagine, spend much time poring over *The Explicator*, that solid, dull little publication where poems are processed into monthly exegesis. Analysis is necessary for teaching poems, and for student papers. Still, somehow, nothing very fresh or to the point is said. One knows ahead of time how the machine will grind. Conventionality has overtaken the industry; nothing new is set up, nothing bad is destroyed. There is even a kind of modern poem, now produced in bulk, that seems written to be explained. Training and labor are required for such efforts, but this can't be the way good poems are written. Inspiration, passion, originality, and even technical assurance must be something that can't be produced in bulk, or merely by training and labor. Nor can good criticism be produced by training and labor and conventionality.

Dullness and the sad, universal air of the graduate schools have descended on close literary criticism. Once it was far otherwise. I can remember when the early essays on *The Waste Land*, the first editions of the Brooks and Warren *Understanding Poetry*, and Blackmur's pieces on Stevens and Marianne Moore came as a revelation. The world was being made anew. Nothing, it seemed, had ever really been read. Old writings, once either neglected or simplified and bowdlerized into triteness, were now for the first time seen as they were. New writing that met the new challenges was everywhere painfully wrestling itself into being. Poetry was still unpopular, but it seemed as though Arnold's "immense future" for literature and particularly poetry was being realized. Here, for a few, was religion and reality.

Perhaps all this was only my adolescent fever. A glow seems to be gone, but perhaps this was just my illusion. Perhaps there never was a glow; more likely, it is still there and yearly seizes new writers and new critics. For me, anyway, the fever is a chronic malaria. I will never quite disbelieve that the world is being remade by the new ways of writing and careful reading. With this admission, I feel in the right mood of warmth and naïveness to start looking closely at Stanley Kunitz's poem "Father and Son." However, I really doubt the possibilities of the method, and even more my own talents for it.

"Father and Son" is a modern poem, one that has obviously been through the new mill and the new training. Yet when read, say twice, there seems to be an embarrassing lack of difficulty. The theme, a son looking for his dead father, must have existed in the time of Cain. The fact of the experience seems so closely joined and identical with its unavoidable symbolic reverbera- tions that it would be banal and schoolteacherish to point them out. The pathos and dignity of expression are as open and ap- parent as such things are in ordinary conversation. The meter is a tolerably regular blank verse.

My first questions are cheating personal ones that mean much to me, but which are no doubt uncritical and unanswer- able by careful reading. I want to know if Kunitz and his own father are the father and son. Is the countryside the country around Worcester, Massachusetts, where Kunitz grew up and I went to boarding school? What happened to the sister? What's the point of the pond? Did the father drown himself, or was his favorite sport fishing or wading for water bugs? *Gemara* seems to be some Torah appendage to the Bible. Some sort of lonely pilgrimage? An experience of bitter purging? But I really don't know, and have no books or knowledgeable people to consult. The word *Gemara* and the poem's tone seem to say it is per- sonal. So, I say yes to most of my questions except the suicide. The pond must somehow touch on the remembered father, and is a puff of blue smoke from everyone's childhood, when ponds, water lilies, and nature were closer and more demandingly mys- terious. The sister is nowhere, an intentional question mark.

A few hard expressions stand out. "A sweet curdle of fields!" Fields don't curdle, curdle is somehow the opposite of sweet. Here is the journey in a phrase. The pathos is in its hard sterility, it's a curdle because no such journey can really be made. Finding the dead father is a pipe dream. Nothing could be more natural or idly futile. The only sand on such a road must be like "bone-dust." "The secret master of my blood" is a stern expression of filial piety. This, too, is hard, unconfessable, tyrannical, and in the terrible nature of things. And this particular father in life loved with a kind of love that was indomitable for him but "chains" for his son. Then several natural and impossible things happen: one strides down years, the fields are fields of childhood, the silence unrolls. Then comes an odd, violent phrase, the night nailed like an orange to the son's brow. Perhaps this is Baudelaire's "old orange squeezed dry," but oranges can be squeezed, they are not nailed. I think of the kind of contradiction I am now familiar with, a mush of obscurity and impossibility nailed to one by necessity, the inescapably absent and unshakable father. Is the orange a sop for a headache savagely nailed to the brow it is supposed to soothe? A grim, jocular reference to the Crucifixion, the torture that saves for believers, and here made low and foolish?

In the next section, three things stop me: the life that has become so unreal and meaningful that it is a *fable*, the hill so figuratively easy and literally impossible to climb *under* (Is it for warmth? Is it to get totally away from the light that is now gone, a kind of death for the son and one that has long been hinted at?), and the somehow reproachful, stoical hysteria of "I'm alone and never shed a tear."

In the last section, the son "whirling between two wars" reminds me of a remark made by Mary McCarthy in an essay. She says that in our nuclear age it is impossible to write as Jane Austen and Tolstoy did about what we know. A house is no longer simply a house, a man is no longer simply a man in a town. The inhuman, unreal, smashing universal is always at our elbow. All must signify and ache with the unnatural and necessary nightmare. The "white ignorant hollow of his face" is the skull, the always known unattainableness of the search and a kind of answer and reassurance. The search must be tried, though one knows that nothing solid can be touched.

Many of the things I like about this poem are simple things hardly worth remarking on but genuine and precious. They are the suburbs, the stucco house, the sister who marries as a matter of course and is not heard of as a matter of course. There's a curious distance, vagueness, and dignity about the house on the hill with light but not enough warmth, and whose light fails, marriage in our wandering world perhaps and no doubt. This is our world, none of it can be put away or expunged any more than boyhood, the need to yearn, and the fact that we are all sons of someone, who is as he was. There's a boyish coziness, innocence, and hopelessness to the turtles and water lilies. The lines after *Gemara* have the vulnerable openness of a prayer. The poem is as much a struggle to recover childhood, or the prayer once held in childhood, as it is about the father.

The other things that make this poem are of a kind that take great art and passion to accomplish. They are matters of rhythm and syntax, all that is the life blood of a poem when we read it to ourselves. These are what Paul Valéry meant when he said a poem was some huge weight carried to some height or the top of a skyscraper and dropped on the reader. The reader feels the simple brute impact, but is ignorant of the sweat and science that carried the weight into position. In the working out of a poem, I look for two things: a commanding, deadly effectiveness in the arrangement, and something that breathes and pauses and grunts and is rough and unpredictable to assure me that the journey is honest. In the first sentence, I like plums that actually do drop one by one in their ripeness, the way they round off the sentence, and their good-natured illusory reference to the father's dropping off. There's a fine careless loosening up of the rhythm in the "odor of ponds" line. The three verbs "strode," "stretched," and "raced" are strong in their position, movement, and pauses. The two participial lines at the end of the first section are authoritatively placed.

So is the last line of section 2. So is the whole artful, broken simplicity of the speech in this section. Also the very different speech and prayer in section 3. Just right is the confused rhythm describing the ferns, turtles, and lilies.

Are there flaws and limitations? I am not sure. I blink a little at a certain overresolute, petrified firmness here and there, in the "master of my blood," the nailed orange, the "never shed a tear," and the "white ignorant hollow of his face." Perhaps these are just characteristics of the experience, and the binding that makes the poem a poem and not an improvisation. Certainly there's authority and honesty, a noble hallucination.

I have written under disadvantages, far from books, and in a rush to make a deadline. I haven't Kunitz's *Selected Poems* at hand to refer to. He has never published an unfelt and unfinished poem. Each line shows his fine touch and noble carefulness.

[1962]

Randall Jarrell

I /

On *The Seven-League Crutches*

Randall Jarrell is our most talented poet under forty, and one whose wit, pathos, and grace remind us more of Pope or Matthew Arnold than of any of his contemporaries. I don't know whether Jarrell is unappreciated or not—it's hard to imagine anyone taking him lightly. He is almost brutally serious about literature and so bewilderingly gifted that it is impossible to comment on him without the humiliating thought that he himself could do it better.

He is a man of letters in the European sense, with real verve, imagination, and uniqueness. Even his dogmatism is more wild and personal than we are accustomed to, completely unspoiled by the hedging "equanimity" that weakens the style and temperament of so many of our serious writers. His murderous intuitive phrases are famous; but at the same time his mind is essentially conservative and takes as much joy in rescuing the reputation of a sleeping good writer as in chloroforming a mediocre one.

Jarrell's prose intelligence—he seems to know *everything* —gives his poetry an extraordinary advantage over, for instance, a thunderbolt like Dylan Thomas, in dealing with the present;

Jarrell is able to see our whole scientific, political, and spiritual situation directly and on its own terms. He is a tireless discoverer of new themes and resources, and a master technician, who moves easily from the little to the grand. Monstrously knowing and monstrously innocent—one does not know just where to find him . . . a Wordsworth with the obsessions of Lewis Carroll.

The Seven-League Crutches should best be read with Jarrell's three earlier volumes. *Blood for a Stranger* (1942) is a Parnassian tour-de-force in the manner of Auden; nevertheless, it has several fine poems, the beginnings of better, and enough of the author's personality for John Crowe Ransom to write in ironic astonishment that Jarrell had "the velocity of an angel." *Little Friend, Little Friend* (1945), however, contains some of the best poems on modern war, better, I think, and far more professional than those of Wilfred Owen, which, though they seem pathetically eternal to us now, are sometimes amateurish and unfinished. The determined, passive, sacrificial lives of the pilots, inwardly so harmless and outwardly so destructive, are ideal subjects for Jarrell. In *Losses* (1948) and more rangingly in *The Seven-League Crutches*, new subjects appear. Using himself, children, characters from fairy stories, history, and painting, he is still able to find beings that are determined, passive, and sacrificial, but the experience is quiet, more complex, and probably more universal. It's an odd universe, where a bruised joy or a bruised sorrow is forever commenting on itself with the gruff animal common sense and sophistication of Fontaine. Jarrell has gone far enough to be compared with his peers, the best lyric poets of the past: he has the same finesse and originality that they have, and his faults, a certain idiosyncratic willfulness and eclectic timidity, are only faults in this context.

Among the new poems, "The Orient Express," a sequel, I think, to "Dover Beach," is a brilliantly expert combination of regular and irregular lines, buried rhymes, and sestina-like repeated rhymes, in which shifts in tone and rhythm are played off against the deadening roll of the train. "A Game at Salzburg" has the broken, charmed motion of someone thinking out loud. Both, in their different ways, are as skillful and lovely as any short poem I know of. "The Knight, Death, and the Devil" is a careful translation of Dürer's engraving. The description is dense; the generalizations are profound. It is one of the most remarkable word pictures in English verse or prose, and comparable to Auden's "Musée des Beaux Arts."

"The Contrary Poet" is an absolutely literal translation from Corbière. The original is as clearly there as in the French, and it is also a great English poem. "The Night before the Night before Christmas" is long; it is also, perhaps, the best, most mannered, the most unforgettable, and the most irritating poem in the book. Some of Jarrell's monologues are Robert Frost for "the man who reads Hamlet," or rather for a Hamlet who had been tutored by Jarrell. In "Seele im Raum," he masters Frost's methods and manages to make a simple half-mad woman speak in character, and yet with his own humor and terror.

My favorite is "A Girl in a Library," an apotheosis of the American girl, an immortal character piece, and the poem in which Jarrell perhaps best uses both his own qualities and his sense of popular culture. The girl is a college student, blond and athletic.

> *(But not so sadly; not so thoughtfully)*
> *And answer with a pure heart, guilelessly:*
> I'm studying . . .

I quote the ending:

> *Sit and dream.*
> *One comes, a finger's width beneath your skin,*
> *To the braided maidens singing as they spin;*
> *There sound the shepherd's pipe, the watchman's rattle*
> *Across the short dark distance of the years.*
> *I am a thought of yours: and yet, you do not think . . .*

The firelight of a long, blind, dreaming story
Lingers upon your lips; and I have seen
Firm, fixed forever in your closing eyes,
The Corn King beckoning to his Spring Queen.

"Belinda" was once drawn with something of the same hesitating satire and sympathy.

[1957]

II /
Randall Jarrell, 1914 – 1965

When I first met Randall, he was twenty-three or -four, and unsettlingly brilliant, precocious, knowing, naïve, and vexing. He seemed to make no distinction between what he would say in our hearing and what he would say behind our backs. If anything, absence made him more discreet. Woe to the acquaintance who liked the wrong writer, the wrong poem by the right writer, or the wrong lines in the right poem! And how those who loved him enjoyed admiring, complaining, and gossiping about the last outrageous thing he had done or, more often, said. It brought us together—whispering about Randall. In 1937, we both roomed at the house of John Crowe Ransom in Gambier, Ohio. Ransom and Jarrell had each separately spent the preceding summer studying Shakespeare's *Sonnets*, and had emerged with unorthodox and widely differing theories. Roughly, Ransom thought that Shakespeare was continually going off the rails into illogical incoherence. Jarrell believed that no one, not even William Empson, had done justice to the rich, significant ambiguity of Shakespeare's intelligence and images. I can see and hear Ransom and Jarrell now, seated on one sofa, as though on one love seat, the sacred texts open on their laps, one fifty, the other just out of college, and each expounding to the other's deaf ears his own inspired and irreconcilable interpretation.

Gordon Chalmers, the president of Kenyon College and a disciple of the somber anti-romantic humanists, once went skiing with Randall, and was shocked to hear him exclaiming, "I feel just like an angel." Randall *did* somehow give off an angelic impression, despite his love for tennis, singular mufflers knitted by a girlfriend, and disturbing improvements of his own on the latest dance steps. His mind, unearthly in its quickness, was a little boyish, disembodied, and brittle. His body was a little ghostly in its immunity to soil, entanglements, and rebellion. As one sat with him in oblivious absorption at the campus bar, sucking a fifteen-cent chocolate milk shake and talking eternal things, one felt, beside him, too corrupt and companionable. He had the harsh luminosity of Shelley—like Shelley, every inch a poet, and like Shelley, imperiled perhaps by an arid, abstracting precosity. Not really! Somewhere inside him, a breezy, untouchable spirit had even then made its youthful and sightless promise to accept—to accept and never to accept the bulk, confusion, and defeat of mortal flesh . . . all that blithe and blood-torn dolor!

Randall Jarrell had his own peculiar and important excellence as a poet, and outdistanced all others in the things he could do well. His gifts, both by nature and by a lifetime of hard dedication and growth, were wit, pathos, and brilliance of intelligence. These qualities, dazzling in themselves, were often so well employed that he became, I think, the most heartbreaking English poet of his generation.

Most good poets are also good critics on occasion, but Jarrell was much more than this. He was a critic of genius, a poet-critic of genius at a time when, as he wrote, most criticism was "astonishingly graceless, joyless, humorless, long-winded, niggling, blinkered, methodical, self-important, cliché-ridden, prestige-obsessed, and almost autonomous."

He had a deadly hand for killing what he despised. He described a murky verbal poet as "writing poems that might have been written *on* a typewriter *by* a typewriter." The flashing reviews he wrote in his twenties are full of such witticisms and barbs, and hundreds more were tossed off in casual conversation, and never preserved, or even repeated. Speaking of a famous scholar, he said, "What can be more tedious than a man whose every sentence is a balanced epigram without wit, profundity, or taste?" He himself, though often fierce, was incapable of vulgarity, self-seeking, or meanness. He could be very tender and gracious, but often he seemed tone-deaf to the amenities and dishonesties that make human relations tolerable. Both his likes and dislikes were a terror to everyone, that is to everyone who either saw himself as important or wished to see himself as important. Although he was almost without vices, heads of colleges and English departments found his frankness more unsettling and unpredictable than the drunken explosions of some divine *enfant terrible*, such as Dylan Thomas. Usually his wit was austerely pure, but sometimes he could jolt the more cynical. Once, we were looking at a furnished apartment that one of our friends had just rented. It was overbearingly eccentric. Life-size clay lamps like flowerpots remodeled into Matisse nudes by a spastic child. Paintings made from a palette of mud by a blind painter. About the paintings Randall said, "Ectoplasm sprinkled with zinc." About the apartment: "All that's missing are Mrs. X's illegitimate children in bottles of formaldehyde." His first reviews were described as "symbolic murders," but even then his most destructive judgments had a patient, intuitive, unworldly certainty.

Yet eulogy was the glory of Randall's criticism. Eulogies that not only impressed readers with his own enthusiasms, but which also, time and again, changed and improved opinions and values. He left many reputations permanently altered and exalted. I think particularly of his famous Frost and Whitman essays, and one on the last poems of Wallace Stevens, which was a dramatic reversal of his own earlier evaluation. His mind kept moving and groping more deeply. His prejudices were never the established and fashionable prejudices of the world around him. One could never say of one of his new admirations, "Oh, I knew *you* would like that." His progress was not the usual youthful critic's progress from callow severity to lax benevolence. With wrinkled brow and cool fresh eye, he was forever musing, discovering, and chipping away at his own misconceptions. Getting out on a limb was a daily occurrence for him, and when he found words for what he had intuited, his judgments were bold and unlikely. Randall was so often right that sometimes we said he was always right. He could enjoy discarded writers whom it was a scandal to like, praise young, unknown writers as if he were praising and describing Shakespeare's tragedies, and read Shakespeare's tragedies with the uncertainty and wonder of their first discoverers.

He once said, "If I were a rich man, I would pay money for the privilege of being able to teach." Probably there was no better teacher of literature in the country, and yet he was curiously unworldly about it, and welcomed teaching for almost twenty years in the shade or heat of his little-known Southern college for girls in Greensboro, North Carolina. There his own community gave him a compact, tangible, personal reverence that was incomparably more substantial and poignant than the empty, numerical long-distance blaze of national publicity. He grieved over the coarseness, unkindness, and corruption of our society, and said that "the poet has a peculiar relation to this public. It is unaware of his existence." He said bitterly and lightheartedly that "the gods who had taken away the poet's audience had given him students." Yet he gloried in being a teacher, never apologized for it, and related it to his most serious criticism. Writing of three long poems by Robert Frost, poems too long to include in his essay, he breaks off and says, "I have used rather an odd tone about [these poems] because I feel so much frustration at not being able to quote and go over them, as I so often have done with friends and classes." Few critics could so gracefully descend from the grand manner or be so offhand about their dignity. His essays are never encrusted with the hardness of a professor. They have the raciness and artistic gaiety of his own hypnotic voice.

Randall was the only man I have ever met who could make other writers feel that their work was more important to him than his own. I don't mean that he was in the habit of saying to people he admired, "This is much better than anything I could do." Such confessions, though charming, cost little effort. What he did was to make others feel that their realizing themselves was as close to him as his own self-realization, and that he cared as much about making the nature and goodness of someone else's work understood as he cared about making his own understood. I have never known anyone who so connected what his friends wrote with their lives, or their lives with what they wrote. This could be trying: whenever we turned out something Randall felt was unworthy or a falling off, there was a coolness in all one's relations with him. You felt that even your choice in neckties wounded him. Yet he always veered and returned, for he knew as well as anyone that the spark from heaven is beyond man's call and control. Good will he demanded, but in the end was lenient to honest sterility and failure.

Jarrell was the most readable and generous of critics of contemporary poetry. His novel, *Pictures from an Institution*, whatever its fictional oddities, is a unique and serious joke book. How often I've met people who keep it by their beds or somewhere handy, and read random pages aloud to lighten their hearts. His book *A Sad Heart at the Supermarket* had a condescending press. When one listened to these social essays, they were like *dies irae* sermons, strange ones that cauterized the soul, and yet made us weep with laughter. A banal world found them banal. But what Jarrell's inner life really was in all its wonder, variety, and subtlety is best told in his poetry. To the end, he was writing with deepening force, clarity, and frankness. For some twenty-five years he wrote excellent poems. Here I only want to emphasize two of his peaks: what he wrote about the war, and what he completed in the last years of his life.

In the first months of the war, Jarrell became a pilot. He was rather old for a beginner, and soon "washed out," and spent the remaining war years as an aviation instructor. Even earlier, he had an expert's knowledge. I remember sitting with him in 1938 on the hill of Kenyon College and listening to him analyze in cool technical detail the various rather minute ways in which the latest British planes were superior to their German equivalents. He then jokingly sketched out how a bombing raid might be made against the college. Nine-tenths of his war poems are Air Force poems, and are about planes and their personnel, the flyers, crews, and mechanics who attended them. No other imaginative writer had his precise knowledge of aviation, or knew so well how to draw inspiration from this knowledge.

> *In the turret's great glass dome, the apparition, death,*
> *Framed in the glass of the gunsight, a fighter's blinking wing,*
> *Flares softly, a vacant fire. If the flak's inked blurs—*
> *Distributed, statistical—the bombs' lost patterning*
> *Are death, they are death under glass, a chance*
> *For someone yesterday, someone tomorrow; and the fire*
> *That streams from the fighter which is there, not there,*
> *Does not warm you, has not burned them, though they die.*

More important still, the soldiers he wrote about were men much like his own pilot-students. He knew them well, and not only that, peculiarly sympathized with them. For Jarrell, the war careers of these young men had the freshness, wonder, and magical brevity of childhood. In his poetry, they are murderers, and yet innocents. They destroyed cities and men that had only the nominal reality of names studied in elementary geography classes.

> *In bombers named for girls, we burned*
> *The cities we had learned about in school—*
> *Till our lives wore out*

Or

> *In this year of our warfare, indispensable*
> *In general, and in particular dispensable*

Finally, the pilot goes home for good, forever mutilated and wounded, "the slow flesh failing, the terrible flesh / Sloughed off at last . . . / Stumbling to the toilet on one clever leg / Of leather, wire, and willow." There, knowledge has at last come to him:

> And it is different, different—you have understood
> Your world at last: you have tasted your own blood.

Jarrell's portraits of his pilots have been downgraded sometimes as unheroic, naïve, and even sentimental. Well, he was writing beyond the war, and turning the full visionary powers of his mind on the war to probe into and expose the horror, pathos, and charm he found in life. Always behind the sharpened edge of his lines, there is the merciful vision, *his* vision, partial like all others, but an illumination of life, too sad and radiant for us to stay with long—or forget.

In his last and best book, *The Lost World,* he used subjects and methods he had been developing and improving for almost twenty years. Most of the poems are dramatic monologues. Their speakers, though mostly women, are intentionally, and unlike Browning's, very close to the author. Their themes, repeated with endless variations, are solitude, the solitude of the unmarried, the solitude of the married, the love, strife, dependency, and indifference of man and woman—how mortals age, and brood over their lost and raw childhood, only recapturable in memory and imagination. Above all, childhood! This subject for many a careless and tarnished cliché was for him what it was for his two favorite poets, Rilke and Wordsworth, a governing and transcendent vision. For shallower creatures, recollections of childhood and youth are drenched in a mist of plaintive pathos, or even bathos, but for Jarrell this was the divine glimpse, lifelong to be lived with, painfully and tenderly relived, transformed, matured—man with and against woman, child with and against adult.

One of his aging women says:

When I was young and miserable and pretty
And poor, I'd wish
What all girls wish: to have a husband

But later, thinking of the withering present, she says:

How young I seem; I am exceptional;
I think of all I have.
But really no one is exceptional,
No one has anything, I'm anybody,
I stand beside my grave
Confused with my life, that is commonplace and solitary.

In so reflecting, she is a particular woman—one sad, particular woman reaching into Jarrell's universal Everyman, poor or triumphant. Speaking in his own person and of his own childhood, he says:

  ... As I run by the chicken coops
With lettuce for my rabbit, real remorse
Hurts me, here, now: the little girl is crying
Because I didn't write. Because—
        of course,
I was a child, I missed them so. But justifying
Hurts too ...

Then, in a poem called "Woman," the speaker, a man, addresses the woman next to him in bed:

Let me sleep beside you, each night, like a spoon;
When, starting from my dreams, I groan to you,
May your I love you send me back to sleep.
At morning bring me, grayer for its mirroring,
The heavens' sun perfected in your eyes.

It all comes back to me now—the just under thirty years of our friendship, mostly meetings in transit, mostly in Greensboro,

North Carolina, the South he loved and stayed with, though no agrarian, but a radical liberal. Poor modern-minded exile from the forests of Grimm, I see him unbearded, slightly South American-looking, then later bearded, with a beard we at first wished to reach out our hands to and pluck off, but which later became him, like Walter Bagehot's, or some Symbolist's in France's *fin de siècle* Third Republic. Then unbearded again. I see the bright, petty, pretty sacred objects he accumulated for his joy and solace: Vermeer's red-hatted girl, the Piero and Donatello reproductions, the photographs of his bruised, merciful heroes: Chekhov, Rilke, Marcel Proust. I see the white sporting Mercedes-Benz, the ever better cut and more deliberately jaunty clothes, the television with its long afternoons of professional football, those matches he thought miraculously more graceful than college football . . . Randall had an uncanny clairvoyance for helping friends in subtle precarious moments—almost always as only he could help, with something written: critical sentences in a letter, or an unanticipated published book review. Twice or thrice, I think, he must have thrown me a lifeline. In his own life, he had much public acclaim and more private. The public, at least, fell cruelly short of what he deserved. Now that he is gone, I see clearly that the spark from heaven really struck and irradiated the lines and being of my dear old friend—his noble, difficult, and beautiful soul.

[1965]

Dylan Thomas

Nothing could be more wrongheaded than the English disputes about Dylan Thomas's greatness. The inarticulate extravagance of Edith Sitwell and Herbert Read was hardly disinterested, and it has harmed Thomas's reputation; but compared with the methodical, controversial blindness of Symons, Grigson, and the reviewer in *Scrutiny*, it has a certain charm. I suppose, of the other living English poets, the best are Graves, Auden, MacNeice, and Empson. The bulk and brilliance of Auden's work puts him in a place by himself. Of the remaining three, I think, only MacNeice can be considered as a serious rival to Thomas.

He is a dazzling obscure writer who can be enjoyed without understanding. When the critics discovered that he made sense and was not a Shakespeare, they were disillusioned. The heavy-handed obtuseness of their attacks on Thomas is reminiscent of the manner in which they dismissed Ezra Pound ten or fifteen years ago. The cases are similar. Both poets are superior stylists; but they tend to be fragmentary, overingenious, and to have difficulty in finding a subject. Several of Thomas's best poems have the childlike directness and magic of "Cathay." Everything that I have said of Pound could be said of Hart Crane, whose resemblance to Thomas is even closer. Like Thomas, Crane is subjective, mystical, obscure, and Elizabethan in his rhetoric.

Both long for their childhood and use sexual symbols. "Rip van Winkle" and "Repose of Rivers" are like "Fern Hill"; "Black Tamborine" is like "The Hunchback in the Park"; and "Wine Menagerie" is like Thomas when he is most labored and obscure. As he was not influenced by Crane, comes from another world, and has a very different personality, the similarity is remarkable.

Thomas is famous for his recitals on the radio, and one can understand why this is so. As a formal metrician, Wallace Stevens is the only living poet who can hold a candle to him. His ear is infallible, and the splendor of his devices reminds one of Hopkins. Anyone who has read Bridges's *Study of Milton's Prosody* must admire the strange skill with which Thomas varies the strict iambic lines of his earlier poems. The easy and loose movement of his later syllabic stanzas is just as remarkable. These have a singing rush that is unlike the suave accentual flow of Auden's syllabics, or Marianne Moore's personal, almost prosy rhythm. The rhythmical surface is surprisingly interesting even in passages where the meaning is awkwardly expressed or commonplace. And there are lines whose meaning is sustained that are almost Shakespearean:

> *I make a weapon of an ass's skeleton*
> *And walk the warring sands by the dead town,*
> *Cudgel great air, wreck east, and topple sundown,*
> *Storm her sped heart, hang with beheaded veins*
> *Its wringing shell, and let her eyelids fasten.*
> *Destruction, picked by birds, brays through the jawbone,*
> *And, for that murder's sake, dark with contagion*
> *Like an approaching wave I sprawl to ruin.*

It is metrics and rhetoric, as well as imagination, that lifts this from the slipshod rant of its innumerable American, English, and Welsh imitations.

The poems are about light—the ecstasy of experiencing it, the agony of its deprivation, and the agony of its attainment. A handful of simple situations are used to express this: seed and ground, child and womb, sexual fulfillment and sexual frustration, sin and purity, and life and death. There is also the ecstasy of the child, the poet, and the idiot. Thomas usually develops his action by means of Freudian or Christian symbols, or by variants on these that he has invented. Icons and natural objects are often hard to tell apart. A final characteristic of Thomas's machinery is its repeated use of about twenty typical words. One is surprised that he has never written a sestina with *locks, keys, sun, grains, fire,* and *death* as the repeated words.

No one should overlook Thomas's faults, for they are not the result of carelessness or flippancy, but of method. Few poets have wasted as many fine lines on unsuccessful poems. To make this explicit, I shall enumerate and give examples.

Repetition and Redundancy: (a) Self-imitation. Thomas often appears to be rewriting with the same symbols and language a poem that he has already written. (b) Lyrical façades. "The force that through the green fuse" uses a beautiful repetitive structure to conceal parts that are clumsy and uninspired. "And death shall have no dominion" has twenty indifferent lines supported by a magnificent refrain. (c) Substitution of repeated symbols or description for logic or narrative. Because of this, the three longest poems are swamped in rhetoric and never develop. (d) Insertion of matter that merely repeats or echoes other parts of the poem. The loose structure of "I make this in a warring absence" and many of the obscurer poems is made "water-tight," as Thomas would say, by plugging.

Overloading: (a) Words or phrases that disrupt their context. There is always a meaning of some sort, but unexpected words are thrown in to heighten a passage that is unredeemably flat and useless. No good poet is guilty of this expedient as often as Thomas, and it is needless to give examples. He is sometimes brilliantly successful. (b) Symbols unsupported by their context. "The Death of a Man Aged One Hundred" confuses and destroys its action by introducing *locks* and *keys.* By a reversal of this process, the clarity of the symbols is often muddied by their particularization. (c) Omission of numb or supporting lines. Almost all the parts of "In Memory of Ann Jones" are powerful and necessary, but the whole gives a somewhat crowded and muscle-bound impression. In this case one hardly cares, for, as Dryden said of Oldham, it is seldom that a poet is betrayed by so much force. But in other places the betrayal is real, and great lines are thrown away because they lack a context in which their force can function.

If Thomas kept his eye on his object and depended less on his rhetoric, his poems would be better organized and have more to say. In his later poems, he has been moving in this direction, but I agree with Empson that the process is still incomplete.

I assume that Thomas is a very good poet. Although one feels that he has the equipment to grow immeasurably, it would be foolish to minimize what he has already accomplished. Several of his poems will last. "In Memory of Ann Jones" is thoroughly seen and felt. The density, magnificence, and honesty of its language make it one of the best short elegies in English. "A Hunchback in the Park" (the reviewers who have objected to the omission of "Light breaks where no sun shines" have been right, but no one has missed "The Hunchback," a much finer poem) is free from overwriting and is perfectly organized.

> The hunchback in the park
> A solitary mister
> Propped between trees and water
> From the opening of the garden lock
> That let the trees and water enter
> Until the Sunday sombre bell at dark
> Eating bread from a newspaper
> Drinking water from a chained cup
> That the children filled with gravel
> In the fountain basin where I sailed my ship
> Slept at night in a dog kennel
> But nobody chained him up.

Only a few poems are more sensitive and magical than these stanzas or the five that follow. In this poem, and in the much slighter "In my craft and sullen art," metrics, rhetoric, and imagination are one. Their formal perfection and their elaborate directness will seem just as remarkable in a hundred years as now. Among the imperfect poems with fine sections are "Especially when the October wind," "I make this in a warring absence," "How shall my animal," "If my head hurt a hair's foot," "Holy Spring," "Poem in October," "A Winter's Tale," and "A Refusal to Mourn." There are also the stories (especially "Peaches," which should be read with "In Memory of Ann Jones") which, though less intense than the poems, often have a good structure, wit, and a subject. The best of Thomas's later poems is "Fern Hill," which reminds one of Wordsworth's pastorals of childhood. Although small and simple in comparison with the older poet, Thomas has the advantage in this case of really being something of a bewildered, dazzled child. "Fern Hill" is well composed, although line by line the writing is intentionally loose. The shock of its conclusion, and a little of the wonderful momentum of its exuberance, will come through in my quotation:

> *Nothing I cared in the lamb-white days, that time would*
> > *take me*
> *Up to the swallow-thronged loft by the shadow of my hand,*
> > > *In the moon that is always rising*
> > > > *Nor that riding to sleep*
> > > *I should hear him fly with the high fields*
> *And wake to the farm forever fled from the childless land.*
> *Oh as I was young and easy in the mercy of his means,*
> > > *Time held me green and dying*
> > > *Though I sang in my chains like the sea.*

[1947]

John Berryman

I /
The Poetry of John Berryman

Groups of John Berryman's *Dream Songs** have been coming out in magazines for the last five years. They have been talked about, worried over, denounced, adored. They are puzzling, not quite intelligible—and beyond a doubt fun to read or hear. When they don't make you cry—these poems will make you laugh. And that is news.

In many ways, Berryman is typical of his generation, a studious generation, stuffed with new conventions, and squeezed by the pressure of the unconventional. As soon as he began to publish, one heard of his huge library, his phonograph installed by Bernard Haggin, his endless ability to quote poetry, and his work on a conclusive text of *King Lear*. In his twenties, he was already a keen critic and a distinguished scholar; from the first he wrote with vehemence and calculation. He was disciplined yet bohemian; unorthodox in the ardor of his admirations and yet so catholic and generous that he was hampered in finding his own voice. He seemed to throb with a singular rhythm and pitch. One felt the fierce charge of electricity and feared that it might

---

* *77 Dream Songs* by John Berryman. New York: Farrar, Straus and Giroux, 1964.

burn out the wires. He vibrated brilliantly to all significant in-
fluences and most of all to the new idiom of Auden. His proper
bent seemed toward an intense and unworldly symbolic poetry.

In the beginning, Berryman might have grown into an
austere, removed poet, but instead he somehow remained deep
in the mess of things. His writing has been a long, often backbreaking search for an inclusive style, a style that could use his
erudition and catch the high, even frenetic, intensity of his
experience, disgusts, and enthusiasm. And how wonderful the
enthusiasm! What stirred him most then were the late plays of
Shakespeare. He would recite magical, little-known speeches,
remarkable for their exploratory syntax and dramatic flights of
psychology. Syntax and psychology—in his new poems, each
sentence and stanza seemed to clutch after all the twists and
experiments spread over many pages of the late Shakespeare.

It is a temptation in poetry to jump from style to style—
sometimes without advance and with so little connection to
previous work that change is monotony. With Berryman, each
succeeding book is part of a single drive against the barriers of
the commonplace. Before writing about his *Dream Songs*, I want
to look briefly at his earlier work. A definite pattern or lurch of
alteration goes through it all.

Consider the following lines from "The Statue":

Where I sit near the entrance of the Park,
The charming, dangerous entrance of their need,
Dozens, a hundred men have lain till morning,
And the preservative darkness waning . . .

The poem is about destitute bums sprawling by a statue of
Humboldt. It is an impressive effort to give a pang of squalor to
the monumental and a breath of grandeur to the miserable.
What else could make either tolerable? I have selected rather
meanly, trying to indicate the Audenesque.

My favorite Berryman poem of this period is "Winter Land-
scape," a symbolic description of Brueghel's painting. It is
written in one sentence that loops through five five-line stanzas,

as if it were trying to make a complete poem out of Keats's pictorial and next-to-last stanza in the "Grecian Urn." The old meaning is repeated by a darker, more imperiled voice. The music and imagery move with a relentless casualness. Like the painting, all is simultaneous, and flows in a timeless circle of calm, overshadowed beauty.

> *These men, this particular three in brown*
> *Witnessed by birds will keep the scene and say*
> *By their configuration with the trees,*
> *The small bridge, the red houses and the fire,*
> *What place, what time, what morning occasion*
>
> *Sent them into the wood . . .*

If Berryman had gone on composing with such gentleness and delicacy and clarity, he would at the least have been notable as a technician. He chose, however, a more reckless and tortured line. Lucid, cool, Parnassian description vanished and new methods were felt out. In "Canto Amor," one of his most eloquent and high-flown poems, he tried, like Rossetti and Pound, but with a difference, to adapt the speculative *stile nuovo* of Dante's shorter poems.

> *Dream in a dream the heavy soul somewhere*
> *struck suddenly & dark down to its knees . . .*
> *And then that other music, in whose sake*
> *all men perceive a gladness but we are drawn*
> *less for that joy than utterly to take*
> *our trial, naked in the music's vision . . .*

The power of these lines comes from the difficulty of the task, the brave labor to give music and nobility to a bare, archaic style, full of elbows, quaintness, and stops. If Berryman's later work seems idiosyncratic, one should remember that he had the humility and stamina to pass all the hardest standard tests. Elsewhere, about this time, he was working at simpler, more broken and prosaic effects. Here are the opening lines from "The Song of the Tortured Girl":

After a little I could not have told—
But no one asked me this—why I was there.
I asked. The ceiling of that place was high,
And there were sudden noises, which I made . . .

The poem in which everything flowers for Berryman is his long *Homage to Mistress Bradstreet*. It is wonderfully wrung and wrought. Nothing could be more high-pitched, studied, and in-flamed. One can read it many times and still get lost in it; with each renewal, it becomes clearer and more haunting. In part, it is a biography of Anne Bradstreet that reproduces the grammar, theology, and staid decor of the period. The poet, however, heightens the action by imagining his heroine with the intensity of a seizure of hallucination. He is in her presence, she seems inside him. In what is almost a love declaration, she speaks to him in a language that is a strange mixture of hers and his. Somehow, the story of her landing, her pious and despairing moments, the bearing of a child, the death of a daughter, and her own aging and wavering relations with her husband and family get told with a passionate fullness. Here Berryman's experiments with music and sentence structure find themselves harnessed to a subject and trial that strain them to the limit. His lovely discordant rhythms ride through every break, splutter, archaism, and inversion. The old rustic, seventeenth-century, provincial simplicity survives and is greatly enriched by the jagged intellectual probing and techniques of the modern poet. *Homage to Mistress Bradstreet* is the most resourceful historical poem in our language.

Dream Songs is larger and sloppier. The scene is contempo-rary and crowded with references to news items, world politics, travel, low life, and Negro music. Its style is a conglomeration of high style, Berrymanisms, Negro and beat slang, and baby talk.

The poem is written in sections of three six-line stanzas. There is little sequence, and sometimes a single section will explode into three or four separate parts. At first the brain aches and freezes at so much darkness, disorder, and oddness. After a while, the repeated situations and their racy jabber become more and more enjoyable, although even now I wouldn't trust myself to paraphrase accurately at least half of the sections.

The poems are much too difficult, packed, and wrenched to be sung. They are called *songs* out of mockery, because they are filled with snatches of Negro minstrelsy, and because one of their characters is Mr. Bones,* who keeps questioning the author and talking for him. The dreams are not real dreams but a waking hallucination in which anything that might have happened to the author can be used at random. Anything he has seen, overheard, or imagined can go in. The poems are about Berryman, or rather they are about a person he calls *Henry*. Henry is Berryman seen as himself, as *poète maudit*, child and puppet. He is tossed about with a mixture of tenderness and absurdity, pathos and hilarity that would have been impossible if the author had spoken in the first person.

Berryman is very bookish and also very idiosyncratic. The bookishness shows up as a fault in a certain echoing hardness, yet it tempers his quirkiness and lets him draw on whatever models will serve him and are extended by his undertaking. Here is a bit of Pound:

> *I seldom go to films. They are too exciting,*
> *said the honorable Possum.*

Here is Stevens:

> *Pleased at the worst, except with man, he shook*
> *the brightest winter sun.*

---

* Lowell corrected this error in a later issue: "Mr. Bones is not 'one of their characters,' but the main character, Henry."

And here is a passage that would have pleased Cummings:

This is the lay of Ike.
Here's to the glory of the great white—awk—
who has been running—er—things in recent—ech—
in the United—if your screen is black,
ladies & gentlemen, we—I like—
at the Point he was terrific . . .

Berryman's debt to these three authors is much deeper and more imaginative than such verbal similarities would suggest. From Pound he learned the all-inclusive style, the high spirits, the flitting from subject to subject, irreverence, and humor. I say "learned," but it is really a question of resemblance. I feel the presence of Stevens in sonorous, suggestive, nuance-like, often not quite clear lines; in cloudy anecdotes about fanciful figures, such as *Quo*, or in the section about Clitus and Alexander the Great, Henry has much the same distance and identification with his author as Crispin in "The Comedian as the Letter C." The resemblance to Cummings is in the humor, verbal contortion, and pathos. There is also Joyce.

Several of the best poems in this sequence are elegies to other writers. His elegies are eulogies. By their impertinent piety, by jumping from thought to thought, mood to mood, and by saying anything that comes into the author's head, they are touching and nervously alive.

Bless Frost . . .

His malice was a pimple down his good
big face, with its sly eyes . . .
He had fine stories and was another man
   on the whole in private.
He apologize to Henry off & on
for two blue slanders, which was good for him . . .
      For a while here
we possessed an unusual man.

Henry's queer baby talk was at first insufferable to me, and yet I soon surrendered to the crazy joy, the wildly personal use of minstrel language.

I could quote many funny and many sad lines from *Dream Songs*. Instead, I will select one entire section, one of the best and most unified:

There sat down once a thing on Henry's heart
so heavy, if he had a hundred years
& more & weeping, sleepless in all them time
Henry could not make good.
Starts again always in Henry's ears
the little cough somewhere, an odour, a chime.

And there's another thing he had in mind
like a grave Sienese face a thousand years
would fail to blur the still profiled reproach of. Ghastly
with open eyes, he attends, blind.
All the bells say: too late. This is not for tears;
thinking.

But never did Henry, as he thought he did,
end anyone and hacks her body up
and hide the pieces, where they may be found.

He knows: he went over everyone, & nobody's missing.
Often he reckons, in the dawn, them up.
Nobody's ever missing.

The voice of the man becomes one with the voice of the child here, as their combined rhythm sobs through remorse, wonder, and nightmare. It's as if two widely separated parts of a man's life had somehow fused. It goes through the slow words of "*Henry could not make good*," to the accusing solemnity of the Sienese face, to the frozen, automatic counting of the limbs, the counting of the bodies, to the terrible charm and widening meaning of the final line.

77 *Dream Songs* is a hazardous, imperfect book. One would need to see the unpublished parts to decide how well it fills out as a whole. As it stands, the main faults of this selection are the threat of mannerism, and worse—disintegration. How often one chafes at the relentless indulgence, and cannot tell the what or why of a passage. And yet one must give in. All is risk and variety here. This great Pierrot's universe is more tearful and funny than we can easily bear.

[1964]

II /

For John Berryman, 1914–1972

I sit looking out a window at 3:30 this February afternoon. I see a pasture, green out of season and sunlit; in an hour more or less, it will be black. John Berryman walks brightly out of my memory. We met at Princeton through Caroline Gordon, in 1944, the wane of the war. The moment was troubled; my wife, Jean Stafford, and I were introduced to the Berrymans for youth and diversion. I remember expected, probably false, images, the hospital-white tablecloth, the clear martinis, the green antiquing of an Ivy League college faculty club. What college? Not Princeton, but the less spruce Cambridge, England, John carried with him in his speech rhythms and dress. He had a casual intensity, the almost intimate mumble of a don. For life, he was to be a student, scholar, and teacher. I think he was almost *the* student-friend I've had, the one who was the student in essence. An indignant spirit was born in him; his life was a cruel fight to set it free. Is the word for him courage or generosity or loyalty? He had these. And he was always a performer, a prima donna; at first to those he scorned, later to everyone, except perhaps students, his family, and Saul Bellow.

From the first, John was humorous, learned, thrustingly vehement in liking . . . more adolescent than boyish. He and I preferred critics who were writers to critics who were not writers. We hated literary discussions animated by jealousy and pushed by caution. John's own criticism, mostly spoken, had a poetry. Hyper-enthusiasms made him a hot friend, and could also make him wearing to friends—one of his dearest, Delmore Schwartz, used to say no one had John's loyalty, but you liked him to live in another city. John had fire then, but not the fire of Byron or Yevtushenko. He clung so keenly to Hopkins, Yeats, and Auden that their shadows paled him.

Later, the Berrymans (the first Berrymans, the first Lowells) stayed with us in Damariscotta Mills, Maine. Too many guests had accepted. We were inept and uncouth at getting the most out of the country; we didn't own or drive a car. This gloomed and needled the guests. John was ease and light. We gossiped on the rocks of the millpond, baked things in shells on the sand, and drank, as was the appetite of our age, much less than now. John could quote with vibrance to all lengths, even prose, even late Shakespeare, to show me what could be done with disrupted and mended syntax. This was the start of his real style. At first he wrote with great brio bristles of clauses, all breaks and with little style to break off from. Someone said this style was like Emily Dickinson's mad-dash punctuation without the words. I copied, and arrived at a manner that made even the verses I wrote for my cousins' *bouts rimés* (with "floor," "door," "whore," and "more" for the fixed rhymes) leaden and unintelligible. Nets so grandly knotted could only catch logs—our first harsh, inarticulate cry of truth.

My pilgrimage to Princeton with Randall Jarrell to have dinner with the Berrymans was not happy. Compared with other poets, John was a prodigy; compared with Randall, a slow starter. Perpetrators of such misencounters usually confess their bewilderment that two talents with so much in common failed to jell. So much in common—both were slightly heretical disciples of Bernard Haggin, the music and record critic. But John jarred the evening by playing his own favorite recordings on an immense machine constructed and formerly used by Haggin.

This didn't animate things; they tried ballet. One liked Covent Garden, the other Danilova, Markova, and the latest New York Balanchine. Berryman unfolded leather photograph books of enlarged British ballerinas he had almost dated. Jarrell made cool, odd evaluations drawn from his forty, recent, consecutive nights of New York ballet. He hinted that the English dancers he had never seen were on a level with the Danes. I suffered more than the fighters, and lost authority by trying not to take sides.

Both poet-critics had just written definitive essay-reviews of my first book, *Lord Weary's Castle*. To a myopic eye, they seemed to harmonize. So much the worse. Truth is in minute particulars; here, in the minutiae, nothing meshed. Earlier in the night, Berryman made the tactical mistake of complimenting Jarrell on his essay. This was accepted with a hurt, glib croak, "Oh, thanks." The flattery was not returned, not a muscle smiled. I realized that if the essays were to be written again . . . On the horrible New Jersey midnight local to Pennsylvania Station, Randall analyzed John's high, intense voice with surprise and coldness. "Why hasn't anyone told him?" Randall had the same high, keyed-up voice he criticized. Soon he developed chills and fevers, ever more violent, and I took my suit coat and covered him. He might have been a child. John, the host, the insulted one, recovered sooner. His admiration for Randall remained unsoured, but the dinner was never repeated.

Our trip a year later to Ezra Pound at St. Elizabeths Hospital near Washington was softer, so soft I remember nothing except a surely misplaced image of John sitting on the floor hugging his knees, and asking with shining cheeks for Pound to sing an aria from his opera *Villon*. He saw nothing nutty about Pound, or maybe it was the opposite. Anyway, his instincts were true—serene, ungrudging, buoyant. Few people, even modern poets, felt carefree and happy with Pound then . . . When we came back to my room, I made the mistake of thinking that John was less interested in his new poems than in mine . . . Another opera. Much later, in the ragged days of John's first divorce, we went to the Met Opera Club, and had to

borrow Robert Giroux's dinner jacket and tails. I lost the toss
and wore the tails.* I see John dancing in the street shouting, "I
don't know you, Elizabeth wouldn't know you, only your
mother would."

Pound, Jarrell, and Berryman had the same marvelous and
maddening characteristic: they were self-centered and unselfish.
This gave that breathless, commanding rush to their amuse-
ments and controversies—to Jarrell's cool and glowing critical
appreciations, to Berryman's quotations and gossip. His taste for
what he despised was infallible; but he could outrageously hero-
worship living and dead, most of all writers his own age. Few
have died without his defiant, heroic dirge. I think he sees them
rise from their graves like soldiers to answer him.

Jarrell's death was the sadder. If it hadn't happened, it
wouldn't have happened. He would be with me now, in full
power, as far as one may at fifty. This might-have-been (it's a
frequent thought) stings my eyes. John, with pain and joy like
his friend Dylan Thomas, almost won what he gambled for. He
was more eccentric than Thomas, less the natural poet of natural
force, yet had less need to be first actor. He grew older, drier,
more toughly twisted into the varieties of experience.

I must say something of death and the *extremist poets*, as
we are named in often pre-funerary tributes. Except for Weldon
Kees and Sylvia Plath, they lived as long as Shakespeare, outlived
Wyatt, Baudelaire, and Hopkins, and long outlived the forever
Romantics, those who really died young. John himself lived to
the age of Beethoven, whom he celebrates in the most ambitious
and perhaps finest of his late poems, a monument to his long
love, unhampered expression, and subtle criticism. John died
with fewer infirmities than Beethoven. The consolation somehow doesn't wash. I feel the jagged gash with which my con-

---

* Lowell misremembers details of this occasion, which occurred before he himself
had joined the Metropolitan Opera Club, then housed in the old Met. They
were both my guests and the rules required us to wear evening clothes. I loaned
Lowell my dinner jacket (his was in Boston) and Berryman wore his own tails,
dating from our college days and still fitting him perfectly. The opera, beautifully
sung by Licia Albanese, was *La Traviata*.   R.G.

temporaries died, with which we were to die. Were they killed, as standard radicals say, by our corrupted society? Was their success an aspect of their destruction? Were we uncomfortable epigoni of Frost, Pound, Eliot, Marianne Moore, etc.? This bitter possibility came to us at the moment of our *arrival*. Death comes sooner or later, these made it sooner.

I somehow smile, though a bit crookedly, when I think of John's whole life, and even of the icy leap from the bridge to the hard ground. He was springy to the end, and on his feet. The cost of his career is shown by an anecdote he tells in one of the earlier *Dream Songs*—as a boy the sliding seat in his shell slipped as he was rowing a race, and he had to push back and forth, bleeding his bottom on the runners, till the race was finished. The bravery is ignominious and screams. John kept rowing; maybe at the dock no one noticed the blood on his shorts—his injury wasn't maiming. Going to one of his later Minnesota classes, he stumbled down the corridor, unhelped, though steadying himself step by step on the wall, then taught his allotted hour, and walked to the ambulance he had ordered, certain he would die of a stroke while teaching. He was sick a few weeks, then returned to his old courses—as good as before.

The brighter side is in his hilarious, mocking stories, times with wives, children, and friends, and surely in some of the sprinted affairs he fabled. As he became more inspired and famous and drunk, more and more John Berryman, he became less good company and more a happening—slashing eloquence in undertones, amber tumblers of bourbon, a stony pyramid talking down a rugful of admirers. His almost inhuman generosity sweetened this, but as the heart grew larger, the hide grew thicker. Is his work worth it to us? Of course; though the life of the ant is more to the ant than the health of his anthill. He never stopped fighting and moving all his life; at first, expert and derivative, later the full output, more juice, more pages, more strange words on the page, more simplicity, more obscurity. I am afraid I mistook it for forcing, when he came into his own. No voice now or persona sticks in my ear as his. It is poignant, abrasive, anguished, humorous. A voice on the page, identified as my friend's on the telephone, though lost now to mimicry. We should hear him read aloud. It is we who are labored and private, when he is smiling.

I met John last a year or so ago at Christmas in New York. He had been phoning poems and invitations to people at three in the morning, and I felt a weariness about seeing him. Since he had let me sleep uncalled, I guessed he felt numbness to me. We met one noon during the taxi strike at the Chelsea Hotel, dusty with donated, avant-garde constructs, and dismal with personal recollections, Bohemia, and the death of Thomas. There was no cheerful restaurant within walking distance, and the seven best bad ones were closed. We settled for the huge, varnished unwelcome of an empty cafeteria-bar. John addressed me with an awareness of his dignity, as if he were Ezra Pound at St. Elizabeths, emphatic without pertinence, then brownly inaudible. His remarks seemed guarded, then softened into sounds that only he could understand or hear. At first John was ascetically hung over, at the end we were high without assurance, and speechless. I said, "When will I see you again?" meaning, in the next few days before I flew to England. John said, "Cal, I was thinking through lunch that I'll never see you again." I wondered how in the murk of our conversation I had hurt him, but he explained that his doctor had told him one more drunken binge would kill him. Choice? It is blighting to know that this fear was the beginning of eleven months of abstinence . . . half a year of prolific rebirth, then suicide.

I have written on most of Berryman's earlier books. 77 Dream Songs are harder than most hard modern poetry, the succeeding poems in His Toy are as direct as a prose journal, as readable as poetry can be. This is a fulfillment, yet the 77 Songs may speak clearest, almost John's whole truth. I misjudged them, and was rattled by their mannerisms. His last two books, Love & Fame and Delusions, Etc., move. They may be slighter than the chronicle of dream songs, but they fill out the frame, alter their speech with age, and prepare for his death—they almost bury

John's love-child and ventriloquist's doll, Henry. *Love & Fame* is profane and often in bad taste, the license of John's old college dates recollected at fifty. The subjects may have been too inspiring and less a breaking of new ground than he knew; some wear his gayest cloth. *Love & Fame* ends with an intense long prayer sequence. *Delusions* is mostly sacred and begins with a prayer sequence.

Was riot or prayer delusion? Both were tried friends. The prayers are a Roman Catholic unbeliever's, seesawing from sin to piety, from blasphemous affirmation to devoted anguish. Their trouble is not the dark Hopkins discovered in himself and invented. This is a traditionally Catholic situation, the *Sagesse*, the wisdom of the sinner, Verlaine in jail. Berryman became one of the few religious poets, yet it isn't my favorite side, and I will end with two personal quotations. The first is humorous, a shadow portrait:

> *My marvelous black new brim-*
> *rolled felt is both stuffy and raffish.*
> *I hit my summit with it, in firelight.*
> *Maybe I only got a Yuletide tie*
> *(increasing sixty) & some writing paper*
> *but ha(haha) I've bought myself a hat!*
> *Plus strokes from position zero!*

The second is soberly prophetic and goes back twenty-six years to when John was visiting Richard Blackmur, a few days before or after he visited me:

UNDERSTANDING

> *He was reading late, at Richard's down in Maine,*
> *aged 32? Richard and Helen long in bed,*
> *my good wife long in bed.*
> *All I had to do was strip & get in my bed,*
> *putting the marker in the book, and sleep,*
> *& wake to a hot breakfast.*

Off the coast was an island, P'tit Manaan,
the bluff from Richard's lawn was almost sheer.
A chill at four o'clock.
It only takes a few minutes to make a man.
A concentration upon now and here.
Suddenly, unlike Bach,

& horribly, unlike Bach, it occurred to me
that one night instead of warm pajamas,
I'd take off all my clothes
& cross the damp cold dawn & totter down the bluff
into the terrible water & walk forever
under it out toward the island.

[1972]

Andrei Voznesensky

We have come here to listen to Andrei Voznesensky, both in his own voice and in translation, because he is a good poet. We are here too because he is a Russian poet. In this chafing and often terrifying moment for his country and ours, a yearning is felt on both sides to break through. We are dissatisfied with the present lull, surly, torpid, distrustful. We wish to go beyond the tense stances and slump of the higher levels—the old bear and old Uncle Sam with his goatee and red-and-white-striped flag-waving trousers—two big powers with the power to hurt, disturbingly alike in their problems and temptations, disturbingly different in their ideological logic and idiom. Sometimes each country seems like an invention of the other, a blessed outlet for invective, an excuse to rally its citizens' morale, until even the shyest and most unpolitical bristles with a fierce readiness, and each sentence of innocent recollection becomes an act of accusation. We long to meet another human being.

Andrei Voznesensky is such a man, an emissary because he is not an emissary, representative because he represents no official dogma or policy, not even a rival literary position, but simply Russian writing at its best. His voice has rung around the world. We are glad that what makes it carry is the difficult mastery of his art, and not a message. We are glad he has not come here to convert us, glad that he has protested and been in trouble with his government, and glad too that this protest was complicated, obscure, and human, that it was made at home, and that he comes here as a visitor, not as an exile, to show what can be done in Russia, and not to expose.

Andrei Voznesensky is a difficult writer, who writes in a language that few of us, including all his translators tonight, can understand, yet he is peculiarly easy for us to like and admire. He comes to us with the careless gaiety of the twenties and Apollinaire, with a flippant magic, effervescent intensity, and an imagination so boisterous and high-spirited that only a Russian could survive it. He says, "We do not burn to survive, but to step on the gas." Voznesensky is not likely to burn out, he is not Mayakovsky. When he looks at himself, I think he is glad he is only life-size, or a bit smaller. Everywhere in his poetry is something fine-boned, fragile, and sensible. With humor, with shrewd amazement, with rushes of defiance, he is able to be himself, a gift no one is born with, and which is only acquired by the most heroic patience and ingenuity.

He has a large vocabulary, and larger interests: architecture, Paris, New York, machines, bureaucrats, and people. Every other poem is a love poem or about women. He is much too fascinated in surprising and in striking from bold, unexpected angles to be often obscure. Surrealism sprouts from his finger ends: a hundred anti-worlds, aluminum birds with women's heads, pink-candled birthday cakes stuck to a ceiling, houses without walls, men without skins, and noses that go on growing all night. Each imaginary toad lives in a real garden. Each invention is made of real material, and has behind it the deftness of a real hand, heart's blood, and an unsleeping wit and intelligence. Sometimes he seems like the universal young man in revolt, impatient with the tame, the conventional, or merely the old, out to smash the gilded chairs of the academicians for fresh kindling. But at other times, and often shifting from line to line, he has the steady sorrowing sympathy of Pasternak or Chekhov.

Auden has written, "As a fellow maker, I am struck first and foremost by his craftsmanship. Here at least is a poet who knows that, whatever else it may be, a poem is a verbal artifact that must be as skillfully and solidly constructed as a table or a motorcycle." Voznesensky is lucky in drawing this praise from our own most resolute craftsman, and lucky too in attracting Auden and the other poets who are here as his translators. How far they have deviated, I cannot tell, but each of their English poems has an edge, some witty, others somber and poignant. That such a professional and poet's poet as Voznesensky should ring through Russia and now here is a sobering and delicate surprise. By his moderation and fineness, he comes off for us and gives us his little world of the lover, his slang, his country scenes, and his war of the artist against "the crude archangel made of nuts and bolts," "the cybernetic robot who says to his creator, 'Give me your wife.' "

This is a hard time to be a poet, and in each country it is hard in different ways. It is almost impossible, even where this is permitted, to be directly political and remain inspired. Still the world presses in as never before, prodding, benumbing. We stand in a sort of international lull. Like a cat up a tree, we want to climb down without falling. It's too much, we've lost our foothold. The other night, I found myself shaving. An impatient, just-lit cigarette was sighting me down from the soap dish, and the bathroom door was ajar to catch messages from the world news roundup. It's too much, it's too tense. We want another human being. We want Andrei Voznesensky with his antiworlds to juggle us back to the real world for a moment. We are glad he is our guest.

[1967]

Sylvia Plath's *Ariel*

In these poems, written in the last months of her life and often rushed out at the rate of two or three a day, Sylvia Plath becomes herself, becomes something imaginary, newly, wildly, and subtly created—hardly a person at all, or a woman, certainly not another "poetess," but one of those super-real, hypnotic, great classical heroines. This character is feminine, rather than female, though almost everything we customarily think of as feminine is turned on its head. The voice is now coolly amused, witty, now sour, now fanciful, girlish, charming, now sinking to the strident rasp of the vampire—a Dido, Phaedra, or Medea, who can laugh at herself as "cow-heavy and floral in my Victorian nightgown." Though lines get repeated, and sometimes the plot is lost, language never dies in her mouth.

Everything in these poems is personal, confessional, felt, but the manner of feeling is controlled hallucination, the autobiography of a fever. She burns to be on the move, a walk, a ride, a journey, the flight of the queen bee. She is driven forward by the pounding pistons of the heart. The title *Ariel* summons up Shakespeare's lovely though slightly chilling and androgynous spirit, but the truth is that this Ariel is the author's horse. Dangerous, more powerful than man, machine-like from hard training, she herself is a little like a racehorse, galloping relentlessly with risked, outstretched neck, death hurdle after death hurdle topped. She cries out for that rapid life of starting pistols, snapping tapes, and new world records broken. What is most heroic in her, though, is not her force, but the desperate practicality of her control, her hand of metal with its modest, womanish touch. Almost pure motion, she can endure "God, the great stasis in his vacuous night," hospitals, fever, paralysis, the iron lung, being stripped like a girl in the booth of a circus sideshow, dressed like a mannequin, tied down like Gulliver by the Lilliputians . . . apartments, babies, prim English landscapes, beehives, yew trees, gardens, the moon, hooks, the black boot, wounds, flowers with mouths like wounds, Belsen's lampshades made of human skin, Hitler's homicidal iron tanks clanking over Russia. Suicide, father-hatred, self-loathing—nothing is too much for the macabre gaiety of her control. Yet it is too much; her art's immortality is life's disintegration. The surprise, the shimmering, unwrapped birthday present, the transcendence "into the red eye, the cauldron of morning," and the lover, who are always waiting for her, are Death, her own abrupt and defiant death.

> *He tells me how badly I photograph.*
> *He tells me how sweet*
> *The babies look in their hospital*
> *Icebox, a simple*
> *Frill at the neck,*
> *Then the flutings of their Ionic*
> *Death-gowns,*
> *Then two little feet.*

There is a peculiar, haunting challenge to these poems. Probably many, after reading *Ariel*, will recoil from their first overawed shock and painfully wonder why so much of it leaves them feeling empty, evasive, and inarticulate. In her lines, I often hear the serpent whisper, "Come, if only you, too, could have my rightness, audacity, and ease of inspiration." But most of us will turn back. These poems are playing Russian roulette with six cartridges in the cylinder, a game of "Chicken," the wheels of both cars locked and unable to swerve. Oh, for that heaven of the humble copyist, those millennia of Egyptian artists repeating their lofty set patterns! And yet Sylvia Plath's poems are not the celebration of some savage and debauched existence, that of the "damned" poet, glad to burn out his body for a few years of continuous intensity. This poetry and life are not a career; they tell that life, even when disciplined, is simply not worth it.

It is poignant, looking back, to realize that the secret of Sylvia Plath's last irresistible blaze lies lost somewhere in the checks and courtesies of her early laborious shyness. She was never a student of mine, but for a couple of months, seven years ago [1959], she used to drop in on my poetry seminar at Boston University. I see her dim against the bright sky of a high window, viewless unless one cared to look down on the city outskirts' defeated yellow brick and square concrete pillbox filling stations. She was willowy, long-waisted, sharp-elbowed, nervous, giggly, gracious—a brilliant tense presence embarrassed by restraint. Her humility and willingness to accept what was admired seemed at times to give her an air of maddening docility that hid her unfashionable patience and boldness. She showed us poems that later, more or less unchanged, went into her first book, *The Colossus*. They were somber, formidably expert in stanza structure, and had a flair for alliteration and Massachusetts's low-tide dolor:

> *A mongrel working his legs to a gallop*
> *Hustles the gull flock to flap off the sand-pit.*

Other lines showed her wit and directness:

> *The pears fatten like little Buddhas.*

Somehow none of it sank very deep into my awareness. I sensed her abashment and distinction, and never guessed her later appalling and triumphant fulfillment.

[1966]

Two

Art and Evil

First I want to confess that I intend to run far and at a breakneck speed from my title. *Art* and *Evil*: these words have a somewhat savagely neon-lighted, newly baptized, neo-art-for-art's-sake, Naughty Nineties severity to them. They are the shell that covers old weakness and a heart of gold. I admit that I come before this immense audience with fear and trembling. I hope to tempt rather than to accuse. I hope to amuse you, and show how art can make even ill things a joy. I want to talk about the pleasure we all take in the company of bad men and bad women.

During the last twenty years [1936–1956], the earth's surface seems to have sagged and cracked. These have been the years of Hitler, Stalin's purges, Buchenwald, the atomic bomb, the threat of nuclear war. During this period our graver and more high-powered critics have had to attempt a massive reappraisal; they have pretty well agreed that writers can be too healthy for their own good. Today we are all looking for darkness visible, and we know that a realistic awe of evil is a mighty valuable thing for the writer to have. Our literary models at first were the most violent Elizabethan tragedians, the French *poètes maudits*, and our own madcap experimental writers of the nineteen-twenties. Old classics no longer pleased; but presently we discovered with relief that supposedly sound authors were much worse than they seemed. We discovered the black nihilistic, homosexual, almost disintegrating Shakespeare of *Measure for Measure, Troilus, Hamlet,* and *Timon.* We discovered a black gin-drinking Tennyson. We discovered a black wolfish, wife-deserting Dickens, whose grotesque Hieronymus Bosch world struck us as God's plenty, a richer dramatic creation than any English writer's since Shakespeare. Then a funny thing happened: just as we had labeled our times the Age of Anxiety, and had managed to point out an ample and redeeming shadow of darkness in just about every writer who had ever lived—just at this point we suddenly found we were midway in a second solid, sensible, wealthy, optimistic, child-bearing era, one not unlike the times of Queen Victoria and Prince Albert. Out of the black earth of our evil authors and evil visions, we have somehow rebuilt our own booming 1970s, '80s, and '90s, complete with their dynasties of Republican Presidents.

Today, when I look back some twenty years, I think I can say with very little exaggeration that my once polemical and rebellious loyalties have become such dim truisms that I can no longer understand them. In 1933 T. S. Eliot published a little book on the modern temper entitled *After Strange Gods.* Eliot was writing in the full greenness of his recent conversion to Catholicism, classicism, and conservatism. His book has lost none of the freshness, magic, and one-sidedness of its occasion. Eliot had of course by this time published his long poem, *The Waste Land.* He had written "Let us go then, you and I, / When the evening is spread out against the sky / Like a patient etherized upon a table." And he had written many other lines which authoritative critics had considered as touchstones of the anti-poetic. So Eliot may have had a chip on his shoulder. He may have had a delicious sense of turning the tables when he wrote the following sentences on the subject of arbitrary evil in the stories of Thomas Hardy. Eliot said, "I am concerned with the intrusion of the diabolic in modern literature as a consequence of the limiting and crippling effect of a separation from orthodoxy and tradition." Eliot went on—his tone had the somewhat tearful, somewhat rising note of a true preacher: "But I am afraid that even if you can entertain the notion of a positive power for evil working through human agency, you may still have a very inaccurate notion of what Evil is, and may find it difficult to believe that it may operate through men of genius and excellent character. I doubt whether what I am saying will convey much to anyone for whom the doctrine of Original Sin is not a very real and tremendous thing." This passage at first struck many of us as a little stiff and silly, as being itself a bit diabolic. Later the point came across; such sentiments had their vogue, and many imitations. And now, in 1956, we are older than the Eliot of 1933; we are older than the aged eagle himself; Original Sin has lost its old shine for us; we no longer possess that simple faith, that straightforward sophistication, and that angry bounce that allowed T. S. Eliot to call Original Sin *tremendous*.

At this point I want to stop, and breathe, and turn around for a moment so I can attack my subject in a lighter and perhaps more colorful style. I want to tell you two stories of my own personal contacts with the diabolic. The trouble with writing poetry is that you have readers, and the trouble with readers is that you have to listen to them after they have spent their time reading you. Mine, unless they are young poets or teachers of English, usually say one of three things. If they are relatives, they ask me why I choose such sordid downhill subjects. If they are strangers who want to be cordial yet dislike what they have read of me, they admit that some of the things I have published are over their heads. If they are not sure that they want to be cordial, they overemphasize that they are not intellectuals. They confess that all they can do is run a brokerage, make money, have five children, build a house from their own plans, and run, say, the Boston Museum of Natural Science as a hobby. The final blow is to ask me in a harsh, clear, incredulously polite voice about the Pulitzer Prize. "You won the *Nobel* Prize, didn't you? Everyone can't do that." Now, at the time when I was choosing "Art and Evil" as a title for this talk, I was spending many evenings with a favorite relative, an elderly lady who had recently been through a landslide of sorrows, but yet managed to be more observant, more lighthearted, more full of talk, and more all there than anyone I have known. We would listen to the lavishly anguished music of Schubert's *Winterreise* sequence, a work in which naïve and morbid lyrics are made sublime by the music. My cousin enjoyed every drop of this work, but then she would talk to me about being more positive. "You mustn't mislead younger people," she would say, "with your verses." Though a moderate drinker herself, my cousin believed with A. E. Housman that malt could do more than Milton. She would hold out a huge pale cylinder of martinis. "This will do you good," she would say. She would urge me to take siestas after lunch, knowing that sloth is the safest cure of all vices. Finally she would hand me an armful of fierce whodunits with horrifying covers. Nothing in this line was too rough for her: I still feel wounded when I think of how my cousin found my poems gloomier than the *Winterreise*, more inflammatory than martinis, duller than detective stories, and deader than sleep.

Now, when Eliot was cautioning us about the intrusion of the diabolic in modern literature, I don't imagine he was taking up arms against Agatha Christie, Eric Ambler, Graham Greene, and the Crime Club. Indeed, nothing could be less mysterious and more aboveboard than the means by which a mystery pleases. Here the author is selfless, he must plot every inch, he must do all the work, and consequently no reader ever complains that the most ingenious and farfetched plot is unintelligible. Once the detective has struck his trail of blood, he can gayly revel in all the needless and whimsical erudition that modern poets aspire to. How many lives have been deadened and blanked by the necessity of reading and teaching literature; how many lives have been saved by crime books. There is something philanthropic and almost sugary about a good horror plot: secure in the cool soothing arms of horror, we accept even the travelogues of Melville, the encyclopedic researches of Mann, the astronomy of Dante. In the Gospels, perhaps it is the horror and the scandal of the

Cross that beguiles intellectuals to read through the Sermon on the Mount. I like to think that Plato was a reader of thrillers, and after banning Homer from his Republic, he would have declared thrillers innocent of Original Sin and given them the keys to his Athens.

Now, one of the hopeful characteristics of our human nature is that we cannot even put up with *evil* for long, unless it is made exciting, and we cannot put up with excitement unless it is true. All parties agree on this, but from there on, the approach is classical or romantic. The romantic approach is that man is the victim of the gods; this is on the whole the position of Greek classical drama, a position which the imagination will never quite disown. The classical approach is man's abuse of God's love; this is the position, on the whole, of Plato and the world religions, a position they can never quite get rid of. Both sides call on Christ. Here I am tempted to overreach myself and address you for a half minute as a theologian and Christian apologist. I would like to say that I see being as made up of hierarchical elements: nature, man, society, the angels perhaps, and God. We see each element from time to time as good, indifferent, or bad, as black, white, or gray. The war of God and creation, of classicist and romantic goes on forever. What is special about Christ is that he takes both sides at once.

I am now ready to start on the real subject of my paper and talk about my villains. I have chosen eight examples: two criminals, Rimbaud and Milton's Satan; two cold men, George Eliot's Grandcourt and Vergil's Aeneas; two comics, Dickens's Sarah Gamp and Faulkner's Popeye; and two manipulators, Goethe's Mephistopheles and Shakespeare's Iago. Of all these, the only Christ-like characters are, of course, the criminals. Heroes of this sort are admired by all who want either to ruin or to reform the world. The criminal is called Cain, but he has other names which often suit him better. He is called Lucifer, Prometheus, Orestes, Christ, and each name stands for a different reality. According to orthodox theology, Christ is God, he is God the Son, so at peace with God the Father that the Love that unites them is itself

God. Now theological formulas may not seem to signify much to us, all that has been said about the Three persons in one Substance may strike us as childishly unpragmatic. What I want to say here is that Three persons in one Substance is the strongest imaginable way of stating that there is no celestial strife, no tyrant father, no son in revolt, no mutual incomprehension in heaven, and no new order. The Gospel story, far from being the story of revolt, is not even the story of a reconciliation. Nevertheless, Christ dies; he is mistaken for a criminal and executed, perhaps in good faith by a world that is itself at war with God, and perhaps doesn't know it. Now, the society that executed Christ as a criminal and blasphemer is not very unlike other societies— we will therefore have to put up with this muddle: there will always be something of God the Father's goodness about society, and something of God the Son's goodness about each rebel. Natural history shows us that there is a good deal of the lamb in the wolf and a good deal of the wolf in the lamb. The same is true of persons, to come to my heroes. Cain is perhaps the story of the man who tries to be reconciled with God by sacrificing his brother; Prometheus is the story of seemingly hopeless defiance of a tyrant; Orestes is the story of purging society by murdering the tyrant; Satan is the story of spirit trying to commit suicide in order to be God; Christ is the mystery of how accepting death and dying is life.

In actuality, these stories intermingle, and in the life and writings of Arthur Rimbaud they were exceptionally mixed up and intense. At the age of nineteen, Rimbaud wrote and published a forty-page prose poem called A *Season in Hell*. It is a symbolic autobiography, a confession, a series of delirious visions, and also a piece of experimental writing that gives the contradictory impression of being completely contrived and yet haphazard; of reciting a memorized part, and of telling all without fear or artifice. Rimbaud seems to be reading over the stories of all the world's scapegoats, and in each case saying, "No, this is too simple, this doesn't fit me." Here is Rimbaud as Cain, who says: "While still quite a child I used to admire the incurable convict on whom the prison doors were always shutting. I would look up the inns and lodgings which such a man might have hallowed with his presence. With a convict's vision I saw the blue sky and blossoming labor of the countryside. I smelled his fatality in the cities. The criminal had more strength than the saint, more good sense than a traveler—he alone was the sole witness of his glory and rightness." Then Rimbaud is like the Wandering Jew, a victim driven across the face of the earth. "I know not where I go, nor why I go," he says. "I enter everywhere. I answer everything. They will not kill me any more than they would kill a corpse. In the morning I had so lost a look that those whom I met perhaps did not see me." Or again Rimbaud is a kind of Barabbas cursing the Pharisees. He says, "I have no moral sense. I am an animal. But I can be saved; whereas you—maniacs, butchers, misers—you are animals in disguise. Magistrate, you are a savage; merchant, you are a savage; Emperor, old itching scab, you are a savage—you have drunk contraband whiskey." Then a little later, but not permanently, and not as a climax, Rimbaud is the repentant sinner. He says, "I am no longer in love with boredom. I am not a prisoner of my intellect. The world is good. I love my brethren. God is my strength. These," he declares, "are not the promises of a child, nor are they made in the hope of escaping old age and death." Boy, poet, magician, tramp, tough, explorer of the Orient—half of Rimbaud always seems to be running headlong to knock his brains out, the other half is a shrewd, commonsensical, businesslike person—someone much like his mother, that proud, respectable peasant woman who went on running farm and family after being abandoned by her drifting husband, the soldier. Defiant, humble, practical, terrified, foolhardy: Rimbaud is always picking himself up to find new ways of running in the same direction. Rimbaud's precosity —no one his age has ever written better poetry—his precosity made him both accomplished and impatient; his peasant character allowed him to look out for himself and yet remain awkward. All these qualities show up in his humor. "From my ancestors, the Gauls," he says, "I got my blue eyes, narrow brainpan, and clumsiness in battle. My clothing is as barbarous as theirs, but I don't butter my hair." He says, "I don't suppose

I have set out for a wedding feast with Jesus Christ as my father-in-law." He imagines himself as an African savage. "Dance, dance, dance," he says. "I can't even imagine the hour when the white man shall land and I will collapse into nothingness." In one section Rimbaud invents a character called the Foolish Virgin. The Foolish Virgin is Verlaine, the poet who, though twenty years older, left his wife to follow Rimbaud. Verlaine is made to say, "Oh yes, I was a respectable woman in those days. Rimbaud was almost a child; his mysterious tenderness seduced me. I forgot all my human obligations to follow him. I have heard him boasting of his infamy. He would say, 'My forefathers were Scandinavian. I will make gashes all over my body. I will tattoo myself. I will never work!' Often at night the boy would lie in wait for me when he was drunk in order to scare me. Then he would go about with the pretty airs of a little girl at Sunday school." Rimbaud's comment on this passage is *drôle de ménage*: a queer couple!

In the literature of the world, Rimbaud has many cousins. He is the violently tender Propertius meeting the ghost of his mistress and saying, "*Sunt alaquid Manes*: a ghost isn't nothing." He is both the obscenely raving Lear and the famous simple Lear who holds up the strangled Cordelia and says, "Pray you undo this button." He is both a parody and a sequel to the Napoleon of boys' books. He is one more Faust undergoing a planned derangement of his senses in order to write entertainingly about himself. French literature, however, seems almost to have a patent on underworld Christs. The criminal Christ is subtly related to another character in French fiction who is even more commonly met with and who is not at all a criminal. This character is the woman-shy man. His first appearance is historical and noble; he is King Louis IX in Joinville's memoirs. After that there is Hypolite in *Phèdre*, Molière's *Misanthrope*, Benjamin Constant's Adolphe; Flaubert's Charles Bovary, the Gide of Gide's journals and much of his fiction, and the narrator-hero in Proust's *Search for Lost Time*. How this character changes into a criminal is well shown by Stendhal's Julian Sorel. English authors—but this is perhaps an illusion—seem to stand more outside their rogues. Villon's *Testament* is at the heart of French literature, in a way that Chaucer's Wife of Bath and Shakespeare's Falstaff are not at the heart of English. What other literature has dark autobiographical works that can compare with those by Villon, Sade, Rousseau, Stendhal, Baudelaire, Saint-Beuve, Tristan Corbière, Céline, Genet? One thinks of the eighteenth-century philosopher Diderot writing about Rameau's disreputable nephew, and of our own twentieth-century philosopher Sartre writing on Jean Genet, the criminal novelist. But to come back to Rimbaud; we enjoy his humor, his passion, his honesty; we enjoy his toughness and his panic; we enjoy the power and newness of his language. *A Season in Hell* is the work of a religious and ignited man; it is completely concrete, and yet everywhere bursting at the seams with a meaning that cannot be formulated but that is intense to the point of being a parable.

But if we can like the artist criminal as Satan, what shall we say of Satan as Satan? In Milton's Lucifer, it would seem that we have no human foothold, here there is nothing for tears, no human weakness to knock our breasts over. C. S. Lewis has written a brilliant scolding little book on *Paradise Lost*. In his preface he pays tribute to another critic, Charles Williams, for rediscovering "after over a hundred years of misinterpretation" that Satan really is diabolic. C. S. Lewis attacks Milton's Satan waspishly. Rather as though he were the devil's advocate, he demonstrates that Satan is a liar, a bad logician, a self-deceiver, a bluff, a creature sleeplessly thinking about himself, and one whose speeches are interminable autobiography. Now, this really does seem to have something of Milton's intention, but what are we to say of the nineteenth century, and such intelligent readers as Blake, Shelley, Lord Macaulay, Sir Walter Raleigh, and even T. S. Eliot, who not only appear to have missed so block-like and advertised a fact as Satan's diabolism, but to have thought that Milton was giving us a perhaps disastrously heroic version of himself. Now, C. S. Lewis admits, as he must, that Satan is by far Milton's best character; his explanation is an adroit one: bad persons, Lewis says, are always easier to portray than good ones, for, although none of us knows anything much about men who are better than we, yet on the other hand evil is always faithful to us, always at our elbow, always below us; to characterize a bad man we have only to release our own bad passions, hatreds, suppressions, confusions. I suppose it would be a little cheap for us to jeer at this explanation, and to say sarcastically that Milton must have been extraordinarily rich in evil-controlled passion, since he was to succeed better than all others in raising the devil, in making Satan live. When Milton writes of God, creation, the history of man, and even of Eve and Adam, a certain paralysis, a certain coldness, a certain vagueness and unease seem to strike him. Yet, with Satan, Milton's energy never fails, and his epic justifying God's ways lives principally by virtue of the devil. I don't think we should say with Blake that Milton was secretly of the devil's party, for his devil is undoubtedly cruel, a positive power with its will set on absolute destruction, and only veiling destruction from itself by more destruction, a creature living on the void and breathing it in with relentless gluttony as a drug addict might smoke opium. Satan declares, in his great speech at the beginning of Book IV, "Evil be thou my good." Thenceforth, all hope is excluded, he *is* hell, and within his hell another opens, and so on, ad infinitum, and each hell compared to its successor is a heaven; but at least Satan holds divided empire with God: He knows that his own and not another's will is being done. Yet once we have made all possible allowance for Satan's bad role, we must admit he plays it with almost infinite courage, intelligence, fire, unwillingness to set his course by formulas, and perhaps above all with unfailing rhetorical adequacy, pith, and variety. The Father of Lies is very appropriately a master of words. He also knows how to act, in the sense both of taking action and of playing a part.

We live in a hard and cracked world. If there was ever a positive power for evil at work through human agency, that power is still at work. But meanwhile, in science, philosophy, art, and even theology, Satan is for the moment a dead letter, he is unverifiable. Wallace Stevens has written in a sequence of poems called *Esthétique du Mal*, "The death of Satan was a tragedy for the imagination." Satan was "himself denied." According to Stevens, Satan should have known that this was in the cards, for, still quoting Stevens, "negation begets filial negation, negation is eccentric." But as we look on the infinitely diminishing returns of Satan's denial, we too may regret the withdrawal of so skillful and cutthroat an opponent and say, also with Stevens, that "under every *no* lay a passion for *yes* that had never been broken." This is the devil's epithet, the best that can be said of him.

At this point I wish to return to realism, and take a character who has nothing supernatural about him, and who has never probably tempted even the silliest reader to feel even the most mistaken and silly admiration. I am speaking of Mr. Mallinger Grandcourt in George Eliot's last novel, *Daniel Deronda*. Grandcourt is like his name: rich, impressive outwardly, cold, bored. He is too wealthy, too cold, too bored, and too scared not to be hard and sadistic when he has the chance, but even in this he is not extreme; he is not picturesquely horrible, he is not a lost violent soul in any visible and dramatic manner; he is merely true to life. Though a breathing lifelike person and in no way a symbol, he is also mainly a burnt place, a hole without a doughnut, a void for George Eliot's heroine, Gwendolyn Harleth, to fall into. The novel *Daniel Deronda* is the story of Gwendolyn's fall, a fall in its way as significant as Eve's and as realistically and as lovingly told as Anna Karenina's. The reasons why Grandcourt is so burnt-out and low-spirited are not altogether clear; he is largely passive, and perhaps today we would send him to a doctor rather than sit by and let him drown in the Mediterranean as George Eliot and Gwendolyn finally do. However, there *is* one moment when Grandcourt is active and makes what might be called his tragic choice. This is when he proposes to Gwendolyn, is accepted, and consequently can*not* marry his mistress, Mrs. Glasher, whom he has been keeping in dangling uncertainty for many years and who has borne him four children. Just before his marriage, and not long before the close of his life, Grandcourt pays Mrs. Glasher a visit which is one of the iciest in fiction. Grandcourt has to tell her about his marriage and ask her to return his family diamonds. Both these duties bore and embarrass Grandcourt. Here Grandcourt is cold-blooded, poisonous, languid, a lizard sunning its cold body and idly staring its victim into petrifaction—or rather, in George Eliot's words, "not caring a languid curse for anyone's admiration yet fond of looking stonily at smiling persons, and requiring that those persons be there and that they must smile." Grandcourt describes his journey: "I rested at the Junction, a hideous hole. These railroad journeys are always a confounded bore. But I had coffee and smoked." He leads up to announcing his marriage by saying, "The time has gone on with rather a rattling pace with me; generally it is slow enough." We next see Grandcourt annoyed at the scene which follows his announcement and annoyed that no imperiousness can save him *from* the scene. He leaves feeling deucedly sorry for himself for having had to watch Mrs. Glasher's misery, he is gnawed by a sense of imperfect mastery. Henceforth, Grandcourt is doomed; he can only enjoy life by commanding and understanding nothing; that is, by torturing. Why we enjoy or at least tolerate Mr. Mallinger Grandcourt, I cannot quite say. Perhaps it is because we like Gwendolyn, and want to hear about even the void she falls into, the knife blade she cuts her hand on. But Grandcourt's inner life is like a dentist's drill hitting a nerve twenty-four hours a day. If he had written a book it would have been a gentleman idler's version of Dostoevsky's *Notes from the Underground*; but Grandcourt is too bored and imperious to lacerate himself or to write his confession.

My next illustration is the Fourth Book of *The Aeneid*. It is also about a desertion, but the meaning is very different. Erich Auerbach in his powerful critical book *Mimesis* has shown that certain characters in Dante's Hell, Purgatory, and Paradise are so immediate and fully and inexhaustibly human that they shatter the author's great pattern of justice at the very moment when they fully bring it to actuality. Perhaps Dido does this with Aeneas and his epic destiny. Certainly, Aeneas has to get away: Dido is a roaring fire; she burns, she wanders raging through the entire city of Carthage, she is like a deer with a deadly arrow in its side; she becomes Aeneas' mistress. Clearly, Aeneas must get away or be unmanned. He can't loiter as a sort of prince consort —this neither his own manhood and ambitions nor the balloon-like, massive Titianesque passions of Dido will allow. Yet the way Vergil presents the story is hard for us to swallow. We don't like the gods infatuating Dido; we don't see why they have to entangle her with Aeneas; we don't believe that he believes that he is leaving Dido to found the Roman Empire; how could anyone know or even want to imagine such things? We don't believe that Aeneas, a simple Bronze Age chief, could have the least conception of Roman administration, Roman military methods, Roman senatorial procedure, Roman road-making. Aeneas is not eloquent in his final interview with Dido. When he says *"Italiam non sponte sequo*r: not by my own will do I go on to Italy," we don't believe him. We know he is leaving a real woman of flesh and blood to follow the empty abstract fantasy of becoming a figurehead in an epic poem. Aeneas is a myth without fictional or historical reality. He is almost as bad as Grandcourt, who wants nothing at all but to assuage his boredom by domineering. But when we reach the end of Book Twelve and the entire epic, the story of Dido and her desertion seems neces-sary and at the heart of Vergil's story. Aeneas, the founder of the republic and the public servant, is doomed to die many times. He dies with the fall and burning of Troy, he dies with the mislaying of his wife in the burning city, he dies with the death of his father, he dies symbolically by descending into the underworld, and finally in the death of his dearest friends and in the agony of civil war—a war in which, in order to be loyal to his faith that he will ultimately save and establish the state, he is first forced almost to ruin the state. He is like that other ancestor, Abraham, so searchingly described by Kirkegaard. Abra-ham, forced to slaughter his son Isaac in order that paradoxically, through this same Isaac, his seed may be as numerous as the sands of the desert. Aeneas, in tearing himself away from Dido, comes to know the full torture of seeming to be, of all but believing himself to be, cold, dead, calculating, serpentine. *The Aeneid* is perhaps like Proust's novel, the story of what one must give up to write a book.

It is a far cry from the contemptible laconic Grandcourt and the heroic laconic Aeneas, or even the flaming Ciceronian Dido to my next character, Sarah Gamp in Dickens's *Martin Chuzzlewit*—Sarah, the midwife, the layer-out of the dead, who therefore loves both young and old, Sarah with her teapot filled with gin, requiring her pint of porter to be brought regular and drawn mild, Sarah Gamp, who orders a little bit of pickled salmon, a little sprig of fennel, a sprinkling of white pepper, some new bread, a pat of butter, the cowcumber she is partial to, her Brighton Old Tipper Ale, her not more than a shilling's worth of gin, and water warm when she rings the bell; Sarah, who feeds her patient by clutching his windpipe so as to make him gasp, Sarah, who wears a prodigious nightcap, yellow, and in the shape of a cabbage, with a watchman's coat tied around her neck by the sleeves, so that "from behind" she looks "as though she were being embraced by one of the patrol"; Sarah, who lives "above a bird-shop where the birds dance their little ballets of despair and where one unhappy goldfinch lives outside a toy red villa with his name on the door, and draws water for his own drinking and mutely appeals to some good man to drop a penny's worth of poison into it." Gluttonous, filthy, drunken, colorful, sordid, incoherent, an ocean of words: Sarah is fascinating and moves through the plot of *Martin Chuzzlewit* like a huge refuse-splattered rat, or like the man changed into a bug in Franz Kafka's *Metamorphosis*. She is wonderfully awful, perhaps the most gorgeous of all Dickens's talkers. In the end the author cannot bring himself to punish her, and merely leaves her where her drinking will be curtailed—yet she really is bestial, monstrous like life, only bigger and better, and she is a blood-relation to other less charming persons, the Tartuffian hypocrite Pecksniff, to the murderous, possessed Jonas Chuzzlewit. If Dostoevsky had rendered Sarah Gamp, she would have been horrible and incidentally comic; in Dickens she is comic and incidentally horrible.

My next example is also a gargoyle, but this time one that

is definitely meant to make our flesh creep—Popeye, the homicidal, impotent little creature in Faulkner's *Sanctuary*, who murders two important characters, and is finally hanged for the
murder of a man he didn't kill because he was in another town
killing another man. He has no chin at all, his face just goes
away like the face of a wax doll set too near a hot fire and forgotten. At the end Popeye cannot rise out of his immaculate
self, or in any way understand defending his life. "Them durn
hicks," he says about the small-town jailers, "Jesus Christ!" On
the night before his death, the minister says, "Will you let me
pray for you?" "Sure," Popeye answers, "don't mind me." When
he is ready to be hanged, only one thing worries him. "Fix my
hair, Jack," he says to the hangman.

Finally, I want to touch briefly on another kind of villain,
the manipulator. In Goethe's *Faust*, that perhaps greatest of
education books, the endless dialogue between Faust and Mephistopheles tells a father-and-son story, where Faust—young, passionate, poetic, selfish, and blind—is forever having to talk to
his almost Hegelian antithesis, middle-aged, apathetic, prosy,
clear-headed, and clear-sighted Mephistopheles—who at least has
the virtue of being more interested in his victim than in himself.
As for that other, far different manipulator, Iago, he rises to new
heights in that dark scene in which he gives his lying description
of how Cassio mistook him in his sleep for Desdemona. "Sweet
Desdemona! O sweet creature!" he makes Cassio say. Then, says
Iago, "He kissed me hard, as if he would pluck up kisses by the
roots that grew upon my lips; then laid his leg over my thigh,
and sighed." The celebrated handkerchief spotted with straw-
berries is now described. Othello screams, "O blood, blood,
blood! . . . Even so my bloody thoughts with violent pace shall
ne'er look back, ne'er ebb to humble love till that capable and
wide revenge swallow them up." Othello kneels and swears,
"Now by yond marble heaven . . . I here engage my words."
Then comes that final driving-in of the nail, the moment when
lion and fox, when toreador and bull, when Iago and Othello are
doomed together. Iago, carried beyond his machinations and
ultimately beyond any possibility of his own survival, says, "Do

not rise yet." *He* kneels and says, "You elements that clip us round about, witness that here Iago doth give up the execution of his wit, hands, heart to wronged Othello's service . . . What bloody business ever." This is perhaps a version of that old and still popular moralist's practical joke, the joke of the torturer boiled . . . [*The manuscript breaks off at this point.*]

[*1955–6*]

The *Iliad*

[*This essay, which Lowell wrote at eighteen, is the earliest example of his prose in this book. It appeared in the June 1935 issue of the school magazine, while he was a senior at St. Mark's.*]

Seldom equaled and never surpassed, Homer has lived through the ages as the creator of the epic and the father of poetry. His only rivals are Shakespeare and Dante, and many consider him to be greater than either. Generations have admired the *Iliad* chiefly for its beautiful similes, its stately verse, its grand style, and its magnificent passages. All these, however, are secondary; for it is quite natural that so great a genius as Homer should take a tremendous subject and that his technique in expressing it should be almost perfect. Many lesser works have all these qualities, yet most of them have been forgotten long ago, and the few that have survived are seldom read. We do not judge a painting by its anecdote or its pretty colors, nor should we judge a piece of writing by its style. We should ask only two questions about a work of art: "What has it created that exists now?" and "How deeply does it express life?" None of the forgotten authors has ever approached the depth and the universality of Homer.

I shall first state briefly Homer's original contribution to literature, in order to treat at greater length the far more important question of his message. He molded the epic into its present form. This form or scheme has been followed religiously by all his successors, including Vergil and Milton. Future Greek oratory, in all its forms, is predicted and almost surpassed in the great speeches of Diomed, Phoenix, and Achilles, in the ninth book. The dramas of Aeschylus, the odes of Pindar, and the abstract philosophy of Socrates are but fuller expressions of different sides of the *Iliad* and the *Odyssey*. Even classical architecture is suggested by some of their descriptions.

To understand any work that has been accepted as great, one must go on the assumption that it brings some vital message and that it expresses some mighty ideal, or else the work would not have survived. The magnitude and the depth of the *Iliad* make it almost as difficult to understand as life. But by reading intelligently and carefully, at the same time making use of the researches of other scholars, one can comprehend the bulk of what is said. A strong desire to see light and a vivid imagination are, of course, necessary, or the reader will not be able to escape the error of the German critic Wolfe, who tried to prove that not one but twenty authors wrote the *Iliad*. The books are not a series of disconnected ballads but parts of a unified whole whose sections are very subtly joined. The *Iliad*, as we have it now, undoubtedly differs widely from its original form. There are numerous interpolations, and small fragments have probably been lost, but considering that its only means of transmission for over two centuries was by mouth, one must be astounded by its completeness. More contradictions are to be found in *Macbeth* alone than in the entire twenty-four books of the *Iliad*.

Homer aims to show how all mortal strife finally ends in the infinite power of Zeus. To obtain this effect, he divides the *Iliad* into seven oppositions, all of which are limited; but in the end they lead up to and are united in the limitless Zeus. The men on earth are arrayed against each other in two groups, the Greeks and the Trojans, or the West and the East. Each group is again subdivided internally. The resistance of the individual to authority and established law becomes a problem in both armies. Hector and Antenor give Paris very little opposition, for in the East power is more or less passively accepted. In the West, on the other hand, where the individual is all-important, the problem of Achilles assumes alarming proportions, and for a while seriously threatens the success of the entire Greek expedition. There is a general opposition of men of thought to men of action. The similiarity of Nestor and Ulysses on one side to Antenor and Glaucus on the other reminds one of the common bonds which hold men of learning together throughout the world.

Parallel to the situation on earth is that in heaven, on Olympus. This brings up the question as to what is the place and the importance of the gods. They should be considered as abstract qualities, or even better as human characteristics personified. Homer, of course, never intended to make his epic an allegory, for no form of abstract philosophy existed in his day. He did, however, think in terms of symbols and unconsciously personified his thoughts. Venus and Mars are opposed to Juno and Pallas. Polygamy and the disorderly, purposeless Eastern warfare are contrasted with the sanctity of the home and the military discipline of the more objective wars of the West. The Greek champion, Diomed, in the third book, puts both Mars and Venus to flight. For, although they are not very great obstacles, Troy cannot fall until they are met and vanquished. The Trojans are somewhat redeemed by their high culture, which is personified in Phoebus Apollo, the god of light. Though the Greeks will eventually absorb most of the learning of the Orient, all physical strength turns out to be impotent against so intangible a force. Neptune, representing the maritime superiority of the Hellenes, to a certain extent opposes Apollo, but the two have little in common and seldom clash. The gods are different sides of Zeus and not independent powers, for only when humored can they accomplish anything.

By far the most important character in the *Iliad* is Zeus. He is the spirit of the universe, unfathomable and eternal: the irresistible force that makes the world go round, crushing all opposition, and the petty, meaningless power that seems to delight in doing strange things with our destinies. The two sides might be called fate and caprice, although caprice is entirely subordinate. Even when circumstances appear to be working most strongly against any established order, they are in reality under complete control. Occasionally, when Zeus falls asleep, lesser gods rule for a short period. Then everything goes wrong on earth; but as soon as the supreme god awakens, all is readjusted and recovered. Thus, the march of humanity continues in spite of numerous obstacles. The fates should be regarded as scales, which as such can be used by Zeus at will. Even when they are consulted, their decisions are not necessarily binding. It is possible to consider Zeus as controlled by the fates; but if this were so, the all-powerful would be restricted, the infinite would be limited, and an enlightened and advanced philosophy would become blind fatalism. Our whole system would crumble, and the finely constructed *Iliad* would be turned into a chaotic jumble.

The key to Homer's greatness lies in the perfection with which he reconciled the human with the divine. The decrees of Zeus must be executed, yet man is independent and his individual actions cannot be controlled. He has a free will. When this will is in harmony with Zeus, man will be just and great; when it is out of harmony, he becomes ignoble and small. The divine dreams and the supernatural appearances of the gods on earth can affect mortals only through their minds. If Agamemnon had not believed himself able to conquer Troy, the deceitful dream from Jove would have been ineffectual. If Pandarus had not been ready to violate the treaty, Minerva's materialistic offers of wealth and glory would have had no influence. If Hector had not been confident in his own skill, he would not have rushed headlong into combat with Achilles. Occasionally in the latter part of the *Iliad* the deeds of the gods cannot be explained in this manner, but these instances are very rare and probably spurious. The strength of Zeus is not in his absolute power over pawns but in the ability with which he invariably accomplishes his ends through the agency of free men, whom he is unable to control except indirectly.

We can understand how the divine and the human are interwoven by studying two of the principal characters and perceiving their condition. Hector is by no means the hero of the *Iliad*, but his condition is very interesting. He might be called the Greek in Troy, for his sympathies and his beliefs were Occidental. He believed that the Trojans were wrong in starting the war; he hated polygamy and despised his brother Paris. Out of harmony with himself and Zeus, he must, no matter what the outcome of the war, see either the destruction of his ideals or the downfall of his kinsman.

Whether we like Achilles or not, we must admit that he is a giant. Not only his physical actions, which are unimportant, but also his mental passions are tremendously enlarged. Homer has taken the most extreme case to show that this titan must conform to the will of the universe, and that even he can accomplish nothing when he is out of harmony. The plot, so to speak, of the *Iliad* depicts the two terrible wraths of Achilles, and how in each case the hero's wrath is completely overcome. In the first book, Agamemnon selfishly takes away Achilles' captive, Briseis. Authority misuses its power and wrongs the individual; consequently, the individual is perfectly justified in passively refusing to cooperate with a force which he believes to be acting unfairly toward him. It is now necessary for Agamemnon to be humbled. To accomplish this end, Zeus afflicts the Greeks with a series of almost unparalleled disasters. But after Achilles scornfully refuses the more than ample offers of the commander's ambassadors, he is no longer in the right and must himself be subjugated. If Achilles had become reconciled with Agamemnon at this point, he would certainly have been a more sensible man and probably a better man, but he would not have been heroic; nor could the *Iliad* ever have been written if he had not been what he was. The hero's punishment will be in proportion to his wrath, for during the next nine books, sulking in his tent, he is no longer the hero. His place is taken by Ajax, Diomed, and a score of lesser men. The long period of suffering from inaction is finally climaxed by the death of his great friend, Patroclus. It is significant that at this time Thetis, the mother of Achilles, again makes her appearance. She symbolizes some external force acting on the will of her son. The irresistible laws of Zeus working informally on Achilles at last force him to make peace with Agamemnon.

Now the second and greater wrath begins. The Trojans, and above all Hector, must suffer for the death of his friend. It is to be expected that Achilles should do everything in his power to overcome and kill the conqueror of Patroclus. No possible moral code, however, can permit the dragging of Hector's corpse around the walls of Troy or the refusal to allow it a decent burial. A sort of undercurrent runs through the celebration of the games and the funeral, in the next-to-last book. We cannot but contrast the magnificent oration to Patroclus with the unworthy neglect of his rival. The unreasoning hate of Achilles cannot continue. His smoldering anger is actually more harmful to himself than to the Trojans. Then Thetis appears to him for the last time. The hero gradually softens and repents his cruelty, so that, when the inspired Priam comes before him to ask for the return of Hector's body, he is quite willing to grant the father's wish. The story is now ended. The strongest and the most violent character in literature is once more at harmony with the world, having become reconciled to authority and forgiven his enemy.

The *Iliad* will be read as long as there are people on this earth. Here we find, eight centuries before Christ and five hundred years before Plato, a man whose philosophy is as mature and complete as that of either. We are told that the accomplishments of man are unlimited, and that when he places all the strength of his mind and his body to the task, a new almost divine power takes possession of him. Homer's heroes continually pray to the gods and always seek to obey and execute their commands. This is but a symbol of an enlightened mind always questioning itself, always seeking means of self-improvement, and always striving for something higher. Homer's principle of placing oneself in harmony with the universe and executing to the best of one's ability the decrees of the gods is just as binding and as seldom carried out today as it was twenty-seven hundred years ago, when the Grecian bard compressed the entire world with all its mysteries into his epic.

[*1935*]

Ovid's
Metamorphoses

A. E. Watts's translation* of the *Metamorphoses* into
five-foot couplets is admirable, steady, civilized—and impossible.
Watts, you have to conclude, has chosen the wrong poem in the
Metamorphoses because this work, as he says in his preface, is
"the most complete exploration in verse of the resources of
rhetoric." Unfortunately, the resources of rhetoric cannot be
explored by academic piety and a photostat exhibition of devices
and tropes. Once started on the job, however, Watts chose the
wrong meter. No English poet has ever translated hexameters
into adequate pentameter couplets. No poet since Chaucer has
done a translation even of couplets into couplets that has turned
out to be comparable to the original. No one *not* a poet has ever
written readable couplets. No one in our century has written an
interesting long poem in couplets. To make sure of mortally
crippling himself, Watts has chosen to mix a gushing run-on line
with the divided, antithetical, and end-stopped line of Pope and
Dryden. The Watts couplet is freakishly stiff and floppy, a Minotaur, uneasy in both its natures; it brays without emphasis. The
translation was then doomed from the start. But Watts has also
picked a perverse idiom for Ovid; he speaks breezily about

---

* *The Metamorphoses of Ovid*, English version by A. E. Watts. University of
California Press, 1955.

writing as a contemporary and yet "enjoying the freedom of the language from Shakespeare to the present day." Instead, he builds a mammoth dump heap stacked with pre-Wordsworthian poeticisms. Watts is not a rhetorician; he is not a metrist; it cannot even be said that he has given us a new Ovid, or a literal Ovid.

By using some of Picasso's drawings as illustrations, Watts or his publisher has made an unstrategic choice—Picasso is fine for Ovid, but he is death on Watts. Left to itself, Watts's untimely performance has an air of modest and stubborn blitheness. As we read on and on in Watts, we are far from the diseased humors of fashion, far from Picasso's two-headed roosters, far from the pressure and patronage of the Dictator Augustus, far, perhaps, from Ovid; but we are very near to an innocent and perished nobility of amateurs. We are near to the never-never land of Ovid's nineteenth-century translators, Orger, Rose, Howard, and King, whose works "fashion, not an impartial estimation, has consigned to oblivion." Here is how Watts renders the death of the Calydonian boar:

> *And while the beast spun round in frenzied wrath,*
> *Bleeding afresh, and spilled the hissing froth,*
> *Hard on his shaft, the marksman, hastening near,*
> *Pricked him to rage, and with his glittering spear*
> *Between the shoulders dealt the killing blow.*

These lines are like tapestry; they should have been *been* tapestry. They should have been done into strangely spelled French. Their irregular and indistinct letters should have been deciphered one by one, as they unwound like a dragon on some tapestry huntsman's tapestry banner. Instead, they have been coupled with Picasso. On the facing page, Picasso—lithe, steely, classical, outrageous—has drawn his pig-like hounds, Thurberish and all mouths; a Meleager part gangster, part peer of France, part bearded Louis-Philippe French sailor—a Meleager naked, glorious, surgical, who probes with his spear at a brute, suffering, drooping muskrat of a wild boar.

So much for pig-sticking and Watts-baiting. I turn now to an affable and bludgeoning man. In the dedication to his translations from the *Metamorphoses*, Dryden writes that he considers his own versions as "perhaps, the best of my endeavors in this kind," and that Ovid, "the most palatable to us of the Roman wits," is "perhaps, the most according to my genius." This is sensible. Deciding to write in couplets was also sensible, for in Dryden's age this meter was the lingua franca for all such translations—Dryden's English Augustan couplets for Ovid were as to-be-expected as Constance Garnett's Georgian prose for Tolstoy. Yet Dryden is loaded down with a backbreaking bag of ready-made tricks for giving clarity and finish to his lines. They roar like an unmuffled Vespa, and leave behind them much of Ovid's subtlety, his placed and displaced words, his delicately varied sentences, his always attentive and changing voice. Dryden the translator is not Dryden the author of the portrait of Shaftesbury; he is a smaller man caught between rapid self-imitation and impressionistic imitations of his originals. Dryden's *Metamorphoses* is a period piece. Still, Dryden is bland, fluent, and spirited; he seldom writes without dash and a stately amusement. Here is his death of the boar:

> *The wound's great author close at hand provokes*
> *His rage, and plies him with redoubled strokes;*
> *Wheels as he wheels, and with his pointed dart*
> *Explores the nearest passage to his heart.*
> *Quick and more quick, he spins in giddy gires.*

Ezra Pound has written that he doesn't think anyone can know anything at all about the art of lucid narrative in English if he hasn't seen all fifteen books of Ovid's Elizabethan translator, Arthur Golding. This is a good way of putting it, and yet I imagine Golding has rarely been read from cover to cover. The reason for this, at least in my own case, is metrical. Even if one is careful not to tub-thump, and reads Golding's huge, looping "fourteeners" for "sense and syntax" as Pound advises, even then one trips; often the form seems like some arbitrary and wayward hurdle, rather than the very backbone of what is being said. One longs to change rhyme words, cut superfluous filler-words, and reduce Golding to paragraphs. Another defect, though not one that prevents good reading, is Golding's lack of rhetorical expertness and interest. A *Metamorphoses* without rhetoric is as unimaginable as a *Lear* in basic English. But Golding, a translator of Calvin, whose single original work was a disquisition on the Earthquake of 1580 as a sign of God's wrath against Sunday theatrical performances, belongs to the tradition of those medieval monks who preserved Ovid's text and canonized the author. Gracefully, directly, and with a diction as lively as the Latin, Golding retells the *Metamorphoses*, as if he had made them. Here he is on a boar, not Meleager's, but the one that mangles Adonis:

> *By chance his hounds in following the track, a boar did see*
> *And roused him; and as the swine was coming from the*
>   *wood*
> *Adonis hit him with a dart askew, and drew the blood.*
> *The boar straight with his hooked groin the hunting staff*
>   *withdrew.*

The boar then has its tusks "in Adonis's cods as far as it could thrust, and laid him all along for dead." Here is Golding calling attention to his caesuras and line endings, and writing an equally beautiful lyrical invocation to Bacchus:

> *Thy youthful years can never waste, there dwelleth aye in*
>   *thee*
> *A childhood, tender, fresh and fair; in heaven we do thee*
>   *see*
> *Surmounting every other thing in beauty and in grace;*
> *And when thou standst without the horns, thou hast a*
>   *maiden's face.*

Here is Watts:

Unfading boyhood, Liber, youth eterne
Are yours; in heaven the fairest star you burn,
Or laying by your horns, on earth you tread,
And like a girl's appears your comely head.

A final note on the translators and their verse forms. In Golding, on the whole, meter follows sentence music, and sentence music follows sense. Golding can hardly write ten lines without making one feel that meter offers fewer impediments to him than almost any narrative poet in the language. Paradoxically, one feels that a series of small but numerous alterations would have made Golding's translation either perfect verse or perfect prose. To say this is, of course, saying that Golding's translation is a major accomplishment. It often resembles and equals the great long poem of its age. But *The Faerie Queen* moves without a hitch, because stanza, sentence music, and sense exist only dimly in themselves; each furthers the others, and lives by surrender. Spenser is supreme in his combinations. Still, the defective Golding is profounder and fresher; his methods should have been copied by Ovid's later translators. These, instead of the story, give us the buzz of their style. They write libretti without orchestras or actors. In these versions, Ovid's airy, worldly, fabulous persons become embalmed in their makeup. I can think of three useful ways of translating Ovid for *us*. The first is Pound's magical echoes of the Bacchus episode; the second is Richmond Lattimore's strong line-for-line, almost word-for-word *Iliad*; the third is Professor Pharr's *Aeneid*, untranslated but with vocabulary and notes at the foot of each page of text. Ovid is different from any of the men I have mentioned. His hexameters, his sentences, and his sense have furious separate existences; they come at each other on foot, on horseback, with swords, forks, and nets, like gladiators they grapple for the kill, and then . . . there is harmony.

Ovid's simplest successes, even, are untranslatable. Here is the beginning of the *Metamorphoses*:

In nova fert animus mutatas dicere formas corpora . . .

The word placing gives almost the impression of a child waking up and talking. Though meticulously ordered, the words seem to drop where they will in their hurry to announce themselves. The mind (*animus* is difficult to translate) bears, or is carried, into new things; not until we get to *corpora* do we know what these new things are. *Mutatas dicere formas* is a conventional arrangement, but in this setting the three words seem italicized, as if Ovid wished to accent the drama of his stumbling by accident on the grand style, his great theme. Is this encounter, though, an accident or a calculated carelessness? Isn't it that Ovid is both too modest and too self-confident to prepare for his meeting? Ovid is curiously intimate and impersonal; there is even here a suggestion of that shy, flirtatious self-concern and gingery vagueness which make Ovid's *Amores* and *Tristia* so dissimilar to Horace's *Epistles*. How much Ovid gives of himself, how little he tells! There are mirrors on the wings of the stage; Ovid takes a deft, impatient look, then, tremblingly aware of the audience, flies to his story. This knack of flight and return, of magic and familiarity, is Ovid's specialty. None of his translators has been able to catch the manner. Perhaps I am superimposing much on little, but I challenge anyone to superimpose anything on Dryden's

Of bodies changed to various forms I sing.

This flattens and simplifies, as is usual with Dryden, and it leaves out *in nova fert*. One might praise *various*, and like the line's ring and swing. Justus Miller's Loeb Classic prose puts in everything, and gives almost the literal meaning: "My mind is bent to tell of bodies changed to new forms." But Miller gives no hint of a voice or a style. Golding lumbers and doesn't bother. His

> *Of shapes transformed to bodies strange I purpose for to
>   sing*

sounds like Miller done into a "fourteener." Watts's

> *Change is my theme*

gets Ovid's hurried, intent, jumping start, but is so terse that it loses the original's hushed, confiding, surprised courtesy.

Ovid's wonderful speeches and stories are too long for quotation, so my second example must also be a trifle. In Book XIII, Polyphemus, the Cyclops, is courting the nymph Galatea. He pleads his suit in a long, touching, absurd song filled with dairy products. Wide-eyed with enthusiasm, the monster declaims that he offers Galatea not common pets, such as kids, fawns, and turtledoves, but two identical bear cubs. Here's how Ovid phrases this detail:

> *Inveni geminos, qui tecum ludere possint,*
> *inter se similes, vix ut dignoscere possis,*
> *villosae catulos in summis montibus ursae:*
> *inveni et dixi "dominae servabimus istos."*

Polyphemus is not a ladies' man, but he has been to the schools. Suspecting, perhaps, that Galatea is a good-for-nothing boy-crazy nymph, he offers her not only the cubs but a geometrically perfect lesson in elocution. Each ungainly descriptive item is isolated, each is hammered home with immense pauses; the stress grows more and more foolish and climactic; finally, Polyphemus lets his cat out of the bag, and says URSAE, bears! The Watts version is clownish doggerel:

> *Twin cubs the nurslings of the shaggy bear,*
> *So like, the which is which you could not swear.*

When first I found them on the hillside steep,
These for my mistress then I swore to keep.

The *Metamorphoses* ends in a rush of apotheoses: first
Julius Caesar's, then Augustus' (prophesied), and then Ovid's
own, immortalized by his verse. The passages are peculiarly
Italian in their grandiosity, humility, naïveté, and wiliness. Here
is grandiloquence:

> *Iamque opus exegi, quod nec Jovis ira nec ignis*
> *nec poterit ferrum nec edax ebolere vetustas.*

This is impeccable, but almost glib in its impudent closeness to
the *Exegi monumentum* of Horace. I don't think, however, that
this is one of those famous instances of slapdash, Ovidian languor; nor is Ovid trying his hand exactly at parody or rivalry. He
is saying something like this: "If you want to hear immortality
asserted in immortally carefully contrived words, read Horace.
Look, I pay tribute to Horace; but my lines, by their volume, by
their naturalness, and by the lightning rapidity with which they
follow my will, are also immortal." After the grandiloquence,
Ovid shifts to deadly directness:

> *Nomen erit indebile nostrum . . .*
> *ore legar populi . . .*
> *vivam.*

Somehow the various styles move together—generously, quickly,
carelessly, unapproachably.

But what did the prodigious and up-to-date Ovid see in his
notorious, magical, and very stale Greek mythological anecdotes?
He was too knowing, too amused, too much a man of the Great
City to have been swept off his feet into Arcadia. He wasn't
writing to the dictation of Milton's Spirit, or to entertain his
children, or to get at the *philosophy* of myth, or to lend the state
a hand in its religious revival. He is *the* writer of all the writers
of the world who followed his own bent in writing a very long

poem. For this, though so immensely derivative and so immensely influential, Ovid has had neither models nor disciples. Not even Chaucer, our one English poet to tell stories in a clear, distinguished, witty, absorbing style, can step in as Ovid does. Ovid is always there, cutting, dawdling, hurrying, throwing in speeches; and yet carried away, wonderstruck *by* his stories and wonderstruck at knowing that *he* is telling them. His style, as no other's, shifts from Vergilian wonder to the flippant, forceful, jabbing worldliness of a letter writer.

In Book VIII of the *Metamorphoses*, Scylla, Princess of Megara, is infatuated with Minos, the Cretan, who is besieging her father, Nisus. She trembles lest one of her father's soldiers kill Minos "by mistake," for no one in his right mind could injure this enemy, glamorous in purple and on his white horse. She reasons with herself eloquently, then she cuts off her father's "single scarlet hair, on which his kingdom did depend." Minos accepts the hair without a smile, repulses Scylla, takes the city, sails. Scylla stands on the shore. Deserted, desperate, she makes an illogical, devastating harangue. She dwells on the bulls that have plagued Minos' life; there is his mother Europa, wooed by Zeus in the form of a bull (not Zeus, but a real bull, she says); there is his wife, Pasiphaë, who has coupled with a bull (the bull is less of a monster than Minos, she says). Finally, Scylla dives into the sea, and hangs on to Minos' keel; she won't be loosened. Suddenly Nisus, now a "hobby-hawk," hovers in the air; on "nimble wings of iron mail, he souses down on Scylla to seize her where she hung." He would "have torn her fain with bowing beak," but Scylla is already changed to a lark. A "hobby-hawk" hovering in air with "nimble wings of iron mail" and "with bowing beak": this is Ovid.

[1955]

Hawthorne's Pegasus

[*This essay was written as part of a series of children's books conceived and edited by Michael di Capua, in which Lowell chose to introduce young readers to Hawthorne's retelling of the myth of Pegasus.*]

Nathaniel Hawthorne has a magical, carefree touch in describing animals. I can see the winged horse, Pegasus, at the fountain of Pirene. His body is white, just like the body of any good white horse, but Pegasus' tufted, silvery wings flutter and rustle above him. He draws "in the water with long and pleasant sighs and tranquil pauses of enjoyment, and then another draught and another and another." Soon the youth Bellerophon is on his back, and the beautiful horse is five hundred feet aloft, snorting and trembling with anger because he is being ridden for the first time. The sky-voyage has begun.

The stories of the Greek heroes are endless, and almost as endless is the number of their storytellers. Where should one start? For me they began thirty-five years ago [in 1928], when Herbert Hoover was President of the United States, and radios ran on batteries, and ladies were beginning to cut their hair short, and people traveled long distances by train and not by air. My mother used to read to me from a lyre-stamped and wilted tan-covered book of Hawthorne's Greek tales that had been given her as a child. Hawthorne had been dead only about thirty-five years when the book was first bought for her and read to her.

The tales, some of the best in the world, were well told. After all this time, the plots still stick in my mind, and I remember, even more clearly, many small details: an attendant on Circe with "sea-green hair"; the boy Theseus, wrestling "with the big and sluggish stone, as if it had been a living enemy"; Cadmus sowing the dragon's teeth and seeing "the whole surface of the ground . . . broken up by a multitude of polished brass helmets, coming up like a crop of enormous beans"; Lynceus, whose eyes "could see through a millstone." Sometimes when I am trying to go to sleep, I can almost touch these people and talk to them. If I read some false, modern retelling of the old stories, I say to myself, "This isn't the way it happened. I was there. It wasn't a wall that Lynceus could see through, but a millstone!" Hawthorne's fables are history to me, and just as much fact as the earth, the water, and the sky.

For some reason, I had no memory at all of Pegasus, and never knew even that the winged horse and Bellerophon and the monstrous, three-headed Chimaera belonged to one adventure. I feel I should have known. Where else could one learn to travel in the sky? It is sad to have walked on the ground these many years, when one might have had wings.

Pegasus is more than just a sky-flyer; he is also, I think, imagination. Day after day, we walk the same sidewalks, go into the same rooms, see the same people, and drag along in the same hurting leather shoes. Then, in some dream or daydream, imagination catches us and carries us off on the winds of invention. Dragons smoke, gold blazes in rock holes, we stare at the dull old carpet and see a kingdom. Everything has meaning and loveliness; everything shines. To show this, Hawthorne made up an important character of his own: the little boy, the only person who can tell Bellerophon that Pegasus really exists and will some-day come to the fountain of Pirene. Later, the boy will become a storyteller, or a poet. Even now he knows the secret hiding

place of the imagination. He knows he will never find the marvelous winged horse by trying to look directly at it, by gaping
at the sky, or by hiking over the hot Greek hills. Only by letting
his thoughts wander and wonder over the water's surface will he
snatch up a reflection—it is just a common white gull's wing at
first—and this will be the horse. He cannot tell why this is so,
and neither can I.

The other characters around the fountain—the farmer, the
old man, and even the timid maiden—are like most people, like
all of us most of the time. For them, the imagination is a joke,
an old wives' tale, and nothing they will ever see. They know
that horses cannot have wings, and are useful only for plowing.
For them, the birds have no voices, singing is talking, and time
is the clock's stiff finger poking them in the ribs and pointing to
the usual assignments. They are wrong, of course.

Or are they? The story of Pegasus has three leading actors:
Pegasus, Bellerophon, and the Chimaera, the beast with three
heads—a lion's, a goat's, and a snake's. I have said enough about
Pegasus. Bellerophon is the fairy-story prince. We know him well;
he is any young man, only more handsome, more brave. He is
steadier and luckier. He is like us, if we shut our eyes. The
Chimaera is the usual dragon in fairy stories, only dirtier and more
repulsive, because we ourselves could almost make a Chimaera
by taking farm animals apart and sticking them together again.
He is not like us. All three lived so far off in the Greek past that
no one knows when, except that it was at a time when ordinary
life shelves off into a dream.

Much later, just two thousand years ago, at about the time
of Christ, a great writer named Horace was living in Rome. He
was a poet, but he cut his hair, shaved every day, talked clearly,
and wrote sensibly. He shuddered when he saw writers who
didn't do these things, and, like most Romans, he wanted to
see things straight and as they are. He thought about strange
beasts like the Chimaera with distaste. He called them disasters,
and said if a painter were to put a horse's head on a man's body
and then plaster on feathers, he would be laughed at. I don't
know what Horace would have thought of Pegasus. Perhaps he

would have stood glooming by the fountain of Pirene, like the farmer, and muttered that horses can't fly and are meant for plowing. He might have told Bellerophon to go to a hospital. Perhaps Horace was right, and even people of imagination must learn to walk on the ground. I don't know at all, but you may when you are older.

Meanwhile, fly in the air on the back of Pegasus. Later, if you read Hawthorne's other Greek tales, you will find they hang together and spread out into a strange new country that you can live in for months and revisit as long as you live. Later, you will read these stories as the Greeks wrote them, and as others have rewritten them, and you will see scenes from the stories as many artists have painted them. You will be surprised to discover how differently the best minds of the ages saw the same persons and plots. Later, you will read Hawthorne's finer and darker book, *The Scarlet Letter*, and from knowing his Greek stories you will feel on familiar ground, and yet you will learn a thousand new things that will make you rub your eyes. Think of all this as ahead of you now, while you make your journey. Thank Hawthorne for spinning out so many marvelous details, such as Bellerophon's boredom and hopelessness as he waited by the fountain. You may even invent details of your own. In another version of this story, Pegasus' hoofs look like moons, and the Chimaera is finally killed by Bellerophon's pushing a bar of lead down its throat. The bar melts, and the Chimaera chokes on the scalding lead. That's how you finish off a monster, if your feet are on the ground.

[1963]

On the
Gettysburg Address

Abraham Lincoln was the last President of the United States who could genuinely use words. He and Thomas Jefferson are perhaps the only Presidents with this gift.* Without his best speeches, Lincoln would have been less great as a man of action; had he not been a great statesman, he could not have written his speeches. He knew his occasion and sensed that whatever he said must have the gravity and brevity of an act of state.

Last spring I was talking about the Gettysburg Address to a friend who is also a man of letters. He pointed out to me its curious, insistent use of birth images: "brought forth," "conceived," "created," and finally, a "new birth of freedom."

Birth and Death!

The Gettysburg Address is a symbolic and sacramental act. Its verbal quality is resonance combined with a logical, matter-of-fact, legal, prosaic brevity. It is part of the battle, a last military push that alters and adds significance to the previous military maneuvers. In his words, Lincoln symbolically died, just as the Union soldiers really died—and as he himself was soon

* On his copy of this address, delivered at the Library of Congress on January 3, 1964, Lowell added a note: "This sentence was written before I had read President Kennedy's undelivered address." See page 376.

really to die. By his words, he gave the field of battle a symbolic significance that it had lacked. For us and our country, he left Jefferson's ideals of freedom and equality joined to the Christian sacrificial act of death and rebirth. I believe this is a meaning that goes beyond sect or religion and beyond peace and war, and is now part of our lives as a challenge, obstacle, and hope. Lincoln's occasional speech of a hundred years ago still rings today when our country struggles with four almost insoluable spiritual problems: how to join equality with excellence, how to join liberty to justice, how to avoid destroying or being destroyed by nuclear power, and how to complete the emancipation of the slaves.

[1964]

Hopkins's Sanctity

What few writers have stressed sufficiently, and what is difficult to put objectively and with relevance, is the heroic sanctity of Hopkins's life. His inebriating exuberance: the experiments in meter and language, the sketches, the novel musical compositions, the curiously particular and charged observations on nature and the critical obiter dicta, the proposed introductory book to science, the proposed critical edition of Newman's *Grammar of Assent*, the designing a flask for Bridges; all this is balanced by the strict fastidiousness of his religious life, a fastidiousness which, had there been nothing else to Hopkins, might have brought him a sort of small and humorous fame as the absurd Jesuit.

The life, of course, has its analogy in the poetry, in what might be called the éclat of his utterance and technique. Both were so superior and so original that few readers in his lifetime could follow. In almost anyone else this swirl of diversities would have been ruinous, but in Hopkins there was achievement. His daring is sober, his obedience is alive.

Hopkins's sanctity—he would have been a saint had he written nothing—was much more. John Pick in a recent book has shown to what an extent Hopkins's life is based on the exercises of St. Ignatius. I shan't try to specify just what a Jesuit's life is—a soldier's life, close to the physical Incarnation, in some ways rather footloose; it seems to flower most in furious activity, as in the case of the Canadian martyrs. Hopkins's life was short and broken. But like Luigi Gonzaga's it is a complete Christian life and it ended with conquest.

Like other practiced writers, Hopkins was able to use most of his interests and experiences in his poetry. However, if we compare him with his peers in the eighteenth and nineteenth centuries, we see that he was able to do this rather more than the others. Why? This is where the problem of sanctity is relevant. When we examine Pope, Wordsworth, Coleridge, Arnold, or Browning, I think we realize that after a certain point all these men—all of them great writers at times and highly religious in their fashion—stopped living; they began to reflect, to imagine, to moralize: some single faculty kept on moving and fanning the air, but the whole-man had stopped. Consequently, in their writings they mused, they fabled, they preached, they schemed, and they damned. Hopkins is substantially dramatic (*in act* according to the language of scholastic philosophy).

Now, to be thoroughly *in act* is human perfection; in other words, it is to be *thoroughly made*. According to Catholic theology, perfection demands a *substantial transformation*, which is called first sanctifying grace and then beatitude; it involves the mysterious co-working of grace and free will. To go into this question further would be a digression. What I want to emphasize is that for Hopkins life was a continuous substantial progress toward perfection. He believed this, he lived this, this is what he wrote.

I think it can be shown that the beliefs and practices of most modern poets more or less exclude perfection, and that insofar as perfection is shut out the poetry suffers. Writings as well as writers should be judged in terms of substantial action. For writings are dependent on writers, although there never will be any laws for judging one by the other. A number of famous modern poems are specifically about human perfection: "An

Essay on Man," "An Ode to Evening," "The Prelude," "On a Grecian Urn," "The Scholar-Gypsy," "Among School Children," *The Waste Land*. Indeed, there is very little writing on anything else. I think if any of these poems are set against "The Wreck of the Deutschland" or Hopkins's last sonnets, they appear a little abstract and superficial. The reason is not that the writers did not experience what they wrote about, they all did; but their experience is confined to one faculty: reason, imagination, or memory. They are rationalists or romantics.

Hopkins has his faults. (1) He knew nature but he did not know too much about people. He met them sacramentally and at their occupations, but, in his poems at least, he shows little knowledge of their individuality and character. When he writes about the sacramental experiences of occupational types ("Felix Randall") or, better, about his own experiences of nature or God, he is on solid ground. Sometimes he slips. I have never altogether liked his nuns and sailors in "The Wreck of the Deutschland." Perhaps this is why "Harry Plowman" and "Tom's Garland" are so heavy. (2) Hopkins's rhythms, even when he is not writing sprung rhythm, have the effect of a hyperthyroid injection. As we know from the letters and personal anecdotes, he lived in a state of exhilaration. But in some poems we feel that the intensity is mannered; in others, we could wish for more variety. I agree with most of McLuhan's excellent analysis of "The Windhover," but it is perhaps a limitation that the last six lines are forced by their rhythm, almost in spite of themselves, to rival the simple physical intensity of the octet. The versatility, however, of these rhythms within their limitations is miraculous. They are more a personal limitation than a fault. (3) There is something in style that is very close to conversation. The conversation may be either genteel or colloquial, but it must have a supple gravity and scope as well as color. Masterpieces of style are the "Wife of Bath" Prologue, Villon's *Testament*, Shakespeare's great tragedies, the best ballads, Milton's sonnets, the lyrics of Donne, Herbert, Marvell, the later tracts and satires of Pope and Dryden, and some of Hardy; the great recent master is Yeats. Hopkins belongs to this tradition; infrequently his lines collapse in a styleless exuberance:

> *This was that fell capsize*
> *As half she had righted and hoped to rise,*
> *Death teeming in at her port-holes*
> *Raced down decks, round messes of mortals.*

Messes of mortals! This is a murderous example of numb sprung rhythm and alliteration. There are other lines that verge on this and are saved only by their strong, original feeling. In his last letter to Bridges, he writes: "The river is the Barrow, which the old Irish poets called the dumb Barrow. I call it burling Barrow Brown. Both descriptions are true." This sort of thing is common in the nineteenth and even eighteenth centuries, and meter never entirely escapes it, but earlier it would have been uncommon. (4) Enough has been written about Hopkins's awkwardness, obscurity, and syntactical violence. For such an innovator these were probably unavoidable. The best remedy, Hopkins's and Whitehall's, is a sensitive recital.

Hopkins's epitaph, I think, should run something like this: He wrote religious lyrics that are thoroughly of the nineteenth century and yet are unsurpassed by anything written in the great ages of religion. He is probably the finest of English poets of nature; i.e., of inanimate creation. Along with Dante, Villon, Ben Jonson, Donne, Herbert, and Milton, he is one of the very few personal or substantially active poets. Besides being an innovator, he worked at least four different traditions, the alliterative, the Miltonic, the metaphysical, and the Keatsian-romantic. According to Whitehall, he will perhaps be known as the restorer of recited verse. Yet his sermons and letters are as excellent as his poetry; and all his writing is just what he is: the work of his unique personality and holiness.

[1944]

English Metrics

This book* is remarkable for its scholarship, reasoning, and literary taste. These were the three qualities necessary for the undertaking. Few writers possess them, fewer still have been able to combine them, and none that I have read have applied them to this subject with Dr. Thompson's industry and force.

I have nothing to say about the scholarship, except that it is such as only another scholar can adequately admire or profitably dispute. Thompson is also a man of letters. The best contemporary poetry and criticism are not just part of his study, they are the air he breathes, and the style he practices. Most scholars are not men of letters, but statisticians and warehouses. Their research is their own, but their value judgments are secondhand furniture. On the other hand, the literary man's research is also usually secondhand; he seldom has the gifts and patience to become a scholar.

The quality, however, that I most envy in *The Founding of English Metre* is the author's ability to think through and theorize. He does this with great good sense, stubbornness, clarity, freshness, and newness. He sees meter as the conflict and resolution of something definite and something indefinite.

---

* *The Founding of English Metre* by John Thompson. New York: Columbia University Press/London: Routledge, 1962.

The definite is meter itself, everything that is measurable, a priori, and subject to rule. The indefinite is speech rhythm. Here there are no laws, nothing can ever be measurable, and the critic can only depend on his ear, intuition, taste, and knowledge of life. This theory, if we can call it a theory, is so simple and sensible that it almost seems a hoax. Thompson applies it to very complex material, and succeeds where a less steady and energetic mind would have come up with truisms and confusion.

I shall skim through the six chapters separately, because each faces up to different opportunities and problems. Chapter 1 is mostly about Wyatt, one of the supreme English poets at times, but one whose method is contradictory and much debated. We no longer see him as a blundering pioneer who floundered about trying to be correct in the manner of Sidney. Yet more recent critics have made Wyatt too much of a modern, who was careless of rules and allowed his scansion to follow his ear and feeling for speech. Thompson scans every debatable line, describes the old four-beat accentual line, the newer accentual-syllabic line, shows the inconsistencies in Tottel, explains what can be explained, and shrewdly leaves what must ever remain undecided undecided.

The trouble with the poems in *The Mirror for Magistrates* is that they are bulky, undistinguished, and at odds with the standards and desires of any later period. They are rarely read, almost never with care, and never at all, perhaps, with a fresh eye. Essay after essay gives the same perfunctory dismissals and the same perfunctory praise to Sackville. Thompson, however, writes, "Dolman's *Hastings* is quite another thing. He varies the relation of his metrical pattern according to his dramatic intention." In this way, the critic makes an important theoretical point and at the same time offers an original discovery.

The chapter on Gascoigne is perhaps more of a logical link than an exploration. I have always felt that Gascoigne's attempt to make metrical accents and speech accents literally coincide was pedantic and that most of his pieces, except for a handful of accidental triumphs, were more fossils than poetry. Yet today we are troubled by the ways in which strict meter cuts into the naturalness of our speech rhythms. The counterpoint often seems crude and monotonous. After reading Thompson's discussion, I suspect that Gascoigne was concerned with something that is almost the opposite of metronomic regularity, that speech and meter were *equally* important to him, and that he was troubled, as perhaps no later poet was, by the artifice that removes poetry from life. At the same time he knew that the flux of life was not poetry.

Spenser's *Shepheardes Calendar* has a fine reputation as a museum piece, but like *The Mirror for Magistrates*, it is little read and seldom with much joy or profit. The poetry is mostly a sort of dried cake frosting. What is more arresting is the metrical experiment, a mixture of the tame, the confused, the archaic, and the brilliant. Thompson does more than other critics to map this wilderness, show where the theories are significant, and where good poetry comes through in flashes. The chapter on classical meters shows very clearly what these authors tried to do, how they failed, and how they were driven by something living and important that forced them somewhat accidentally to enlarge the possibilities of English rhythm. Finally, Sidney is presented as the first English poet who was a master of strict accentual-syllabic meter and yet able to vary this meter with a deliberate, controlled, and often gorgeous counterpoint of speech rhythms. Thus Wyatt, Gascoigne, and the old accentual poets are brought together in theoretic fulfillment. With this, Thompson's book reaches its own fulfillment. Sidney synthesizes his predecessors, and leaves a mold for the future that was to last for three centuries. Thompson knows also that Sidney was not necessarily as fine a writer as Wyatt and others, and that much was lost as well as won.

I suppose writers of metrical treatises should resign themselves to being almost as ignorant as the poets they write about. This is a great surrender, and one which might seem to rob the metricist of all that makes his pursuit worth the exercise. Gone now that fascinating, allegorical hunt for hidden, secret laws that all poets must follow and none can describe. Writing on meter is impossible. Indeed, A. E. Housman says in a famous passage: "A few pages of Coventry Patmore and a few more of Frederic Myers contain all so far as I know, or all of value, that has been written on such matters." Elsewhere, however, Housman says about meter: "There is indeed one literary subject on which I think I could discourse with profit, because it is also scientific, so that a man of science can handle it without presumption, and indeed is fitter for the task than most men of letters." Thompson is both a man of science, in Housman's sense, and a man of letters. No one is better equipped to go on and write, not just a few passages, but a history and explanation of English meter from *Adam lay aboundin* to Auden, and onwards, and no one else is likely to write it.

[1962]

Poets
and the Theater

The English stage's most terrible affliction is not Milton, its enemy, but Shakespeare, its friend. Here I falter a moment: the trouble with criticism is that it makes points. Shakespeare wasn't injurious to his younger contemporaries, Ford and Webster; or the German Romantic playwrights, Kleist and Büchner; or to artists in other forms—Verdi and his operas, Dostoevsky and his novels. Good poets have written innumerable bad heroic plays modeled on Shakespeare, who has blinded us. In some obscure way he has prevented us from having a new drama. The Ibsen and post-Ibsen imitations are our best acting theater but never seem to reach the inspiration of great literature. I feel that Shakespeare even forced his most famous challenger, Bernard Shaw, our most gifted modern playwright, into the minor mode of Restoration comedy.

Coleridge was perhaps the first critic to suggest that Shakespeare was too great for any stage. He preferred reading Shakespeare to seeing him acted. No one accepts this opinion now. We all know that Shakespeare, an actor and theater owner, was far too practical and unromantic not to write for the market. Yet, in a strange way, Coleridge has prevailed; no serious critic tried to answer him for a hundred years. *King Lear* and *Antony*

and Cleopatra are still unpopular. A. C. Bradley, who wrote
about Shakespeare's characters as if they had actually lived, is
now laughed at, but he is probably less obsolete than his
opponents, Granville-Barker and E. E. Stoll, who explained the
plays as plays. Certainly the studies of Shakespeare's imagery,
rhythms, life-grasping language have little to do with acting.
Eliot's most inspired criticism of Shakespeare shows how his
verse can be transformed into a dramatic monologue in the style
of "Gerontion." Boris Pasternak, Shakespeare's translator and an
artist nearer to him than any modern author, sees him as a sort
of Flaubert or Tolstoy manqué, forced by his times to write
plays and hacking out verse.

Our stage is half fish and half man, half mass culture and
half a thing for the intellect. Perhaps it has the best of both
worlds, but sometimes one looks on it with a yellow eye and
wonders if anyone is really delighted. For all its popularity, it is
not universally popular. The large audiences that spontaneously
love television, movies, baseball, and other sports, seldom go to
the theater. If they do, they feel on leaving that they've been sold
something artificial, expensive, coterie, "improving," and high-
brow. For a hundred and fifty years poets have looked on the
theater with fascination and fury. Often only with fury, as in this
statement of Yvor Winters: "In general I think the world would
be well enough off without actors. They appear capable of any
of three feats—of making the grossly vulgar appear acceptably
mediocre; of making the acceptably mediocre appear what it is;
and of making the distinguished appear acceptably mediocre."
Winters goes further. Realizing that if you don't like actors, you
cannot like plays, he describes the latter as "a bastard form . . . If
a play is read, much of it is dull. If it is acted, a good deal is certain to be badly managed." For him, prose plays come close to
being mere scenarios, while even *Macbeth* often seems a collabo-
ration between Shakespeare and Sergeant Pistol.

Here I am not interested in Winters's theories, but in his
passions and prejudices. What he feels about the stage is moral
nihilism, a nonsensical and perverse attitude of course, but one
that most of us share at times. Poets in particular find it hard to

look at plays with serenity. No two arts are more opposed than our poetry and our theater. In comparison with poetry, theater, even Off-Broadway and even in its losses, is a highly popular medium. Even though the playwright faces much greater difficulties in making the grade than other writers, and even though he is nothing if he fails, yet if he succeeds, the uproar of praise is unbelievable. His hits are almost national events. Yet the literary prestige of our plays is wobbly. Even the great, even O'Neill, even Williams, seem more on the fringe of our high culture than part of it. They are seen rather than read, and are very grudgingly allowed to be writers.

At the other extreme are our poets. They are little read, cause no sensations, and live on grants. Yet, if publication is achieved, though sales are nonexistent, the prizes are many, and poets enjoy a quiet, unquestioned, firm renown. Our poetry may not even be considered American, or even involved with the human race, but at least what poets write is literature.

The voice of the commercial rustic moralist must be the cheapest voice in our society. It's easy to kick New York, but one isn't really happy when theater people predict that Broadway is in grave financial danger. Sometimes one gets the impression that every American play is written, produced, directed, acted, and advertised by a machine, by the machinery of a single city. One dares not admit that the resources and sophistication of New York are dead.

I confess I have always felt splenetic about the stage, known very little about it, and shivered at the suggestion that I write for it. Such suggestions have usually come from theater people, who somehow managed to imply that my poems were private jottings, and a sub-professional form. Perhaps my dark heart misinterpreted, and my remarks may have implied to them that all the current theater hits were nothing but charades. Two years ago, however, I was translating Racine's *Phèdre*, and I found I was much more interested in the drama than in the poetry. Then, last summer, I found I had written a play of my own.* I now

* His dramatization of Melville's "Benito Cereno."

feel double-faced, looking on plays as some barbarian Gaul or Goth might have first looked on Rome, his shaggy head full of moral disgust, plunder, and adaptation.

For ages poets, particularly the English poets, have carried on a morose, obsessive courtship with the theater. It rarely got beyond courtship, only scars and humiliation, never a marriage— therefore, there is something envious, hollow, and polemical in the poet's tone of superiority. I expected to find good examples of this in the preface to *Samson Agonistes*, a play written out of Milton's love of Greek tragedy and his hatred of the actual English stage. After all, it was his fellow Puritans, following the regicide of Charles I, who used long iron hooks to pull down the walls of the London and provincial theaters. But I found no help in his preface. Milton is too intent on hammering home his own playwriting methods and standards to have sarcasm to spare for the downfallen theater. Milton is unlike other poets in proving his point, and *Samson* is supreme on three dramatic counts: it is the last great English play in verse, it is the last great English tragedy in any form, and it is the only great English play that cannot be acted. As perverse and heroic as his own hero, Milton has pulled the temple down on everyone, especially the poet, who might want to attempt anything with drama in English.

One is reminded of Virginia Woolf's story of how Eliot burst in on her, while she was writing *Orlando*, and said with uncharacteristic enthusiasm, "I've just read Joyce's *Ulysses*. I'm afraid the novel is finished in our lifetimes." *Samson Agonistes* should have given everyone pause, but it never has, no more than *Ulysses* has halted the writing of novels, including *Orlando*. Professional prose playwrights have gone on writing delightful comedies and flawed tragedies. And poets have gone on filling the graveyard of letters with inflated verse plays, awkward to act and lethal to read.

[1963–4]

New England
and Further

[*This essay, which was left unfinished and unrevised, has had a strange history. It was begun in the late 1960s, put aside until 1977, and taken up again in the final months before Robert Lowell's death. The first version of the early half of the essay was misplaced, and it had to be started anew. After his death, the earlier version turned up and was found to contain many whole sentences and images identical to those composed more than ten years later.*

It was Lowell's intention to write about the authors of New England from Cotton Mather to Frost, Stevens, and Eliot. Both versions of the essay were written in Maine, where he was separated from his library. He had to rely on memory and planned later to check, expand, and revise for matters of style and expressiveness. The present version is an edited text taken from the two compositions.]

New England: too close to home to give us a living likeness. The ache of looking makes me forget past history, personal intimacy, gossip, accuracy, the present. I reach for what I touch or see. Three variations of architecture: the prodigal turn-of-the-century mansion with its landscaped seclusion and sublime shore front, quietly gnawed away by the clockwork river tides, by the mobility of new building, of life. The big houses, though mostly shabby and uneconomical, instinctively emerge with prosperity to greatness and overshadow the greedy, sun-grasping glass of the small view-thirsting modern bungalows. And inland, still shunning the light of day, though now elmless, stand the white, rectilinear houses, marked 1810—nothing changed without, nothing regained within.

The little towns, the villages—wooden in every sense—but modest, functional in their way without bragging about it, with every dated, dead, and still breeding bad style of architecture at home. Every bad new style dots up, and every good—nothing unique. Still, so many beautiful villages, one after another. The red maples, ocean, lake, mountain. A twisted seacoast. Lots of inscriptions, older dates than anywhere in America—or at least more dates, and more famous names. A sinking feeling that man here is a transient, a tourist, a caretaker, and not the householder; that men live in New England as the Venetian now lives in Venice . . . All this white and green and blue is precariously too perfect.

Two old white churches—one Unitarian, one Congregationalist—on every common; handful congregations still attending. But the old is beginning to have the air of a chain of perfectly restored eighteenth-century Treadway Inns. Two things, however, are sturdily flourishing and need no hothouse protections. No other American region has such oceans of advancing scrub forest; no area except the Rocky Mountains is less cultivated. The provincial flying in from his Quebec or Midwestern farmlands is stunned—it's all woods, weeds, raw life! The other thing is spiritual, or, rather, invisible; it's a kind of carnal gravity. Snobbery, fashion, habit, inertia. Also nostalgia, maybe something nobler: a longing in New England so strong for what is not that what is not perhaps exists. Or maybe something still deeper, a peculiar stain or genius that is unkillable, inescapable.

Spirit, not powder and character, made the shot fired at Concord heard round the world. This spirit is of the soul, oh, intensely, and it was like an ax that drove the splintered bodies of the first settlers through the splintered wilderness, drove them until they made God in its image. Those first Puritans, uxorious, unworldly souls with carpenter's hands. In the New World, husbands who sired twenty-three children and outwore three wives—but no curved inflations of the Jesuit baroque, of Tintoretto's Aphrodite. That spirit's one annual memorial is Thanksgiving Day, a travesty, mostly a thanksgiving for the spirit's departure. And the bad Indians—their extermination as crisp, bracing, and colorful as pheasant shooting. The corpse of King Philip "pulled out of the mire . . . a doleful, great, dirty, naked beast he looked like." All gone, then only the virgin-forest romances of Longfellow, wholesome and exemplary beyond belief, or even with belief, idylls that seem to be acted by and for the orphans of Foxe's *Martyrs*.

The modern nationalist occasionally pays homage, as if passing the plate on Sunday, to the old New England spirit, to that short moment when the New World and God were one, like a couple. Perhaps the old Faith survives in its more gnarled, restyled, and secular descendants: New England virtue, integrity, and aridity are still detectable here and there, and impossible not to endure or rashly obey. The old Faith was something of the mind. Intensely of the mind, the naked ideal hidden in vestments of a life-denying drabness, opposed to display and yet expensive, sensual, baroque disclosures of the flesh. Such the fable. One begins with the Pilgrim—rustic, God-fearing; the unworldly soul with a practical hand. A mysterious union of soul and body producing, always invisibly, the saints' multitude of children with an ecstatic joy that even the most inquiring preacher refused to expound.

Cardboard men silhouetted in the famous steepletop hats and sharp black suits. The Mayflower Compact, the Rock, the matchlocks, the three-day Thanksgiving orgy. Their chorus of Indians, painted like women, and yet to the Pilgrims like Saint

Bernards in a time of dearth. That life was no Pilgrim's Progress. If they should come back, where are the farms they worked? We can accept them only as shadows, or bones, sandpapered down to an unlivable, icon simplicity—stamped in stainless steel, without rust or shadow, invented to delight and taunt us with their unattainable avoidance of dust, vacillation, the manmade apocalypse we ourselves have grown reckless enough to accept.

Cotton Mather

A century passes and the Pilgrim is no longer a simple outdoorsman—not a cutout for children, but an effigy to be trampled on by a dubious Enlightenment. He has grown twisted with subtlety, like the dark, learned, well-connected Cotton Mather, the supreme bookman.

Mather wrote 450 books, all published. It seems a slander that he could have done so much harm, when all his days and nights were spent writing and looking up brilliant quotations. He had charm. About his *Winter Meditations* he wrote: " 'Tis, as I remember, Polydore Virgil who related that when Mathildis was, during the depth of winter, straitly besieged in Oxford, she arrayed herself and her followers all in white, the color of the snow upon the ground, and by the advantage of that color escaped through the besiegers unto a place of safety. That which I desire is a free passage for the truths and the ways and the works of God into the minds of my neighbors; and I have therefore taken the advantage of putting a winter complexion upon them; I have clothed them in the colors of winter." Or be airily flip like a colonial Addison: "An English gentleman has been sometimes the most accomplished thing in the whole world!"

He could be pedantically witty: "The name of a *Lady*! What is it in the original sense of the word? It was first *leafdian*, then *lafdy*; from *leaf*, or *laf*, which signifies 'a loaf of bread.' " Or: "The Pythagorians forbade men's eating their own brains, or keeping good thoughts to themselves." Then, his true hellfire, "dragons whose contagious breath peoples the dark retreats of death."

Mather, the Salem witch hanger, was a professional man of letters employed to moralize and subdue. His truer self was a power-crazed mind bent on destroying darkness with darkness, on applying his cruel, high-minded, obsessed intellect to the extermination of witch and neurotic. His soft, bookish hands are indelibly stained with blood—a black image to set against our white busts of Washington and Lincoln. Yet his hangings were small in number and soon ended in disgust, common sense, and exhaustion. Such things had happened everywhere; and then stopped. Perhaps most in his cross-examinations of the harmless and foolish, Cotton Mather exposed the deep symbolic, incongruous intelligence that nearly made him immortal. His face is not on a postage stamp.

Even in Mather's lifetime, witch hanging grew to be criminal, disgusting, almost the laughable farce we perpetuate on Halloween. The spirited New Englander of another generation wanted less religion, and more glorious, mundane, and idealistic fields of action—bloody, if it must be, but logical. It was in the stars, perhaps, for the American Revolution to have flamed first in Boston. Wasn't the Jamaican rum drunk there spiced with gunpowder to burn the tongue? Here debate was hottest, debate changing to riot, then assuming the Army's anonymous uniform for violence. Petitions, speeches, Sam Adams populism, all that fierceness of the early pre-Revolution that somehow lost momentum, and gained the marmorial dignity of George Washington. Their angry, flat faces are still visible in engravings collected by antique luxury inns.

British scarlet highlights the ruin and outrage: the Boston Massacre, the Boston Tea Party, British regiments staggering home from Concord, a third of their forces picked off by invisible American guerrillas—those losses to be doubled by the oppressor's crippling, victorious storming of Bunker Hill. Three charges led by their general, Sir William Howe, later his Crown's most unaccountably immobile of commanders. Ironic war, finished off at last by the French Army sent by Louis XVI at a cost that brought his reign to bankruptcy and gave the French Revolution its breach.

How calm and serene our revolution is when compared with theirs. No representative in our Philadelphia Assembly guillotined by fellow delegates; no unlucky commander brought before a Committee of Public Safety for treason; no revolution of compassion for the poor, who had none for the fortunate. How tame!

As we look backward now, our eyes mercifully myopic from the temporal distance, how equable, practical, and enduring our early republic appears, the first nation not founded on race, language, class, plunder, or even on revolution—but on the Constitution and the Bill of Rights. Was it worth our blood? Impossible to say or to imagine might-have-beens in this topsy-turvy, tumbling world, where our pattern of dogma and explosion, developed by France, Russia, China, is now almost universal.

Without our Revolution that stately, dangerous organism, the United States, would have been shapeless, without bone structure. Without it for us, another story, another literature. For the whole world, we could once have boasted, another world.

Franklin

Benjamin Franklin is not the father of a country, or the beginning of a literature. There's a question whether his occasional pieces and journalism are art. His face, a little full as if air had been blown into it, offers so little conviction that it seems outside the Revolution he did so much to negotiate.

Franklin grew almost younger with age and lived to rewrite his youth. Now, Mather's *unutterable entertainments of paradise* is changed by Franklin to *leisure is a time to do something useful.* On a couple of pages, and as an exercise, Franklin wrote a modernized and transformed translation of the eighteenth-century Bible.

"But *are* there American authors?" asked Sidney Smith, the Whig man of letters. Then he told his daughters he would disinherit them if they didn't read *all* of Franklin. D. H. Lawrence predictably detested Franklin, "the first American dummy." He wrote: "It has taken me many years and countless smarts to get rid of the barbed-wire enclosure that *Poor Richard* has rigged up."

Franklin, a New Englander whose every breath denied the spirit; an American who wasn't even a colonial but an eighteenth-century European, a prophet whose mild sociable Quakerism was stubbornly worldly, and a writer whose writings sought only ease and clarity and shunned soaring.

"You are young, and have the world before you; stoop as you go through it, and you will avoid many hard thumps." These are not Poor Richard's words but a sentence of warning given Franklin by, of all people, Cotton Mather. Mather, no doubt, hardly heard his own voice, but Franklin heeded well. Too well?

Franklin was moderate in his vices, and moderate in their correction. Toward the end of his life, he looked at himself with amused despair. In his charming dialogue with Madame Gout, Gout has the last word: ". . . You have ate and drunk too freely; and too much indulged those legs of yours in their indolence." He was so bland-spoken in talking of rebellion, science, and his ambitions one had to rub one's eyes to realize he was unusual, and could have savage, Swiftian moments, as in the imaginary letter from the Count de Schaumburg to a subordinate commanding the Hessian troops in America. On the wounded: "I do not mean by this that you should assassinate them; we should be humane, my dear Baron, but you may insinuate to the surgeons with entire propriety that a crippled man is a reproach to their profession, and that there is no wiser course than to let every one of them die when he ceases to be fit to fight."

"His God is one that Andrew Carnegie might have invented," wrote Lawrence. Ah, yes, but he wasn't Andrew

186] ROBERT LOWELL

Carnegie or an industrial tycoon. Lawrence is with the angels; but Franklin was a *real* inventor, one of genius, wanting to make his way, no doubt, but unconcerned with acquiring the income of grandeur. I would rather have the printer, Walt Whitman, or the tough moderation of Horace's Epistles. These flew! Franklin merely coaxed his kite into the lightning. Yet he had their amused, open sense of human limitations, a quality out of fashion in his age.

He is said to have been the only American to have understood women. Frenchwomen? "When I saw a beautiful, sweet-tempered girl, married to an ill-natured brute of a husband, 'What a pity,' says I, 'that she should pay so much for a whistle!' "

Emerson

The first Puritans do not deserve their names in its current meaning. They were English overflow, straight religious sectaries who farmed, bred, multiplied, and had little time for introspection or the hot-air cultivation of scruple. A new mythical or imaginary America harmoniously comes into being with Emerson. It arrived during Europe's high age of function, power, and every variety of intellectual and artistic genius . . . the blindness that still lights our days. It was then that inquiring minds first clearly saw our heritage as something to exploit and evade.

Emerson, the greatest nonfiction writer, the most radiant explorer among our Protestant divines. Even in a later time, as a mind, a philosopher, if he was one, he seems a finer and firmer part of our culture than William James.

He wasn't interested in crime, novels, and pessimism—but can we honestly accuse him of ignoring Original Sin? He was unable to do so: he could write lines with the lovely, complaining, weary music of Matthew Arnold:

> Good-Bye, proud world! I'm going home:
> Thou art not my friend, and I'm not thine.

Long through thy weary crowds I roam;
A river-ark on the ocean brine,
Long I've been tossed like the driven foam;
But, now, proud world! I'm going home.

An innovator in his lectures by inventing a prose-haiku of bright, unforgettable phrases. This he did by sifting gold from his daily journals.

Our fire-bringer Prometheus without the menace of Zeus. The even tenor of his life was in tune with the message of the circuit lecturer, speaking for moral heroism in original words: 1. Words are signs of natural facts. 2. Particular natural facts are symbols of particular spiritual facts. 3. Nature is the symbol of the spirit.

The stubbornness to find his own style—a largeness and geniality almost feared by serious critics. His masterpiece is the extended prose elegy on Thoreau. Many years of companionship, amazed observation, and journal jottings went into the portrait. Emerson knew Thoreau as well as Thoreau knew Walden, a less complex substance. And not afraid of reservation, humor, or poignant intuition. "Misuse finally burned out even his indestructible body." And: "I think the severity of his life interfered to deprive him of a sufficiency of human society."

Passion seldom comes in Emerson to making one's eyes water. Mine do so with the concluding passage comparing Thoreau to the edelweiss:

> There is a flower known to botanists, one of the same genus with our summer plant called "Life-Everlasting," a *Gnaphalium* like that, which grows on the most inaccessible cliffs of the Tyrolese mountains, where the chamois dare hardly venture, and which the hunter, tempted by its beauty, and by his love (for it is immensely valued by the Swiss maidens), climbs the cliffs to gather, and is sometimes found dead at the foot, with the flower in his hand. It is called by botanists the *Gnaphalium leontopodium,* but by the Swiss *Edelweiss,* which signifies *Noble Purity.* Thoreau seemed to me living in the hope to gather this plant, which

belonged to him of right. The scale on which his studies proceeded was so large as to require longevity, and we were the less prepared for his sudden disappearance.

The country knows not yet, or in the least part, how great a son it has lost. It seems an injury that he should leave in the midst his broken task which none else can finish, a kind of indignity to so noble a soul that he should depart out of Nature before yet he has been really shown to his peers for what he is. But he, at least, is content. His soul was made for the noblest society; he had in a short life exhausted the capabilities of this world; wherever there is knowledge, wherever there is virtue, wherever there is beauty, he will find a home.

Emerson's poems, like much poetry perhaps, say different, more secret things than his prose. Maybe the first American poet who gave the rhythms of his own ear. He had faults—more than his expansive, inspiration-serving spirit merited. His most irritating mannerism is garrulity. Wisdom chopped and lashed into rhyme and meter. One is not sorry when the longer poems end, though crackling with *trouvailles*. In verse, too often a Blake in fetters. Still, only the very greatest poets wrote more fortunately. He must be honored, too, as the father or teacher of Whitman, who often alarmingly echoes and enlarges him. Between them a universe.

Who can imagine a sexually indiscreet Emerson invoking comrades, chatting with the drivers of New York horse-drawn streetcars, enjoying opera, or scrapping his laconic seventeenth-century measures to invent free verse? Robert Frost's sweeter, thinner, more celestial forerunner.

Hawthorne

I feel more warmth for Hawthorne than for the more exemplary heroes; yet a certain closeness to his temperament, surely a false dream, makes him a deceptive, even an embarrassing subject.

He was an ironic allegorist, therefore shady and suspect as a moralist. A being of such intermingled gloom and brightness, his mood is hard to find. One of his virtues, possessed by few of his forebears, is that he knew how to dislike, not the lawless and ungodly, but the simple, the tedious, the absurd.

He fought off the Puritans, whose shades he partly invented, that they might sober his dark, imperiled repose. "Grim prints of Puritan worthies hung about . . . worthies who looked strangely like bad angels."

His most confident writing, perhaps, is autobiographical; the account of gauging and weighing in the grime of the Boston Customs House, serving without diversion as American consul to Liverpool. Tired, pondering pilgrimage through Italy, wasting part of a summer in the Concord manse leafing through hundreds of old sermons. Then breathing the asphixiating ether of Transcendental socialism at Brook Farm.

When Hawthorne stung, his style smiled. When he didn't sting, he smiled. What is the truth? Was he intending a eulogy when near the end of his life, and in the depths of frustration, he visited President Lincoln and wrote up the meeting with smarting urbanity?

He was an anti-Puritan, troubled as perhaps no true believer has ever been by the Puritan light, which was darkness—as if he were a child of La Fontaine adopted by Jonathan Edwards. Whenever Hawthorne smiles too much, as in *Tanglewood Tales*, he seems inadvertently to lose his muse.

There is something *fin de siècle* about those young years he spent in his bedroom, never going out, having meals left at the door. A solitary, yet many (like the very green William Dean Howells) must have found repose in him after the Olympian affability of Holmes, Lowell, and Emerson. He could tell tales and discuss technique in the way expected of novelists. And feel nostalgia for the old days at the Atheneum, "when a man could drink heavily, and then sleep deep."

The Scarlet Letter is his masterpiece, because of the simplicity of its allegory and the grandeur of its colonial, Jacobean setting—and because of its shocking subject so nervously handled. Hester and Dimmesdale are sacred and profane love, subjects for Titian, yet conventionally clothed. Tragedy in the costume of pastoral comedy, if such is conceivable. Equally fine is the historic and tragic first chapter of *The House of the Seven Gables*, a still tenable anecdote against New England and American capitalism in twenty or so pages. And, here also, the fly buzzing about the death of the millionaire, another allegory. And his best short stories, "pale tint of flowers," as he dismissed them, "that blossomed in too retired a shade . . . without external life."

"He doesn't patronize the butcher—he needs his roast beef done rare," said Melville. Hawthorne's best prose has the red-claret glow and iron of a villagery saturation, not always at the command of that unsatisfied and much greater friend, Melville.

The myth of the New Englander really comes into being in the nineteenth century. It was then that the great imaginative minds first clearly saw their heritage as something both to admire and to fear. There's nothing coarse, fleshly, or Rabelaisian about those opposed spirits, Hawthorne and Emerson. Both were anti-Puritans, conscious and deliberate about it, yet sure they had inherited the essence.

They may have seen their forebears as British ex-patriots, hardly Americans. But these new men struck their English contemporaries as men of a different species. They strike us as men of a different species, far more haunted, twisted, inspired, and refined by the Puritan character than any of their ancestors or predecessors. Hawthorne, a moderate conservative and given artist, feared big claims, optimism, and preaching. He trusted only the dark geniality of his fictions, and even this trust was rattled with doubts.

Hawthorne and Emerson were friends of a kind, not exactly opposite faces of one coin, but extreme variations of the same theme. There's sadness, and a certain piercing poetic justice in their ends. Hawthorne died depressed; like Mallarmé and many another, he found life too long for comfort and too brief for perfection. Emerson lingered through twenty or more years of amnesia. For one, unlit self-confinement; for the other, a gentle *tabula rasa.* The language they both cherished never entirely deserted them.

Thoreau

Thoreau died at forty-four; it is unthinkable that he could have aged like the patriarchs or, like Franklin, suffered from gout. For him, precept and example were one; his life was a redeemed precept. If Franklin converted Calvinism to politics and to the socially possible, Thoreau reconverted it as never before into spirit, the impossible spirit. We wonder how so good a man could have been so good a writer, and how so good a writer could have been a good man. "I never got my fingers burned by actual possession."

A naturalist of the eternal, the eternal always at his fingertips. The sound of the screech owls: "They are the spirits, the low spirits and melancholy forebodings, of fallen souls that once in human shape night-walked the earth and did the deeds of darkness, now expiating their sins with their wailing hymns or threnodies in the scenery of their transgressions . . . *Oh-o-o-o-o* that I had never been bor-r-r-r-n!* sighs one on this side of the pond . . ."

This ascetic, disciplined man had absolutely no vices, Emerson said, perhaps with reservation. Still, there is a quality of willful negligence—more shiftless and adrift than the metropolitan sauntering, journalism, and scandal of Whitman. Their one meeting: perhaps arching their backs and eyeing each other like cats? Whitman probably much more embracing, yet it was not he who was impressed but the thorny Thoreau who left the meeting overcome and recorded it with his exact language and unqualified enthusiasm. Emerson, rereading his letter of praise to Whitman, regretted not having underlined the *buts.*

Thoreau can be relentlessly perverse. His insistence on the pettiness of man and the largeness of nature, on the triviality of the world and the infinite capacities of Walden, is mannered. His boast that he had seen the whole world in his rambles through Concord seems a morose witticism. Who but St. Anthony or a catatonic really wants to "see the world in a grain of sand"? We long for a little weakness, darkness, and fiction, for the crowded, the smut, the closeness, and malice of things.

He is the American mystic who can write. In the chapter called "Ponds," all is flexibility and fire. The great sinews of syntax move without toil of ornament, page after page lover-eyed, intimate, and flashing. Pure texture becomes the true blue of heaven reflected in his pond.

He had the shy, brief, ascetic life of Pascal, Herbert, and Hopkins. The gods must have doomed all four to die as undergraduates, but then, won over by so much grit and good nature, gave each a total of forty years. Thoreau, no Christian, and unaware of any quarrel with God, is *the* New England saint; no other had his resonance, freshness of mind, his stern spontaneity. His life was wonderful, and nothing about it more wonderful than the hand, surer than an eagle's wing, that wrote it down. He thought it better to have lived than to live on . . . prolonging life by the penalty of science. A simple crystal, too hard for the regimented ant to crack. Dying and pressed to make his peace with God, he announced, "I am unaware we ever quarreled."

Poetry: was he cowed by the artificial nature of it? For me, Thoreau's poetry is spoiled by flatness and piety; it is conventional and thin in language and form, but original in its conviction. Emily Dickinson could have given his lines the carpentry of inspiration. At times he sounds much like her: "Conscience is instinct bred in the house." The poetic timidity of this man of supreme daring.

Lincoln

"Fourscore and seven years ago our fathers brought forth on this continent a new nation, conceived in Liberty, and dedicated to the proposition that all men are created equal."

Poetry, though nearsighted and infected with grandeur, is at home with brevity—like the Gettysburg Address, briefest of Periclean orations, our nation's one prose poem. Lincoln was the last President of the United States with a gift for words, Thomas Jefferson being his contender. Lincoln would have been less great as a man of action without his speeches; had he not been President, an administrator of iron, he couldn't have written the Gettysburg Address or his last Inaugural. He seized the occasion and sensed whatever he said must have the gravity and consequence of an act for the Union.

Is it possible, as Edmund Wilson suggests, that the fury of war changed Lincoln, the freethinker, into an instinctive Christian? His words at Gettysburg are ritual and sacrificial: "The world will little note, nor long remember, what we say here, but it can never forget what they did here. It is for us the living, rather, to be dedicated here to the unfinished work which they who fought here have so nobly advanced." Their excellence is poetic solemnity, words repeated and held in position by a lawyer's dry, prosaic logic. It is part of the battle, an army's last push that alters and gives meaning to earlier butchery. In his words, Lincoln symbolically died, just as his Union regiments actually died, and he himself was soon actually to die. By his words he gave the battle an allegorical amplitude it had lacked.

For us and our country, he enlarged or consecrated Jefferson's eighteenth-century freedom and equality with the Christian sacrificial act of death and resurrection. I believe this to be an assertion that goes beyond sect or religion and beyond peace and war. It is now part of our lives, as a challenge, obstacle, and hope. Lincoln's occasional speech, dashed off on an envelope in 1863, still stings us today when our country wars with three metaphysically insoluble problems: how to join equality with liberty, how to join liberty with excellence, and how to complete the emancipation of the poor, before destroying or being destroyed by our artillery.

J. R. Lowell

A rank, upholstered, Olympian era: Longfellow, Holmes, Field. More informative are the historians, Parkman and Motley, both stylists, yet pioneers of research.

My great-grand-uncle, J. R. Lowell—the delight of his urbane circle of friends, spry deflater of the outsider: Poe, Thoreau, Whitman, and Mark Twain. Our watchdog. His *Fable for Critics*, a landmark of precosity, written in four-foot anapestic couplets, is amiably student-Byronesque—a Tavern Club performance, too good for its table companions, and styled to flatter with condescension. Most of its literary judgments are local and overstated.

On Emerson: "His prose is grand verse, while his verse, the Lord knows, is some of it pr—— No, 'tis not even prose." On Longfellow: "Why, he'll live till men weary of Collins and Gray."

Lowell—the hardest of the Boston–Cambridge group and a better poet than anyone now will admit. Unfortunately, he wrote his best in a Yankee dialect so erudite that one fancies it his invention, like Chatterton's medieval English. Comparing Lowell's idiom with that of Burns, Frost said rightly, "Scots is a language, not a dialect."

Poor Lowell, his satires, once the rage of Boston and *The Atlantic Monthly*, are now lonely *sui generis* things appreciated by neither farmer nor professor. Three of his nephews were killed in the Civil War, one of them the cavalry commander Charles Russell.

> *Rat-tat-tat-tattle thru the street*
> *I hear the drummers making riot,*
> *An' I set thinking o' the feet*
> *That follered once and now are quiet—*

Lowell's war poems are generally his best. (I omit his shrieking denunciation of Jeff Davis's "dripping red hand.") The

poems are more parochial than many by Whitman and Melville
—like him, anxious civilians and just forty years old. Yet, because
of a skeptical melancholy, I am uneasy with the straight patriot-
ism and armchair abolitionism of this future laureate ambassador
to the Court of Saint James's, the spokesman of provincial New
England, then England's best-loved American. Lowell could not
suffer or imagine the two Americas—North and South—and
their million killed, with Melville's ironic and tormented
resignation.

Though he was brilliantly married and lucky in recognition,
the first part of his life was a repetition of disasters. His family
sometimes had to live with an insane father, with three children
dying in as many years, and then his beautiful wife died, Maria,
his radical muse, "a better poet than I."

"After the Burial," written for his dead child, is really an
unconscious anticipation of Maria's death:

> *But after the shipwreck, tell me*
> *What help in its iron thews,*
> *Still true to the broken hawser,*
> *Deep down among the sea-weed and the ooze?*

He lost in Maria perhaps, though gradually, what he could never
recover, the one thing necessary. He became instead the precursor of two now common employments for poets: he became
a poet-teacher and an early example of the professor who leaves
Harvard to serve in the government.

A bubbling stylist, Lowell was the first American literary
critic with anything resembling the reading, wit, and worldliness
of Matthew Arnold.

When I was a freshman in Cambridge I often passed Elm-
wood, Lowell's tall, gaunt, wooden mansion, his enduring box.
Easy to imagine his bohemian velvet jacket, but hard to enter
the life and wonder what conversation I might have had with
the grizzling poet, my most renowned relation, the merry, book-
drunk gentleman of occasions. "Too many gold snuff-boxes,"
John Jay Chapman said—something like that.

In his youth and even in age, Lowell had dazzling humor in conversation. In his poems a humor that was not afraid to hurt— as it often does in the two volumes of *The Bigelow Papers*, one written to lampoon the Mexican War, the other to urge on the Civil. In their nettling minor way they are inspired, though somehow like parchment scrolls and cunning artifacts, best seen under glass. I envy his strenuous grace, and fear affinities with the cold, gone-out fire.

A man with a library, chain-smoking his cigars, free, to his peril perhaps, of the American writer's almost universal prejudice, his irritating, self-congratulatory boast of preferring experience to books.

A strange miscasting of himself that this urbane man of letters, largely derivative except in dialect, should have written like a Minuteman against the British: "The truth is that we are worth nothing except so far as we have disinfected ourselves of them."

Henry Longfellow

Longfellow, universally credited with good nature, had a genuine and modest sweetness. He sent a wire to Whitman on his seventieth birthday, seemed deaf to literary feuds and to New England superiority. Yet a gentleman Harvard professor. A good storyteller, our cultured metrical technician. Tennyson without gin.

Herman Melville

Melville, the poet—not the greatest, not Emily Dickinson, not Whitman. Not a natural as she was, an imaginer of language, writing what had never been written. Her spirit both householdish and agonizingly personal.

Melville covered more ground, knew socially what all men must endure. His obscurities attempt profundity; hers run after the fascinated inebriation of style. Melville understood more clearly than Whitman and with more impartial compassion the desolation of the Civil War, his most ignited subject. Lacked Whitman's power to keep a long poem flowing, singing, expanding like an Italian opera; nor could he reveal himself in a few gentle, unlabored lines, like the later Whitman suddenly delicate and broken by shock.

Instead, Melville's poems are often encumbered with eighteenth-century pomposity, eloquence contending for the compensation of awkwardness. One model may have been Cowper's *The Castaway*, the uttermost of melancholic confessions. A later influence perhaps the prophetic Matthew Arnold; compare Melville's "Monasteries" with "The Grand Chartreuse."

Although a professional seaman, nothing of Whitman's democratic hug—an unbroken friendship with pessimism. In poem after poem one waits, and is seldom disappointed, for lines of annihilating despair. Often takes no trouble to write well. Can be delightfully odd and merry, sometimes so jocular as to seem to be making a donkey of the Muse.

> *Audacity—reverence. These must mate*
> *And fuse . . .*
> *To wrestle with the angel—Art.*

Too much about the faults. Poetry not his medium, yet no other American poet has allowed such glimmers of genius to escape darkness. Many diamonds hidden in the unscrutinized sands of his immense *Collected Poems*. In modern anthologies that begin with Whitman, Melville must be placed second.

Our tragic poet. No other squeezed more out of life: whaling, the seven seas, exotic countries, sex—or more apprehensively studied the omens of our imperial fortune.

Historians

Francis Parkman, nearly blind and yet one from the crusty, honest Boston upper classes—wealthy, healthy, hardened by his daily three-mile walk, a type still extant, though now a regional vestige. Two categories of foreigners he disdained: the French-Canadian priests and the Canadian Indians, particularly those converted and armed and subsidized by France. The Jesuit Father sprinkling the grace of baptism on a dying Huron stirred his dry Bostonian wit and brought shivers of temperate repulsion. His many volumes run counter to historical orthodoxy. Despite the sometimes too musically heightened sentences, errors made inevitable by his times, and the *simpliste* frankness of his education, a pioneer. Old, unable to look beyond his chair and library, he really *saw* his characters, and wrote well enough, like a factually sensitive novelist, to preserve his stinking, murdering Indians from the complacency of a numb, sophisticated Protestant society.

John Lothrop Motley, a close (perhaps the closest) friend to Prince Bismarck, was turned down by President Grant for the post of ambassador to Spain because he, Motley, parted his hair in the middle. Unlike Parkman, Motley was an altogether transatlantic figure—none of the Parkman narrow, plaintive fervor for the Indian. A statesman and a friend of statesmen, he could draw dead ones as if still living. American and English scholars little interested in Motley or his subjects. Yet—Ivor Winters judged him one of the three or four greatest historians in the English language. So he judged, once at least. Few of Winters's enthusiasms survived bitter terminal repudiation. When I was a boy, I could pick up everywhere the handsome, gilt-edged seven volumes of Motley's *The Rise of the Dutch Republic* for two or three dollars. This the eternity of a past classic, once favored enough to have been a best-seller.

The bent of this huge history is toward an undeviating, reasonable, Northern, nineteenth-century Protestant liberalism—pro-Dutch, anti-Spaniard, an interpretation rejected as unsatisfactory by Gheyl and other modern historians. A popular, patriotic war? Holland at the time was at least half Catholic and probably pro-Spanish, even during the days of the occupation. But who else has given these wars a new life, though "improved"? Motley found an animated model in the rebels and Tories of our own Revolution. Motley's history is as accurate as his remorseless research and the mental anachronisms of his mid-nineteenth-century politics would allow. He reads with the excitement of a novel, a very great one, although without romance or fictitious characters. His are real men, once important in power and office, men a novel would fantasize or strangle. William the Silent, Philip II, the Duke of Parma, the Duke of Alva; compare these statesmen—painted with the calm and precision of Dutch seventeenth-century portraits—with Tolstoy's stunted, more available Napoleon. Even Tolstoy, a writer far, far greater than Motley, he too, as a novelist, wrote in fetters when writing history.

Henry James

Henry James, half New Yorker, half New Englander, half uprooted child tutored by the hotels of Europe—and, with it all, Irish. One has read too many essays to have a word to add; interpretation has lost the oil of novelty. His heroes, heroines, and children are the most lovely and morally overscrupulous in English fiction. Or immorally? Well-heeled, usually attractive heiresses thrown to the sharks, to attract male and female European vampires. Lovers who cannot love and instead marry for acquisition. No one, not even the most practical villain, ever reaches the railroads, mills, mines, and stock exchanges that sent the lovely ladies on their pilgrimage.

James mastered, overmastered, English literary practice—

the first American to be unassailably at home with the traditional English novel. Yet he was not English—more of a flashing Celt, alive with strenuous foreign intensity.

No single supreme masterpiece, no best book, like *Madame Bovary*. Nothing quite opens out in fullness like *Anna Karenina*, or even Dreiser's clubfooted *An American Tragedy*. The works have stretches of worrying, concentration, and narrowness—undistracted distinctions—that no courage or ingenuity, not even his, can widen or unknot. "The best English novelist?" "Hélas, Henry James," Randall Jarrell said. Final style as perplexing as Tacitus for a beginner.

Except for Eliot, none of our critics has his reckless urbanity, assurance. Two Jameses: one is Proust's tender, idealized narrator yearning for truth, kindness, eternity; the other is Baron Charlus, a whale in society, overhearing behind the scenes and conspiring. Oh, mountainous Henry James!

Henry Adams

The later Adams tantalizes, befuddles by the clarity of his disguised meanings. He himself seems half lost, yet he was the subtlest and least hollow of American minds. *Education*, the word repeated and hammered with the persistence of a fundamentalist preacher invoking Jesus. And with as little analysis. Education is all Adams pursued and failed to receive. A dark call. What was it? His failure to be President like those Adamses before him?

Living in Washington to be near politics and politicians, he despised the Presidents and complained he couldn't live to see another mediocrity inaugurated. Jealousy? Or was his education what seventeenth-century theologians called *prevenient grace*? Was it sex?

"Anyone brought up among Puritans knew that sex was sin." So he found that whatever he learned from men was false and whatever he learned from women was true. This throws a light as unbalancing as the light of the moon on the one irreparable disaster, the suicide of his wife, Marion Hooper. Though witty and quick as he, she was not Venus. From an early letter: "She is certainly not handsome; nor would she be quite called plain, I think . . . She knows her own mind uncommon well. She does not talk *very* American . . . She talks garrulously, but on the whole pretty sensibly. She is very open to instruction. *We* shall improve her. She dresses badly. She rules me as only American women rule men, and I cower before her."

Her death, of course, is omitted from the *Education*—a decision as ruinous imaginatively as it was harrowingly human. *Twenty years*—only then does she reappear as the Saint-Gaudens statue on her grave. *Reappears*—but never, not even in their marriage, in the autobiography.

I doubt that education can be defined even by the disillusioned irony Adams used so precisely and disingenuously—to reveal himself by overstatements. Perhaps this most skeptical mind and world traveler, who thought Southerners and the English statesmen mindless, was seeking his salvation—a footless, blown-away seed of Calvin and a disharmonious bedfellow for Cotton Mather and Jonathan Edwards, heathen unvisited by Aphrodite. He jeeringly called himself a "conservative, Catholic anarchist"—or atheist.

Not even *Huckleberry Finn* gives a more dramatic and menaced autobiography by a boy than Adams's first and most knowingly sensuous chapters of the *Education*. Their picture of the yearly and bloody snowball fights between the Boston bluebloods and the Irish. The delirious shifts from city winter to New England summer; his reserve and adoration—"a boy recognizes all adults are his natural enemies"—when he meets in his father's den Senator Sumner and the celebrities of the Free Soil Party. All this, all evolving under the extending shadow of the Civil War. This overture, though brief, compares with the saga of the Mississippi, the unsparing feud, the endangered raft, Nigger Jim and even Huck, Twain's unmarried self, the universal uneducated country boy, his genius for adventures.

Failure, the word repeats as relentlessly as its loyal partner, *education*. Yet by this time Adams had written his *History of the Administrations of Jefferson and Madison*, the most intelligent historical work, not only by an American, but in English. This claim is often made by better authorities. His nine volumes sold as little as the first edition of *Moby Dick*.

What could Adams have expected? He quotes his sources as often as possible, writes dryly—not like Walter Scott or any novel. Yet there is no more interesting and intricate portrait of a great man than his of the indefinable Thomas Jefferson. And dozens of other highpoints, among them the Burr Conspiracy; the political duplicity and military genius of Andrew Jackson; Governor Harrison's disgraceful defeat (called by Tecumseh "the great American victory of Tippecanoe.") "Everyone knows that Indians given equal arms could defeat equal their number of whites." The chauvinistic account of the frigate *Constitution*, etc. For Adams, the superiority of our gunnery demonstrated Americans' more economical and accurate use of force.

The history can entertain by dissecting congressional debates—a history-defying problem, although perhaps politicians once could speak. The pendants to the great history are a dull, dead, laudatory two-volume life of Albert Gallatin, and a vicious short book on the half-mad, prophetic, oratorical genius of John Randolph of Roanoke—Adams's weird Virginian alter ego.

His letters almost, artistically, surpass the *Education*, if anything could, in wonder. In them another Adams, happier and boisterous. I like most his London Civil War letters to his brother, Charles Francis Adams, who wrote back still finer ones from the battlefields. One smiles, not without envy, at the ease and assured precosity with which these young men, still in their twenties, could rip to shreds the policies of Lincoln and Secretary Seward.

Also those to Senator Lodge's wife; and, best of all, those to Elizabeth Cameron, written in his cheerful, downbeat decline. These are many, long, and intimate. Most Melvillean is one, chapter-long, that tells of his ritual orgy with naked South Sea Island women. He wrote almost with a lover's affection, but with the security of the detached.

Emily Dickinson

After a parade of unaccompanied males, a woman, an oasis—Emily Dickinson. Colonel Higginson's "little plain woman with two smooth bands of reddish hair and a face with no good feature"—a woman who drained him more than any person he had ever met. She wrote in a letter on a widow whose son had been killed in the war: "Poor little widow's boy, riding tonight in the mad wind back to the village burying ground where he never dreamed of sleeping! Ah the dreamless sleep!" Her writing was in the 1860s—the war no part in it. About her family she wrote Higginson: "They are religious, except for me, and at breakfast worship the great O they call God." When her father died: "His heart was pure and terrible, I think no other like it exists."

In the 1950s, Professor Thomas H. Johnson printed Miss Dickinson's entire text as she wrote and punctuated it; he removed the emendations of previous editors and he has raised, I think, a critical problem. Has anyone the right to retouch an author? (For myself, I have felt that Wordsworth's "Intimations Ode" could be made into his saddest, most finished poem if about forty of the most frivolous and ode-manufacture lines were left out. Having many times shown my cut versions to friends, I have never made even a momentary convert.) Hate to think what three professors from three different American universities might do revising Gray's "Elegy."

The new complete Dickinson text of 1,800 poems, a new Dickinson, great bulk, peculiar, and on fire, lines steadily alive and original—strangely like the late Henry James's recklessly strenuous prose. There are drawbacks to the bulk—the straying into shagginess, purposeless bad grammar, meaningless dashes spread like bird shot. The poems piled up unseen, some of them perhaps never looked at twice. Would she have mailed them in this state to a trustworthy editor? But who was trustworthy? In a nightmare, imagine correcting or rejecting her manuscript.

The Johnson edition gives an impression of greater energy; the edited editions had more unrumpled (almost) masterpieces. The "improvements," of course, did not always improve. Many will feel she is more in character when frayed and mussed and willful. There was good editing, if such is to be allowed. (1) The last fine but structurally irrelevant stanza of "I felt a funeral in my brain"—cut by an earlier editor. (2) The *tulle* and *gossamer* stanza from "Because I could not stop for death"—also previously removed. (3) Stanza 3 in "There's a certain slant of light" —rewritten. Emendations of three of her greatest poems.

She brought poetry not only spoken language but her own self-speaking language. She can be said to have invented imperfect rhymes, a slight but earth-shaking discovery—all the stranger somehow because used to resurrect for serious writing the quatrains of the hymnal.

She knew how to plunder what was handy. Not a modern sensibility in our sense, but an atheist and heretic assailant filled with indignation, mockery, and terror of Calvin's God. The ladder she climbed points to godless eternity; its rungs were carved from Scripture.

A household spirit who wrote best—almost always when inspired—about death in the house, death real, death fore-experienced, death as a parting.

She lived a life of infatuated friendships, and once or twice or more must have had to survive the agony and crucifixion of lost love. Death, changing seasons, those shadows of death. A few partly humorous nature poems and too many pages of forced New England coyness—such were her subjects. A household ghost, the best female poet since Sappho, a precursor of more talented women poets than her own models—and now an omen of many more affirming the future with the arrogance and pleasantry of a prophet.

She revolutionized poetry, but no man or woman has learned much. Her divine waywardness, whose success is impossible to approve or condemn, separates her from the perfection of Marianne Moore and Elizabeth Bishop. It was as if she had applied the subtleties of prose to the alien goal of poetry; she made the language of her contemporaries obsolete—if anyone had heard her.

Santayana

I used to visit George Santayana in 1950 and 1951 in Rome. He was just under ninety, I was just over thirty. He took a fancy to my craggy, dark, apocalyptic poetry because I was both an old Bostonian and an apostate Catholic.

Santayana, a fantastically displaced spirit, Spanish by blood, New England by upbringing, Roman Catholic by birth (inheritance) and even taste, though in belief a pious agnostic, living out his feeble last days in a Roman monastic hospital run by the Irish Blue Sisters.

Longed for an English club, but feared the removal. In his little room, almost without personal belongings, he wore a shabby chocolate-brown dressing gown and resembled an emeritus Franciscan general. His sight was dim, his right hand was paralyzed. On a bare table before him were neat strips of paper which he glued to manuscripts and letters whenever his hand betrayed him and left an infirm scrawl.

Sometimes he held a magnifying glass in his stiff hand and a large red crayon in the other to mark revisions in a magnum opus written at Harvard in the 1910s. Being deaf, though always soft-spoken and hesitant, he was forced to monologue while often regretting.

His conversation went everywhere: Tarn's new book on Alexander, flaws in Aristotle's *Metaphysics*, Bernard Berenson's constipated style, the ugliness of Bertrand Russell's face, the charming debauchery of his friend Lord Russell, Bertie's older brother, their uniform misfortunes in marriage.

Verses were brought out; a long poem by Lorenzo de' Medici translated by himself, and he would recall pre-World War I Boston and Cambridge gossip.

Santayana had spent his youth trying to wall out New England's stiffness, morals, and the reigning pantheon of Harvard philosophers. It is said he was the only man who could dislike William James. During the Second World War he said, "I don't know what is going on in Italy, I have been living with Dickens in the eternal." When the Blue Sisters entreated him to have an audience with the Pope, he said, "I don't care to meet celebrities."

Of the Catholic Church: "It's a pity it has no bottom . . . it's too good to be believed." Gentle, skeptical, faithless, he might have recognized the metaphysical feudal Virgin of Henry Adams.

When crowds of tiresome academics came to see him, he was always polite, signed their books, and declared he "enjoyed writing his life much more than having lived it." I hope always to treasure his kindness, his Montaigne-like moderation, and civilized, philosophic love of scandal.

Robert Frost

A lifetime, a morality ago, my mother warned me off the moderns, Eliot and Tate, and, as a curative, misquoted Robert Frost, thought to be understandable to everyone, even to herself, to be healthy, wise, and no nihilist to the middle class. My personal and critical love of Frost survived this recommendation of everything I hated.

At that time it was possible, and usually only possible, to anthologize him as a flower bed of benign banality. A lost climate?

Elizabeth Bishop, without smiling, called Frost "our bad white poet." Several years before Frost's death, Randall Jarrell wrote two revolutionary critical essays on the poetry, "the other Frost," a writer of dark, tragic imagination. These brought Frost into favor with previously hostile or condescending radical intellectuals, for many of whom writing of the tragic underside of things was like Grace or attending Jonathan Edwards's Great Awakening.

The stream began to run too darkly. For a time, after the publication of Lawrence Thompson's official three-volume biography—a work mediocre, poisonous, tone deaf, unable to animate a single character—one risked one's virtue by insisting that Frost was indeed good, great, unselfish, just those garlands he had worn like habits for forty years. Of course he was wicked— or rather, although on a smaller scale, like the Tolstoy described by Gorky: a Druid shape including good and evil, a balance beyond our common temptation. Must poets, like actors, develop their generic failing? Though removed from fortune, unlike novelists and other celebrities, they are a prey to inwardness, vanity, and a hunger for magnitude beyond the gods' indulgence. Frost had all that, and besides he *was* an actor, one who might have made Yeats seem a model of artless simplicity. He could charm any moderately friendly audience—and which of his audiences wasn't friendly?—he charmed when other poets would have sat sullen, commonplace, and tongue-tied. There was music in his voice; boredom vanished when he entered the room. He could say many perverse things, but no clichés. It was best to be alone with him.

Unlike Valéry, Frost was not a modern intellectual. And yet I imagine he had a more electric and energetic mind than any poet I've known. In his eighties he could talk you dead—and not with monologue, but by carrying on through the night. He was so greatly nervous he could not eat before any of his thousands of readings.

Always you remember the music, and not only in the conversation but in the speaking murmur he cultivated so cunningly in poems and brought out so vividly when he recited Raleigh's "Sonnet on His Son," or the first lines of "Hyperion." His meter was iron, a little like that of Ben Jonson, with every stress consciously displaced, strained, then placed in sonnet, blank verse, and rhymed quatrain. Frost is *the* American formalist, unrivaled even in our nineteenth century, if we take form to mean—and why must we?—controlled measure. Ah, but it's the heart he wrote we must care for—a heart of stonemason darkness . . . This wasn't his secret of calm.

"Back out of this now too much for us . . ." Beautiful staccato rhythm, also like haiku, and the essence of Frost.

> *First there's the children's house of make-believe,*
> *Some shattered dishes underneath a pine,*
> *The playthings in the playhouse of the children.*
> *Weep for what little things could make them glad.*

Surely this is a memory of Frost's own sad children, allegorical and literal. The lines from the end of "The Pauper Witch of Grafton" are the loveliest he ever wrote about a woman, or perhaps about anything.

"Directive"—an aging Frost's "Tintern Abbey"—written as he journeyed to the destroyed homestead of his early marriage, his lost wife and children. His narrative sadly, rurally, and covertly repeats the Legend of the Grail, here only a hidden household drinking cup. "Directive" might be a tribute or rebuke to Childe Roland who to the dark tower came, to Tennyson, or to *The Waste Land*. Its last line is "Drink and be whole again beyond confusion." A pathetic affirmation.

Wallace Stevens

Frost and Wallace Stevens met while on a train going to Florida. The meeting was not an opportunity for friendship. Stevens may have thought Frost too popular and pre-modern. Frost, if he had ever read Stevens, would have thought him recherché and the poetry a distraction from his own. Stevens, perhaps slightly drunk, is supposed to have said, "The trouble with your poems, Frost, is that they have subjects." Frost came back with, "Yours are bric-a-brac." The answer disappoints. Stevens sent one of his books inscribed "Some more bric-a-brac."

Stevens was not pulverized like Pound and Eliot by petty critics, nor like Frost ignored, then belittled by the intelligentsia. His great reputation, beginning some years before his death, and still expanding, is an enigma. He was born in Pennsylvania, educated at Harvard, and lived the long, invisible life of an insurance-company vice president in Hartford—a town like Boston, only worse, and more parochialized, by the insurance companies themselves. Never traveled except for vacations in Florida and the Caribbean. Stevens as provincial and stand-fixed as Thoreau. A Thoreau converted to the Mallarmean *absence.*

As an undergraduate at Harvard, he had frequent meetings with Santayana, read all the best French Symbolists in their language, a language perhaps he had never spoken. Never missed a Harvard–Yale football game, and in later life boasted to William Carlos Williams: "My secretary has to wear a pistol when she enters my office."

More solitary than a Prufrock, but happy to turn our human flesh, and the sun itself, into metaphor, his eternal metaphor. His great cloud of figures and shadows sops up moisture from the earth. Some woman or lovely thing is forever casting its crystal X-ray on him, then vanishing into the drugless reveries of the enraptured soliloquist. "Dreams are hash," he said, and also, "It gives a man character to have daily contact with a job."

Stevens's work might suggest to us that modern New England no longer exists. He writes about nothing; yet he is the alchemist of nature. Continuing subject: is the imagined object or the real object the real? This theme less barren than it might be because of the inexhaustible, charming, fresh variations played on it.

When the lines go wrong—eloquence dictating to idiosyncrasy. The big *Collected Poems* is too long and the poems too similar to read through, as all such things must be. Yet flip to almost any page—there, new and inspired surprises. More selective poets forbid discovery.

Stevens is reputed to have composed in his head while walking home, or after dinner while listening to music. This may have been the source of his ease, his vastness. Thousands of blank-verse lines: absolutely nothing beyond him with strict iambic pentameter or its variations.

> *Shall I uncrumple this crumpled thing?*
> *I am man of fortune meeting heirs;*
> *for it has come that thus I greet the spring.*
> *These choirs of welcome choir for me farewell.*

His music is Tennysonian, I think, and perhaps even more magical, because everything actual and familiarly obvious is sub-tilized by attenuation. This is not writing for the unsophisticated, though many have tried and enjoyed its song. Even those who love him, as I do also, may find intention lost in nuance and high style. No matter; a large poet with the ear of Shakespeare. Could express the inexpressible and loosen the constriction of sense.

T. S. Eliot

I met T. S. Eliot in 1947, then later almost yearly. Once or twice in London, but mostly in Boston or New York. I knew him late in his life and hurriedly. Yet there is no elder or con-temporary, no parent or childhood blood relation, half a cen-tury's memory, that I more yearn to see return alive. He won with slashing, self-effacing witticisms and anecdotes about the mighty—mostly his friends.

Of Pound: Eliot remembered Pound would walk for two hours and then say, "*You* speak." But by then one had abso-lutely nothing to say.

The Waste Land is sex gone haywire—trembling incapaci-ties, disgust, and the brute compulsion to seduction. The women are stronger than the men, women one can touch and smell, flirting, hard to get. In the broken household of *The Waste Land*, Dido is more *varium et mutabile* than the immobile Aeneas.

The tragic, Jacobean delirium of "Gerontion," a miracle of invention and magnificent upholstery to anyone who has tried to write of dejection.

Later the women dwindle and vanish into spirits. Women are mysteriously not vibrant in Eliot's full plays.

"The Hollow Men" is a song of desiccation, grace through abstinence, celibacy as muse. So it is with the mellower *Ash Wednesday*, where the Virgin appears as an emblem of nostalgia and prayer. Both poems depend, more than anything Eliot had done before, on lyricism; they are almost pure poetry, whatever that means. They are desiccation, not, as before, dirges to lust and impotence. More religious and visionary are the lines in part six of *Ash Wednesday*, a recollection of his North Shore boyhood:

> *From the wide windows toward the granite shore,*
> *The white sails still fly seaward, seaward flying*
> *Unbroken wings*
>   *And the lost heart stiffens and rejoices . . .*

Four Quartets also has no characters except for the very much characterized speaker, and the ghostly composite night-walker in "Little Gidding." The sequence is Eliot's furthest stretch, his greatest and most compassionate poem, written in a revolutionary and lax language. Christian contemplation intertwined with the poet's struggle with words. The two themes pursue one another like Dante's wrestlers, walking about, pluming themselves, and then standing off, as if too close. They are reflections—and two of a kind under the disguise of their opposition. Here and there one finds passages that shine with a renewed visual density—moments from the world between the two wars, the night scene from the Second, gentler than *The Waste Land* flashes of London; Bristol, Massachusetts, religious and secular ruins in rural England. A sad, flexible poem, celebrating the egotistical sublime, an ego more evasive and outwardly humble that the *personage* Eliot found distasteful in Wordsworth.

It seems strange, almost one of Eliot's practical jokes, that this solitary, ascetic, mystical poem should have found its outcome in his happy marriage with a happy young wife. Randall Jarrell said that Eliot, when young, must have been cruel and paranoid—this the genius—then became such a good man he had no need to write any longer.

In any case, he knew when to stop, his work completed at fifty-four. He wrote little more than Housman, yet everything he wrote seems longer than it is. *The Waste Land*, some four hundred lines, is a complete novel, made more spacious by the omission of the familiar filler of plot. Little was left for imitators, and he was too meticulously selective and inspired to give anthologists an opportunity for discovery.

Eliot was abused as no other man, either American or British.

[1977]

Epics

[This essay was originally intended to be part of "New England and Further," apparently as the conclusion. It is not clear how it was to fit with New England, apart from the fact that Moby Dick *is included. Perhaps the intention was to publish it separately. After Lowell's death it was edited by Frank Bidart and published in* The New York Review of Books.]

"Poetry makes nothing happen," Auden said; but the great epics, like our own classics, must mean something, not by didactic pedagogy, propaganda, or edification—but by their action, a murky metaphysical historic significance, a sober intuition into the character of a nation—profundities imagined, as if in a dream, by authors who knew what they had written. Even to the Philistine *podestà*, Dante was the soul of Italy.

Homer—hexameters must have slid from his tongue, as easily and artfully as Shakespeare's last blank verse. He had no necessity or license to vary meter, and had less anxiety than even Walt Whitman for the triumphs of overcurious craft. This and narrative genius were his simplicities to celebrate the cycle of Greek radiance, barbarism, and doom with the terrible clairvoyance of a prophet.

The *Iliad* is the epic of Greece, written when Greece was still half Asiatic and tossing in the womb of her brilliance. Here, already foreshadowed, are deviously debating fractious Greek leaders, kings of petty city-states; the bisexual warrior, heroic comradeship, the lonely man of Excellence, unreliable, indispensable, ostracized at the height of his fortune—here, too, the theme of Greek pathos, the young men carved on the stele for Marathon, the victory's *gloria mundi* killed in full flower.

The *Iliad*, unlike other world epics, is dialectical: thesis, antithesis—the synthesis is wearisome to work and transitory . . . fury, then contrition—insensate rage of Achilles forced to relinquish his concubine, Briseis, to Agamemnon, then his recoiling on himself after the death of Patroclus to rejoin the Greek fighting—then his rabid butchery of the Trojans, then gently relenting to return Hector's body to Priam, the helpless father . . . what no other Greek would dare to do. Achilles is the most mercurial and psychic mind in epic narrative—if mind may be defined as wavering, irresistible force, a great scythe of hubris, lethal to itself, enemies, and the slaves—animator of the actual.

Alexander carried the *Iliad* with other Greek classics on his own Asian invasion, and mysteriously relived with greater intelligence, though a Macedonian alcoholic, the impulsive brutality and forgiveness of Achilles. General Fuller writes: "He was both mystical and practical . . . It was in his outlook upon women— in nearly all ages considered the legitimate spoil of the soldier— that Alexander stood in a totally different moral world compared with the one inhabited by his contemporaries . . . Yet, in spite of this extraordinary respect for womanhood, his highest moral virtue is to be discovered in one of the final remarks Arrian makes in *The Anabasis*[:] 'But I do know that to Alexander alone of the kings of old did repentance for his faults come by reason of his noble nature.' " It's the same Achilles, imitated by a long line of Plutarchan Greeks, from Themistocles and Socrates of Athens

down to Philopemon of Megalopolis. What can Homer teach
. . . the generosity in cruelty?

Milton's run-on blank verse is very baroque, but strangely
unlike other ornate verse, it is hard and idiomatic. I believe him
when he boasts that with time his numbers became easy and
unpremeditated, an inspired, various instrument whenever his
plot condescended to him.

"Milton wrote in fetters when he wrote of Angels & God,
and at liberty when of Devils & Hell." Thus Blake, of course, in
the most famous comment on *Paradise Lost*. Blake based a whole
heretical theology on it, many revolutionary *Songs of Experience*
. . . and much distrait sprawling. Blake was right. One can prove
this by running through *Paradise Lost* and marking the good
lines or groups of lines. The only celestial angels are fallen.

I do not understand Milton's intention. Who or what is
Satan? He is not ultimate evil, though in Milton's myth the
origin of human ill. He lacks many of the common vices of tragedy: disloyalty to friends, cowardice, and stupidity. By title
the Father of Lies, he is not provably a liar. What he says to the
rebel angels, Eve, and even Christ might well seem true to the
sage and unorthodox Milton. He is no devil but a cosmic rebellious Earl of Northumberland, Harry Hotspur, with an intelligence and iron restraint. He is almost early American, the cruel,
unconquerable spirit of freedom.

He has great moments—rousing his followers prostrate in
the infernal bog, his great oratory to them, the Cromwellian drill
and parade of his defeated armies. One feels Milton knew more
of military tactics than Shakespeare, whose battles are charade.
This can't be simply the limitations of the Elizabethan stage. Yet
Shakespeare understood most realistically the evil and pestilence
of civil war. In Book Two's great parliamentary speeches, the
devils organize their words like old parliamentarians, less dis-
honest, and more concise. Satan defying the sun at the beginning of Book Four might be Milton addressing his blindness, his
head only ringing now with ideal upheaval. Satan even animates

Eve, though Adam has never been able to, nor she him. He brings out all the good in her, then her ruin. We can't deprive Satan of his power to destroy—". . . yet all his good proved ill in me . . . evil be thou my good." In *Paradise Regained*, a diminished Satan, maybe himself in disguise, makes all the brilliant speeches. Christ is only a rocky, immobile Puritan breakwater— the voice of denial? Which voice rings true? Are both schizoid anti-selves of one person?

Paradise Lost is alone among epics in being without human beings, except perhaps Eve and Adam. Satan is the engineer of ruin.

> *His troubled thoughts . . . stir*
> *The Hell within him, for within him Hell*
> *He brings, and round about him, nor from Hell*
> *One step no more than from himself can fly.*

After twenty centuries of Christianity, we see our ruin is irreparable. Satan cannot be discovered by faith or science. Could he have been plausible to Milton in the 1660s? *Paradise Lost* is of the world's great poems; I do not see the author's intention. Is Satan the hermetic God . . . *Christus Liberator*?

Dante was virtually a Ghibelline, a fanatical one. His *Commedia* is a Ghibelline epic. The Ghibellines looked for a German Emperor, their shadowy hope, who would unify, but not annex, Italy. They loathed popes as principals of disharmony and internecine murder. They had leanings toward heresy. They led lives, as did the Pope's adherents, the Guelphs, that sinned in a hundred common ways: adultery, sodomy, murder, treason, intrigue. In the *Commedia*, they are tortured for these misdeeds—but who is ever hurt in a poem? Almost all Dante's poetically inspired or humanly attractive characters are Ghibelline—if they are not, like Francesca and Ulysses, they seem the Ghibelline underground. There's one arguable exception, Beatrice, but I will come to her in time. The great sinners are imagined with such sympathy that Erich Auerbach believed that they almost crack Dante's theological system.

With saints, Dante is apathetic. They are written with a dry pen, and parsimonious vision. St. Francis, St. Dominic, St. Bonaventure, Cato, etc., seem almost like primitive lives of the saints read in the silence of a Trappist dinner. They are *nature morte*, and hardly nature, though girded in cunning coils of scholastic philosophy.

Dante's unique genius as a writer of epic—I even include Melville's prose—is that his chief characters are not heroically enlarged, but life-size. Masaccio, alone among the old Italian painters, had this wish for human proportion, lost by the grandeur and embellishment of his greater successors. It's in Farinata's "But who are your ancestors?" Or, holding himself upright in his fiery tomb "as if he held the Inferno in disdain." Ugolino's eating his own starving children, who willingly sacrifice themselves to save their father from starvation. Or Manfredi in the *Purgatorio*, a type of the liberator German Emperor and solider than Othello, "*Biondo era e bello*," etc., down to his burial, *a lume spento*, without the rites of the Church. He is the bastard son of Federico Secondo, the *stupor mundi*, and the greatest Ghibelline, who, though only listed in the *Inferno* among those damned for heresy, somehow overshadows the whole *Commedia* with a revered spirit; just as Pope Boniface VIII is its devil, though paradoxically consigned to Purgatory, not Hell. I am suggesting that the *Commedia*, like *Paradise Lost*, is in part hermetic, and means at times the opposite of what it asserts.

I find it hard to consider Dante as entirely orthodox. Much in his political preference and poetic training, in the *dolce stil nuovo* derived from the Provençals, points toward heresy. But Christian Faith is alive in him, not cold as in Milton. The Church gave his writing a dialectical confusion and intensity. Two forces, not one. His dogs of the Church, Hell's torturers, are real dogs. The *Commedia* is not just a political epic but also, perhaps with less ebullience, a religious epic. *Pilgrim's Progress*.

In Canto 100 of the *Paradiso*, by far Dante's greatest purely sacred poem, dogma changes miraculously to mystical contemplation, the most magnifient in Christian literature.

Beatrice? Saving Grace? She was born in Provence, in the heretical Toulouse of the troubadours—the lady, not one's wife, but the one the troubadour truly loves—chastely by necessity with Dante, but not always in the tradition. Where, where, in the whole *Commedia*, are Mrs. Dante and the Dante children? Dante's meeting with Beatrice in the *Purgatorio* burns with a fiercer love than Francesca's for Paolo. Without Beatrice, Dante's *Comedy* wouldn't exist but, as Pound said, would be "a ladder leading to a balloon."

Unlike other epics, *Moby Dick*, though an allegory, is also an exact whaling voyage. It is not hermetic; things are what they are, and do not opaquely suggest the opposite. The plot is as uncomplicated and straight as its harpoons. Ahab, of course, is other things than a veteran Nantucket whaling captain. In "the Guinea-coast slavery of his solitary command," he suggests Melville's copy-clerk, Bartleby, and Pierre crazed on his withdrawal to write—three cut off from society by the wreck of seclusion. Ahab's perverted religious hunt to kill the White Whale is monomaniacal. He is apocalyptic, with a rage that drowns ship, shipmates, and himself. His destiny is analogous to heroes in Norse Saga, Wagner's *Götterdämmerung*, and, in real life, Adolf Hitler. " 'The first thing that but offers to jump from this boat, I stand in, that thing I harpoon' . . . all directed to that fatal goal which Ahab their one lord and keel did point to . . . how they still strove through the infinite blueness to seek the thing that might destroy them." There's no doubt of Ahab's courage and ability—in action he is more subtly alert and correct than his subordinates.

Moby Dick, the Whale, is more ambiguous. Contradictory scholars label and symbolize him as both evil and its opposite, nature. Let him be nature, a Leviathan with the dolphin's uncanny psychic brain—superior, his enthusiasts would claim, to man, whom he never fought except to save his life. His evil is strength to kill the killer whalemen. Indestructible by Ahab, he is not immortal, and is often permanently wounded.

Homer is blinding Greek sunlight; Vergil is dark, narrow, morbid, mysterious, and artistic. He fades in translation, unlike Homer, who barely survives. By combining the plots of the *Iliad* and the *Odyssey*, Vergil has seemed a plagiarist, attempting an epic as a task for rhetoric. He is as original as Milton. Dryden and the Restoration critics were wrong in thinking the *Aeneid* something like their regilding of Jacobean tragedy . . . giving alloy and polish to old gold.

One cannot doubt that Vergil sincerely and deeply admired the Emperor Augustus, not only for personal patronage but for the peace he brought Italy after her ulcerous, unceasing civil wars, from Marius and Sulla, Caesar and Pompey, Marcus Antonius and Brutus, to Marcus Antonius and Octavian . . . to Augustus. Aeneas is a peace-bringer, a bringer of peace through carnage. I feel Vergil, like a more ambivalent and furtive Milton, was also on the devil's side.

The *Aeneid* is the song of Rome's annals in prophecy and hindsight. Aeneas, unlike Achilles and Odysseus, is darkened by destiny—his actions do not emanate in the present, or from impulsive passions. He exemplifies the grit, torture, and sacrifice that made Rome's unification of the Mediterranean possible. One's heart goes to the defeated. How could Vergil, an outlander, sympathize with Rome's bloody, centralizing conquest of Italy? Why does he make us weep for the deaths of Camilla, Mezentius, and Turnus, outlanders like himself? It's interesting how instinctively and without justifying himself, Vergil chose archaic heroes of his country from both Trojan and Italian.

MEZENTIUS:
"nunc vivo neque adhuc homines lucemque relinquo.
sed linquam."   [X, 855–6]

CAMILLA:

"hactenus, Acca soror, potui; nunc volnus acerbum
conficit et tenebris nigrescunt omnia circum . . ." [XI, 823–4]

vitaque cum gemitu fugit indignata sub umbras. [XI, 831]

Aeneas puzzles, a force more than a person—nothing here of Achilles' dialectic, or the crafty, resourceful companionship of Odysseus. He lumbers through his irresistible march in the last books, less a living man than a Patroclus, hit on the head and stunned by Apollo—or Sintram, paranoid, brave, riding half paralyzed by his costly armor through the bedeviled wood of Dürer. He thinks little, thinks up little, though subject to heart-felt depression. Whatever his author was, he is not an *anima naturaliter Christiana.*

Aeneas has a moment or two of imagination and clairvoy-ance—his hallucinated and almost surrealist narrative of the fall of Troy in Book Two—dust, smoke, butchery, deceit, terror, the annihilation of his home and city. Some authentic murmur in Aeneas' voice makes us unwilling to believe this book was ghost-written by Vergil. With Dido too, he is alive. Dido is hell, Phèdre, Madame Bovary, talkative, repetitive—her few words symbolize thousands. Yet our love goes with her, her beauty, her bravery, her misfortune; and Aeneas, her deserter, seems no man. After her suicide, Aeneas must descend to the underworld, a Roman cemetery with shades like statues: the Illustrious, his dead comrades and unborn descendants. Dido alone is alive, when she turns her back and says nothing to Aeneas' false, forced appeals.

Aeneas is sometimes swollen and Rubensesque, as if painted for the peaceful triumphs of Marie de' Medici—I wish he were greater and had more charm. Yet Vergil, like Frankenstein, put a heart and mind, his own, into his Colossus, the triumphant Ro-man general, the soul of his great epic, if not of Rome. He bears all, he suffers all, a man of sorrows, if human . . . He mislays his wife, while himself escaping the ruin of Troy. He ungrapples mighty Dido, though almost as unfitted for this struggle as Pru-frock. Don't doubt him; his soldiers move forward undeflected.

They do not fight helter-skelter like Greeks, but rather as legion-naires drilled by Marius or Caesar to slaughter the barbarian. All Italy is turned on its head by Aeneas for him to marry Lavinia—she must have loved his victim, Turnus, whose plea for life is refused by Aeneas with stoical severity. Turnus' last action is the final line of the *Aeneid*:

vitaque cum gemitu fugit indignata sub umbras. [XII, 952]

Forever, indignation—too many beautiful things were crushed by the conquest. Too much attrition for the slavery to be immortal for the Romans hard as nails. Vergil may have understood his epic, its prophecy that the Empire of the Divine Augustus was inevitably eroding.

Moby Dick, like most of our nineteenth-century master-pieces, was published still-born, and sold so little it soon snuffed out Melville's popular reputation. It's our epic, a New England epic; unless we feel the enchanted discontinuity of Pound's *Cantos* qualifies. *Moby Dick* is also our one epic in prose. Are there epics in prose? I know one, Carlyle's *French Revolution*, also stylized as poetic extravagance. The modern British historian Taylor wrote: ". . . more than five hundred errors, some of them by no means minor. But what does it matter? When you read Carlyle's *Revolution*, you are there." Epics as verifiable history have too many pitfalls, too many to tempt a rival.

Moby Dick is fiction, not history—beside James or Dickens, how thin and few its characters, how heroic and barbarous its adventure. As a librettist once said to me, "Not the faintest whisper of a female voice." Often magnificent rhythms and a larger vocabulary make it equal to the great metrical poems. Parts, of course, are not even prose, but collages of encyclopedic clippings on cetology. It is our best book. It tells us not to break our necks on a brick wall. Yet what sticks in mind is the Homeric prowess of the extinct whaleman, gone before his prey.

Melville had much experience, if sailing on whalers brings more than working like Hawthorne in a Customs House . . .

as Melville himself did for the remainder of his life . . . twenty unfathomable years of marriage, parenthood, customs, whatever —then thinking of the oceans, and possibly allegorizing himself a little, Melville wrote his final and imperfect masterpiece, *Billy Budd*, the blond, innocent young seaman, hanged from the yard-arm by naval law.

[1977]

Three

On "Skunk Hour"

[This is Lowell's response, in a symposium on his poem, to comments by three poet-critics, named below.]

I / The Meaning

The author of a poem is not necessarily the ideal person to explain its meaning. He is as liable as anyone else to muddle, dishonesty, and reticence. Nor is it his purpose to provide a peg for a prose essay. Meaning varies in importance from poem to poem, and from style to style, but always it is only a strand and an element in the brute flow of composition. Other elements are pictures that please or thrill for themselves, phrases that ring for their music or carry some buried suggestion. For all this the author is an opportunist, throwing whatever comes to hand into his feeling for start, continuity, contrast, climax, and completion. It is imbecile for him not to know his intentions, and unsophisticated for him to know too explicitly and fully.

Three papers by three poets [John Berryman, John Frederick Nims, Richard Wilbur] on another's poem! Perhaps they should be considered as short stories and variants on my original. I shall comment on them later; here, I only want to say that I learned much from them. Very little of what I had in mind is untouched on; much that never occurred to me has been granted me. What I didn't intend often seems now at least as valid as what I did. My complaint is not that I am misunderstood but that I am overunderstood. I am seen through.

I am not sure whether I can distinguish between intention and interpretation. I think this is what I more or less intended. The first four stanzas are meant to give a dawdling more or less amiable picture of a declining Maine sea town. I move from the ocean inland. Sterility howls through the scenery, but I try to give a tone of tolerance, humor, and randomness to the sad prospect. The composition drifts, its direction sinks out of sight into the casual, chancy arrangements of nature and decay. Then all comes alive in stanzas V and VI. This is the dark night. I hoped my readers would remember John of the Cross's poem. My night is not gracious, but secular, puritan, and agnostic. An existentialist night. Somewhere in my mind was a passage from Sartre or Camus about reaching some point of final darkness where the one free act is suicide. Out of this comes the march and affirmation, an ambiguous one, of my skunks in the last two stanzas. The skunks are both quixotic and barbarously absurd, hence the tone of amusement and defiance. "Skunk Hour" is not entirely independent, but the anchor poem in its sequence.

II /
How the Poem Was Written

What I can describe and what no one else can describe are the circumstances of my poem's composition. I shan't reveal private secrets. John Berryman's pathological chart comes frighteningly close to the actual event. When I first read his paper, I kept saying to myself, "Why, he is naming the very things I wanted to keep out of my poem." In the end, I had to admit that Berryman had hit a bull's-eye, and often illuminated matters more searchingly and boldly than I could have wished. Is his account true? I cannot decide, the truth here depends on what psychologists and philosophers one accepts. Berryman comes too close for comfort.

"Skunk Hour" was begun in mid-August 1957 and finished about a month later. In March of the same year, I had been giving readings on the West Coast, often reading six days a week and sometimes twice on a single day. I was in San Francisco, the era and setting of Allen Ginsberg and all about, very modest poets were waking up prophets. I became sorely aware of how few poems I had written, and that these few had been finished at the latest three or four years earlier. Their style seemed distant, symbol-ridden, and willfully difficult. I began to paraphrase my Latin quotations, and to add extra syllables to a line to make it clearer and more colloquial. I felt my old poems hid what they were really about, and many times offered a stiff, humorless, and even impenetrable surface. I am no convert to the "beats." I know well, too, that the best poems are not necessarily poems that read aloud. Many of the greatest poems can only be read to one's self, for inspiration is no substitute for humor, shock, narrative, and a hypnotic voice, the four musts for oral performance. Still, my own poems seemed like prehistoric monsters dragged down into the bog and death by their ponderous armor. I was reciting what I no longer felt. What influenced me more than San Francisco and reading aloud was that for some time I had been writing prose. I felt that the best style for poetry was none of the many poetic styles in English, but something like the prose of Chekhov or Flaubert.

When I returned to my home, I began writing lines in a new style. No poem, however, got finished and soon I left off and tried to forget the whole headache. Suddenly, in August, I was struck by the sadness of writing nothing, and having nothing to write, of having, at least, no language. When I began writing "Skunk Hour," I felt that most of what I knew about writing was a hindrance.

The dedication is to Elizabeth Bishop, because rereading her suggested a way of breaking through the shell of my old manner. Her rhythms, idiom, images, and stanza structure seemed to belong to a later century. "Skunk Hour" is modeled on Miss Bishop's "The Armadillo," a much better poem and one I had heard her read and had later carried around with me. Both "Skunk Hour" and "The Armadillo" use short line stanzas, start with drifting description, and end with a single animal.

This was the main source. My others were Hölderlin's "*Brod und Wein*," particularly the moon lines:

Sich! und das Schattenbild unserer Erde, der Mond,
kommet geheim nun auch; die Schwärmerische, die Nacht
 kommt
"vohl" mit Sternen und "wohl" wenig bekummert um uns,

and so forth. I put this in long straggling lines and then added touches of Maine scenery, till I saw I was getting nowhere. Another source, probably undetectable now, was Annette von Droste-Hülshoff's "*Amletzten Tage des Jahres*." She, too, uses a six-line stanza with short lines. Her second stanza is as follows:

's ist tiefe Nacht!
Ob wohl ein Auge offen noch?
In diesen Mauern ruttelt dein
Verrinnen, Zeit! Mir schaudert; doch
Es will die letzte Stunde sein
Einsam durchwacht.

Geschehen all . . .

Here and elsewhere, my poem and the German poem have the same shudders and situation.

"Skunk Hour" was written backward, first the last two stanzas, I think, and then the next-to-last two. Anyway, there was a time when I had the last four stanzas much as they now are and nothing before them. I found the bleak personal violence repellent. All was too close, though watching the lovers was not mine, but from an anecdote about Walt Whitman in his old age. I began to feel that real poetry came, not from fierce confessions, but from something almost meaningless but imagined. I was haunted by an image of a blue china doorknob. I never used the doorknob, or knew what it meant, yet somehow it started the current of images in my opening stanzas. They were written in reverse order, and at last gave my poem an earth to stand on, and space to breathe.

III / The Critics

I don't think I intended either the Spartan boy holding the fox or Satan's feeling of sexual deprivation while he watched Adam and Eve in the Garden. I may have, but I don't remember. The red fox stain was merely meant to describe the rusty reddish color of autumn on Blue Hill, a Maine mountain near where we were living. I had seen foxes playing on the road one night, and I think the words have sinister and askew suggestions.

I can't imagine anything more thorough than Nims's stanza-by-stanza exposition. Almost all of it is to the point. I get a feeling of going on a familiar journey, but with another author and another sensibility. This feeling is still stronger when I read Wilbur's essay. Sometimes he and I are named as belonging to the same school, what *Time* magazine calls "the couth poets." Sometimes we are set in battle against one another. I have no idea which, if either, is true. Certainly, we both in different ways owe much to the teaching and practice of John Crowe Ransom. Certainly, his essay embodies and enhances my poem. With Berryman, too, I go on a strange journey! Thank God, we both come out clinging to spars, enough floating matter to save us, though faithless.

[1964]

On Translating
Phèdre

Racine's plays are generally and correctly thought to be untranslatable. His syllabic alexandrines do not and cannot exist in English. We cannot reproduce his language, which is refined by the literary artifice of his contemporaries, and given a subtle realism and grandeur by the spoken idiom of Louis XIV's court. Behind each line is a for us lost knowledge of actors and actresses, the stage and the moment. Other qualities remain: the great conception, the tireless plotting, and perhaps the genius for rhetoric and versification that alone proves that the conception and plotting are honest. Matisse says somewhere that a reproduction requires as much talent for color as the original painting. I have been tormented by the fraudulence of my own heavy touch.

My meter, with important differences, is based on Dryden and Pope. In his heroic plays, Dryden uses an end-stopped couplet, loaded with inversions, heavily alliterated, and varied by short unrhymed lines. My couplet is run on, avoids inversions and alliteration, and loosens its rhythm with shifted accents and occasional extra syllables. I gain in naturalness and lose in compactness and epigrammic resonance. I have tried for an idiomatic and ageless style, but I inevitably echo the English Restoration, both in ways that are proper and in my sometimes un-Racinian humor and bombast.

My version is *free*, nevertheless I have used every speech in the original, and almost every line is either translated or paraphrased. Racine is said to have written prose drafts and then versed them. We do not have the prose drafts, but I feel sure that necessities of line rhyme, etc., made for changes of phrasing and even of meaning. In versing Racine, I have taken the same liberty. Here and there, I have put in things that no French classical author would have used. Examples are the Amazon in Theramenes' first speech and the *muck* and *jelly* in Phaedra's second-act speech. Such interpolations are rare, however.

No translator has had the gifts or the luck to bring Racine into our culture. It's a pity that Pope and Dryden overlooked Racine's great body of works, close to them, in favor of the inaccessible Homer and Vergil.

Racine's verse has a diamond edge. He is perhaps the greatest poet in the French language, but he uses a smaller vocabulary than any English poet—beside him Pope and Bridges have a Shakespearean luxuriance. He has few verbally inspired lines and in this is unlike Baudelaire and even La Fontaine. His poetry is great because of the justness of its rhythm and logic, and the glory of its hard, electric rage. I have translated as a poet, and tried to give my lines a certain dignity, speed, and flare.

[1961]

On *Imitations*

This book [of translations] is partly self-sufficient and separate from its sources, and should be first read as a sequence, one voice running through many personalities, contrasts, and repetitions. I have hoped somehow for a whole, to make a single volume, a small anthology of European poetry. The dark and against the grain stand out, but there are other modifying strands. I have tried to keep something equivalent to the fire and finish of my originals. This has forced me to do considerable rewriting.

Boris Pasternak has said that the usual reliable translator gets the literal meaning but misses the tone, and that in poetry tone is of course everything. I have been reckless with literal meaning, and labored hard to get the tone. Most often this has been *a* tone, for *the* tone is something that will always more or less escape transference to another language and cultural moment. I have tried to write alive English and to do what my authors might have done if they were writing their poems now and in America.

Most poetic translations come to grief and are less enjoyable than modest photographic prose translations, such as George Kay has offered in his *Penguin Book of Italian Verse*. Strict metrical translators still exist. They seem to live in a pure world untouched by contemporary poetry. Their difficulties are bold and honest, but they are taxidermists, not poets, and their poems are likely to be stuffed birds. A better strategy would seem to be the now fashionable translations into free or irregular verse. Yet this method commonly turns out a sprawl of language, neither faithful nor distinguished, now on stilts, now low, as Dryden would say. It seems self-evident that no professor or amateur poet, or even good poet writing hastily, can by miracle transform himself into a fine metricist. I believe that poetic translation—I would call it an imitation—must be expert and inspired, and needs at least as much technique, luck, and rightness of my hand as an original poem.

My licenses have been many. My first two Sappho poems are really new poems based on hers. Villon has been somewhat stripped; Hebel is taken out of dialect; Hugo's "Gautier" is cut in half. Mallarmé has been unclotted, not because I disapprove of his dense medium but because I saw no way of giving it much power in English. The same has been done with Ungaretti and some of the more obscure Rimbaud. About a third of "The Drunken Boat" has been left out. Two stanzas have been added to Rilke's "Roman Sarcophagus," and one to his "Pigeons." "Pigeons" and Valéry's "Helen" are more idiomatic and informal in my English. Some lines from Villon's "Little Testament" have been shifted to introduce his "Great Testament." And so forth! I have dropped lines, moved lines, moved stanzas, changed images, and altered meter and intent.

Pasternak has given me special problems. From reading his prose and many translations of his poetry, I have come to feel that he is a very great poet. But I know no Russian. I have rashly tried to improve on other translations, and have been helped by exact prose versions given me by Russian readers. This is an old practice; Pasternak himself, I think, worked this way with his Georgian poets. I hope I caught something worthy of his all-important tone.

This book was written from time to time when I was unable to do anything of my own. It began some ten years ago when I read a parallel French translation of Rilke's "Orpheus," and felt that a much better job might be done in English. I had long been amazed by Montale, but had no idea how he might be worked until I saw that unlike most good poets—Horace and Petrarch are extremes—he was strong in simple prose and could be made still stronger in free verse. My Baudelaires were begun as exercises in couplets and quatrains and to get away from the longer, less concentrated problems of translating Racine's *Phèdre.*

All my originals are important poems. Nothing like them exists in English, for the excellence of a poet depends on the unique opportunities of his native language. I have been almost as free as the authors themselves in finding ways to make them ring right for me.

[1961]

An Interview
with Frederick Seidel

[*On one wall of Mr. Lowell's study was a large portrait of Ezra Pound, the tired, haughty outlines of the face concentrated as in the raised outlines of a ring seal in an enlargement. Also bearded, but on another wall, over the desk, James Russell Lowell looked down from a gray, old-fashioned photograph on the apex of the triangle thus formed, where his great-grandnephew sat and answered questions. Mr. Lowell had been talking about the classes he teaches at Boston University. Four floors below the study window, cars whined through the early spring rain on Marlborough Street toward the Boston Public Garden.*]

FREDERICK SEIDEL : *What are you teaching now?*

LOWELL : I'm teaching one of these poetry-writing classes and a course in the novel. The course in the novel is called Practical Criticism. It's a course I teach every year, but the material changes. It could be anything from Russian short stories to Baudelaire, a study of the New Critics, or just fiction. I do whatever I happen to be working on myself.

Has your teaching over the last few years meant anything to you as a writer?

It's meant a lot to me as a human being, I think. But my teaching is part-time and has neither the merits nor the burdens of real teaching. Teaching is entirely different from writing. You're always up to it, or more or less up to it; there's no question of its clogging, of its not coming. It's much less subjective, and it's a very pleasant pursuit in itself. In the kind of teaching I do, conversational classes, seminars, if the students are good, which they've been most of the time, it's extremely entertaining. Now, I don't know what it has to do with writing. You review a lot of things that you like, and you read things that you haven't read or haven't read closely, and you read them aloud, go into them much more carefully than you would otherwise; and that must teach you a good deal. But there's such a jump from teaching to writing.

Well, do you think the academic life is liable to block up the writer-professor's sensitivity to his own intuitions?

I think it's impossible to give a general answer. Almost all the poets of my generation, all the best ones, teach. At present I only know one, Elizabeth Bishop, who doesn't. They do it for a livelihood, but they also do it because you can't write poetry all the time. They do it to extend themselves, and I think it's undoubtedly been a gain to them. Now, the question is whether something else might be more of a gain. Certainly the danger of teaching is that it's much too close to what you're doing—close and not close. You can get expert at teaching and be crude in practice. The revision, the consciousness that tinkers with the poem—that has something to do with teaching and criticism. But the impulse that starts a poem and makes it of any importance is distinct from teaching.

And protected, you think, from whatever you bring to bear in the scrutiny of parts of poems and aspects of novels, etc.?

I think you have to tear it apart from that. Teaching may make the poetry even more different, less academic than it would be otherwise. I'm sure that writing isn't a craft; that is, something for which you learn the skills and go on turning out. It must come from some deep impulse, deep inspiration. That can't be taught, it can't be what you use in teaching. And you may go further afield looking for that than you would if you didn't teach. I don't know, really; the teaching probably makes you more cautious, more self-conscious, makes you write less. It may make you bolder when you do write.

You think the last may be so?

The boldness is ambiguous. It's not only teaching, it's growing up in this age of criticism which we're all so conscious of, whether we like it or don't like it, or practice it or don't practice it. You think three times before you put a word down, and ten times about taking it out. And that's related to boldness; if you put words down they must do something, you're not going to put clichés. But then it's related to caution; you write much less.

You yourself have written very little criticism, haven't you? You did once contribute to a study of Hopkins.*

Yes, and I've done a few omnibus reviews. I do a review or two a year.

You did a wonderful one of Richards's poems.

I felt there was an occasion for that, and I had something to say about it. Sometimes I wish I did more, but I'm very anxious in criticism not to do the standard analytical essay. I'd like my essay to be much sloppier and more intuitive. But my friends are critics and most of them poet-critics. When I was twenty and learning to write, Allen Tate, Eliot, Blackmur, and Winters, and all those people were very much news. You waited for their essays, and when a good critical essay came out it had the excitement of a new imaginative work.

Which is really not the case with any of the critics writing today, do you think?

* See page 167.

The good critics are almost all the old ones. The most brilliant critic of my generation, I think, was Jarrell, and he in a way
connects with that older generation. But he's writing less criticism
now than he used to.

*In your schooling at St. Mark's and Harvard—we can talk
about Kenyon in a minute—were there teachers or friends who
had an influence on your writing, not so much by the example
of their own writing as by personal supervision or direction—by
suggesting certain reading, for instance?*

My school had been given a Carnegie set of art books, and
I had a friend, Frank Parker, who had great talent as a painter
but who'd never done anything systematically. We began reading the books and histories of art, looking at reproductions,
tracing the Last Supper on tracing paper, studying dynamic
symmetry, learning about Cézanne, and so on. I had no practical interest in painting, but that study seemed rather close to
poetry. And from there I began. I think I read Elizabeth Drew
or some such book on modern poetry. It had free verse in it, and
that seemed very simple to do.

What class were you in then?

It was my last year. I'd wanted to be a football player very
much, and got my letter but didn't make the team. Well, that
was satisfying but crushing too. I read a good deal, but had never
written. So this was a recoil from that. Then I had some luck
in that Richard Eberhart was teaching there.

I thought he'd been a student there with you.

No, he was a young man about thirty. I never had him in
class, but I used to go to him. He'd read aloud and we'd talk,
he was very pleasant. He'd smoke honey-scented tobacco, and
read Baudelaire and Shakespeare and Hopkins—it made the
thing living—and he'd read his own poems. I wrote very badly
at first, but he was encouraging and enthusiastic. That probably
was decisive, that there was someone there whom I admired who
was engaged in writing poetry.

I heard that a very early draft of "The Drunken Fisherman"
appeared in the St. Mark's magazine.

No, it was the Kenyon College magazine [*Hika*] that published it. The poem was very different then. I'd been reading
Winters, whose model was Robert Bridges, and what I wanted
was a rather distant, quiet, classical poem without any symbolism. It was in four-foot couplets as smooth as I could write them.
The *Kenyon Review* had published poems of mine and then
stopped. This was the one time they said, if you'd submitted
this we'd have taken it.

Then you submitted other poems to the Review?

Yes, but that poem was rather different from anything else
I did. I was also reading Hart Crane and Thomas and Tate and
Empson's *Seven Types of Ambiguity*; and each poem was more
difficult than the one before, and had more ambiguities. Ransom,
editing the *Kenyon Review*, was impressed, but didn't want to
publish them. He felt they were forbidding and clotted.

But finally he did come through.

After I'd graduated. I published when I was a junior, then
for about three years no magazine would take anything I did.
I'd get hopeful letters—"One poem in this group interests us,
if you can get seven more." At that time it took me about a
year to do two or three poems. Gradually I just stopped, and
really gave it up. I seemed to have reached a great impasse. The
kind of poem I thought was interesting and could work on became so cluttered and overdone that it wasn't really enjoyable.

I was struck on reading Land of Unlikeness *by the difference*
between poems you rejected for Lord Weary's Castle *and the*
few poems and passages that you took over into the new book.

I think I took almost a third, but almost all of what I took
was rewritten. I wonder what struck you.

One thing was that almost all the rejected poems seemed to
me to be those that Tate, who in his introduction spoke about

two kinds of poetry in the book, said were the more strictly religious and strictly symbolic poems, as against the poems he said were perhaps more powerful because more experienced or relying more on your sense of history. What you took seemed really superior to what you left behind.

I took out several that were paraphrases of early Christian poems, and I rejected one rather dry abstraction, then whatever seemed to me to have messy violence. All the poems have religious imagery, I think, but the ones I took were more concrete. That's what the book was moving toward: less symbolic imagery. And as I say, I tried to take some of the less fierce poems. There seemed to be too much twisting and disgust in the first book.

I wondered how wide your reading had been at the time. I wondered, when I read in Tate's introduction that the stanza in one of your poems was based on the stanza in "The Virginian Voyages," whether someone had pointed out Drayton's poem to you.

Tate and I started to make an anthology. It was a very interesting year I spent with Tate and his wife. He's a poet who writes in spurts, and he had about a third of a book. I was going to do a biography of Jonathan Edwards and he was going to write a novel, and our wives were going to write novels. Well, the wives just went humming away. "I've just finished three pages," they'd say at the end of the day; and their books mounted up. But ours never did, though one morning Allen wrote four pages to his novel, very brilliant. We were in a little study together separated by a screen. I was heaping up books on Jonathan Edwards and taking notes, and getting more and more numb on the subject, looking at old leather-bound volumes on freedom of the will and so on, and feeling less and less a calling. And there we stuck. And then we decided to make an anthology together. We both liked rather formal, difficult poems, and we were reading particularly the sixteenth and seventeenth centuries. In the evening we'd read aloud, and we started a card catalogue of what we'd make for the anthology. And then we started writing. It seems to me we took old models like Drayton's Ode

—Tate wrote a poem called "The Young Proconsuls of the Air" in that stanza. I think there's a trick to formal poetry. Most poetry is very formal, but when a modern poet is formal he gets more attention for it than old poets did. We've tried to make it look difficult. For example, Shelley can just rattle off terza rima by the page, and it's very smooth, doesn't seem an obstruction to him—you sometimes wish it were more difficult. If someone does that today and in modern style, it looks as though he's wrestling with every line and may be pushed into confusion, as though he's having a real struggle with form and content. Marks of that are in the finished poem. And I think both Tate and I felt that we wanted our formal patterns to seem a hardship and something that we couldn't rattle off easily.

But in Lord Weary's Castle *there were poems moving toward a sort of narrative calm, almost a prose calm—"Katherine's Dream," for example, or the two poems on texts by Edwards, or "The Ghost"—and then, on the other hand, poems in which the form was insisted upon and maybe shown off, and where in the things that were characteristic of your poetry at that time —the kind of enjambments, the rhyming, the meters, of course— seem willed and forced, so that you have a terrific logjam of stresses, meanings, and strains.*

I know one contrast I've felt, and it takes different forms at different times. The ideal modern form seems to be the novel and certain short stories. Maybe Tolstoy would be the perfect example—his work is imagistic, it deals with all experience, and there seems to be no conflict of the form and content. So one thing is to get into poetry that kind of human richness in simple descriptive language. Then there's another side of poetry: compression, something highly rhythmical and perhaps wrenched into a small space. I've always been fascinated by both these things. But getting it all on one page in a few stanzas, getting it all done in as little space as possible, revising and revising so that each word and rhythm though not perfect is pondered and wrestled with—you can't do that in prose very well, you'd never get your book written. "Katherine's Dream" was a real dream.

I found that I shaped it a bit, and cut it, and allegorized it, but still it was a dream someone had had. It was material that ordinarily, I think, would go into prose, yet it would have had to be much longer or part of something much longer.

I think you can either look for forms, you can do specific reading for them, or the forms can be demanded by what you want to say. And when the material in poetry seems under almost unbearable pressure, you wonder whether the form hasn't cookie-cut what the poet wanted to say. But you chose the couplet, didn't you, and some of your freest passages are in couplets.

The couplet I've used is very much like the couplet Browning uses in "My Last Duchess," in *Sordello*, run-on with its rhymes buried. I've always, when I've used it, tried to give the impression that I had as much freedom in choosing the rhyme as I had in any of the other words. Yet they were almost all true rhymes, and more than half the time there'd be a pause after the rhyme. I wanted something as fluid as prose; you wouldn't notice the form, yet looking back you'd find that great obstacles had been climbed. And the couplet is pleasant in this way— once you've got your two lines to rhyme, then that's done and you can go on to the next. You're not stuck with the whole stanza to round out and build to a climax. A couplet can be a couplet or can be split and left as one line, or it can go on for a hundred lines; any sort of compression or expansion is possible. And that's not so in a stanza. I think a couplet's much less lyrical than a stanza, closer to prose. Yet it's an honest form, its difficulties are in the open. It really is pretty hard to rhyme each line with the one that follows it.

Did the change of style in Life Studies *have something to do with working away from that compression and pressure by way of, say, the kind of prose clarity of "Katherine's Dream"?*

Yes. By the time I came to *Life Studies* I'd been writing my autobiography and also writing poems that broke meter. I'd been doing a lot of reading aloud. I went on a trip to the West

Coast and read at least once a day and sometimes twice for fourteen days, and more and more I found that I was simplifying my poems. If I had a Latin quotation, I'd translate it into English. If adding a couple of syllables in a line made it clearer I'd add them, and I'd make little changes just impromptu as I read. That seemed to improve the reading.

Can you think of a place where you added a syllable or two to an otherwise regular line?

It was usually articles and prepositions that I added, very slight changes, I didn't change the printed text. It was just done for the moment.

Why did you do this? Just because you thought the most important thing was to get the poem over?

To get it over, yes. And I began to have a certain disrespect for the tight forms. If you could make it easier by adding syllables, why not? And then when I was writing *Life Studies*, a good number of the poems were started in very strict meter, and I found that, more than the rhymes, the regular beat was what I didn't want. I have a long poem in there about my father, called "Commander Lowell," which actually is largely in couplets, but I originally wrote perfectly strict four-foot couplets. With that form it's hard not to have echoes of Marvell. That regularity just seemed to ruin the honesty of sentiment, and become rhetorical; it said, "I'm a poem"—though it was a great help when I was revising, having this original skeleton. I could keep the couplets where I wanted them and drop them where I didn't; there'd be a form to come back to.

Had you originally intended to handle all that material in prose?

Yes. I found it got awfully tedious working out transitions and putting in things that didn't seem very important but were necessary to the prose continuity. Also, I found it hard to revise. Cutting it down into small bits, I could work on it much more carefully and make fast transitions. But there's another point about this mysterious business of prose and poetry, form and content, and the reason for breaking forms. I don't think there's any very satisfactory answer. I seesaw back and forth between something highly metrical and something free; there isn't any one way to write. But it seems to me we've gotten into a sort of Alexandrian age. Poets of my generation and particularly younger ones have gotten terribly proficient at these forms. They write a very musical, difficult poem with tremendous skill, perhaps there's never been such skill. Yet the writing seems divorced from the culture. It's become too much something specialized that can't handle much experience. It's become a craft, purely a craft, and there must be some breakthrough back into life. Prose is in many ways better off than poetry. It's quite hard to think of a young poet who has the vitality, say, of Salinger or Saul Bellow. Yet prose tends to be very diffuse. The novel is really a much more difficult form than it seems; few people have the wind to write anything that long. Even a short story demands almost poetic perfection. Yet, on the whole, prose is less cut off from life than poetry is. Now, some of this Alexandrian poetry is very brilliant, you would not have it changed at all. But I thought it was getting increasingly stifling. I couldn't get my experience into tight metrical forms.

So you felt this about your own poetry, your own technique, not just about the general condition of poetry?

Yes, I felt that the meter plastered difficulties and mannerisms on what I was trying to say to such an extent that it terribly hampered me.

This then explains, in part anyway, your admiration for Elizabeth Bishop's poetry. I know that you've said the qualities and the abundance of its descriptive language reminded you of the Russian novel more than anything else.

Any number of people are guilty of writing a complicated poem that has a certain amount of symbolism in it and really difficult meaning, a wonderful poem to teach. Then you unwind it and you feel that the intelligence, the experience, whatever goes into it, is skin-deep. In Elizabeth Bishop's "Man-Moth" a whole new world is gotten out and you don't know what will come after any one line. It's exploring. And it's as original as Kafka. She has gotten a world, not just a way of writing. She seldom writes a poem that doesn't have that exploring quality; yet it's very firm, it's not like the beat poetry, it's all controlled.

What about Snodgrass? What you were trying to do in Life Studies *must have something to do with your admiration for his work.*

He did these things before I did, though he's younger than I am and had been my student. He may have influenced me, though people have suggested the opposite. He spent ten years at the University of Iowa, going to writing classes, being an instructor; rather unworldly, making little money, and specializing in talking to other people writing poetry, obsessed you might say with minute technical problems and rather provincial experience—and then he wrote about just that. I mean, the poems are about his child, his divorce, and Iowa City, and his child is a Dr. Spock child—all handled in expert little stanzas. I believe that's a new kind of poetry. Other poems that are direct that way are slack and have no vibrance. His experience wouldn't be so interesting and valid if it weren't for the whimsy, the music, the balance, everything revised and placed and pondered. All that gives light to those poems on agonizing subjects comes from the craft.

And yet his best poems are all on the verge of being slight and sentimental.

I think a lot of the best poetry is. Laforgue—it's hard to think of a more delightful poet, and his prose is wonderful, too. Well, it's on the verge of being sentimental, and if he hadn't dared to be sentimental he wouldn't have been a poet. I mean, his inspiration was that. There's some way of distinguishing between false sentimentality, which is blowing up a subject and giving emotions that you don't feel, and using whimsical, minute, tender, small emotions that most people don't feel but which

Laforgue and Snodgrass do. So that I'd say he had pathos and fragility—but then that's a large subject, too. He has fragility along the edges and a main artery of power going through the center.

Some people were disappointed with Life Studies *just because earlier you had written a kind of heroic poetry, an American version of heroic poetry, of which there had been none recently except your own. Is there any chance that you will go back to that?*

I don't think that a personal history can go on forever, unless you're Walt Whitman and have a way with yourself. I feel I've done enough personal poetry. That doesn't mean I won't do more of it, but I don't want to do more now. I feel I haven't gotten down all my experience, or perhaps even the most important part, but I've said all I really have much inspiration to say, and more would just dilute. So that you need something more impersonal, and other things being equal, it's better to get your emotions out in a Macbeth than in a confession. Macbeth must have tons of Shakespeare in him. We don't know where, nothing in Shakespeare's life was remotely like Macbeth, yet he somehow gives the feeling of going to the core of Shakespeare. You have much more freedom that way than you do when you write an autobiographical poem.

These poems, I gather from what you said earlier, did take as much working over as the earlier ones.

They were just as hard to write. They're not always factually true. There's a good deal of tinkering with fact. You leave out a lot, and emphasize this and not that. Your actual experience is a complete flux. I've invented facts and changed things, and the whole balance of the poem was something invented. So there's a lot of artistry, I hope, in the poems. Yet there's this thing: if a poem is autobiographical—and this is true of any kind of autobiographical writing and of historical writing—you want the reader to say, This is true. In something like Macaulay's *History of England,* you think you're really getting Wil-

liam III. That's as good as a good plot in a novel. And so there
was always that standard of truth which you wouldn't ordinarily
have in poetry—the reader was to believe he was getting the
real Robert Lowell.

*I wanted to ask you about this business of taking over pass-
ages from earlier poems and rewriting them and putting them
in new contexts. I'm thinking of the passage at the end of the
"Cistercians in Germany," in* Land of Unlikeness, *which you
rewrote into those wonderful lines that end "At the Indian Killer's Grave." I know that Hart Crane rewrote early scraps a great
deal and used most of the rewrites. But doesn't doing this imply
a theory of poetry that would talk much more about craft than
about experience?*

I don't know, it's such a miracle if you get lines that are
halfway right; it's not just a technical problem. The lines must
mean a good deal to you. All your poems are in a sense one
poem; and there's always the struggle of getting something that
balances and comes out right, in which all parts are good, and
which has experience that you value. And so, if you have a few
lines that shine in a poem or are beginning to shine, and they
fail and get covered over and drowned, maybe their real form
is in another poem. Maybe you've mistaken the real inspiration
in the original poem and they belong in something else entirely.
I don't think that violates experience. The "Cistercians" wasn't
very close to me, but the last lines seemed felt; I dropped the
Cistercians and put a Boston graveyard in.

*But in Hart Crane's "Ode to an Urn," a poem about a per-
sonal friend, there are lines which originally applied to something very different, and therefore, in one version or the other,
at least can't be called personal.*

I think we always bring over some unexplained obscurities
by shifting lines. Something that was clear in the original seems
odd and unexplained in the final poem. That can be quite bad,
of course; but you always want—and I think Chekhov talks
about this—the detail that you can't explain. It's just there. It

seems right to you, but you don't have to have it; you could have something else entirely. Now if everything's like that you'd have chaos, but a few unexplained difficult things—they seem to be the lifeblood of variety—they may work. What may have seemed a little odd, a little difficult in the original poem, gets a little more difficult in a new way in the new poem. And that's purely accidental, yet you may gain more than you lose—a new suggestiveness and magic.

Do you revise a very great deal?
Endlessly.

You often use an idiom or a very common phrase either for the sake of irony or to bear more meaning than it's customarily asked to bear—do these come late in the game, do you have to look around for them?
They come later because they don't prove much in themselves, and they often replace something that's much more formal and worked up. Some of my later poetry does have this quality that the earlier doesn't: several lines can be almost what you'd say in conversation. And maybe talking with a friend or with my wife I'd say, "This doesn't sound quite right," and sort of reach in the air as I talked and change a few words. In that way the new style is easier to write; I sometimes fumble in my head a natural sequence of lines that will work. But a whole poem won't come that way; my seemingly relaxed poems are just about as hard as the very worked-up ones.

The rightness and familiarity, though, is in "Between the Porch and the Altar" in several passages which are in couplets.
When I am writing in meter I find simple lines never come right away. Nothing does. I don't believe I've ever written a poem in meter where I've kept a single one of the original lines. Usually when I was writing my old poems I'd write them out in blank verse and then put in the rhymes. And of course I'd change the rhymes a lot. The most I could hope for at first was

that the rhymed version wouldn't be much inferior to the blank verse. Then the real work would begin, to make it something much better than the original, out of the difficulties of the meter.

Have you ever gone as far as Yeats and written out a prose argument and then set down the rhymes?

With some of the later poems I've written out prose versions, then cut the prose down and abbreviated it. A rapidly written prose draft of the poem doesn't seem to do much good, too little pain has gone into it; but one really worked on is bound to have phrases that are invaluable. And it's a nice technical problem: how can you keep phrases and get them into meter?

Do you usually send off your work to friends before publishing it?

I do it less now. I always used to do it, to Jarrell and one or two other people. Last year I did a lot of showing with Stanley Kunitz.

At the time you were writing the poems for Lord Weary's Castle, *did it make a difference to you whether the poet to whom you were sending your work was Catholic?*

I don't think I ever sent any poems to a Catholic. The person I was closest to then was Allen Tate, who wasn't a Catholic at the time; and then later it became Jarrell, who wasn't at all Catholic. My two close Catholic writer friends are prose writers, J. F. Powers and Flannery O'Connor, and they weren't interested in the technical problems of poems.

So you feel that the religion is the business of the poem that it's in and not at all the business of the Church or the religious person.

It shouldn't be. I mean, a religion ought to have objective validity. But by the time it gets into a poem it's so mixed up with technical and imaginative problems that the theologian, the priest, the serious religious person isn't of too much use. The poem is too strange for him to feel at home and make any suggestions.

What does this make of the religious poems as a religious exercise?

It at least makes this: that the poem tries to be a poem and not a piece of artless religious testimony. There is a drawback. It seems to me that with any poem, but maybe particularly a religious one where there are common interests, the opinion of intelligent people who are not poets ought to be useful. There's independence to not getting advice from religious people and outsiders, but also there's a narrowness. Then there is a question whether my poems are religious, or whether they just use religious imagery. I haven't really any idea. My last poems don't use religious imagery, they don't use symbolism. In many ways they seem to me more religious than the early ones, which are full of symbols and references to Christ and God. I'm sure the symbols and the Catholic framework didn't make the poems religious experiences. Yet I don't feel my experience changed very much. It seems to me it's clearer to me now than it was then, but it's very much the same sort of thing that went into the religious poems—the same sort of struggle, light and darkness, the flux of experience. The morality seems much the same. But the symbolism is gone; you couldn't possibly say what creed I believed in. I've wondered myself often. Yet what made the earlier poems valuable seems to be some recording of experience and that seems to be what makes the later ones.

So you end up saying that the poem does have some integrity and can have some beauty apart from the beliefs expressed in the poem.

I think it can only have integrity apart from the beliefs; that no political position, religious position, position of generosity, or what have you, can make a poem good. It's all to the good if a poem *can* use politics, or theology, or gardening, or anything that has its own validity aside from poetry. But these things will never per se make a poem.

The difficult question is whether, when the beliefs expressed in a poem are obnoxious, the poem as a whole can be considered beautiful—the problem of the Pisan Cantos.

The *Pisan Cantos* are very uneven, aren't they? If you took what most people would agree are maybe the best hundred passages, would the beliefs in those passages be obnoxious? I think you'd get a very mixed answer. You could make quite a good case for Pound's good humor about his imprisonment, his absence of self-pity, his observant eye, his memories of literary friends, for all kinds of generous qualities and open qualities and lyrical qualities that anyone would think were good. And even when he does something like the death of Mussolini, in the passage that opens the *Pisan Cantos*, people debate about it. I've talked to Italians who were partisans, and who said that this is the only poem on Mussolini that's any good. Pound's quite wily often: Mussolini hung up like an ox—his brutal appearance. I don't know whether you could say the beliefs are wrong or not. And there are other poems that come to mind: in Eliot, the Jew spelled with a small j in "Gerontion," is that anti-Semitism or not? Eliot's not anti-Semitic in the evil sense, but there's certainly a dislike of Jews in those early poems. Does he gain in the fierceness of writing his Jew with a small j? He says you write what you have to write and in criticism you can say what you think you should believe in. Very ugly emotions perhaps make a poem.

You were on the Bollingen Committee at the time the award was made to Pound. What did you think of the great ruckus?

I thought it was a very simple problem of voting for the best book of the year; and it seemed to me Pound's was. I thought the *Pisan Cantos* was the best writing Pound had ever done, though it included some of his worst. It is a very mixed book: that was the question. But the consequences of not giving the best book of the year a prize for extraneous reasons, even terrible ones in a sense—I think that's the death of art. Then you have Pasternak suppressed and everything becomes stifling. Particularly in a strong country like ours you've got to award things objectively and not let the beliefs you'd like a man to have govern your choice. It was very close after the war, and anyone must feel that the poetry award was a trifling thing compared with the concentration camps. I actually think they were very distant from Pound. He had no political effect whatsoever and was quite eccentric and impractical. Pound's social credit, his Fascism, all these various things, were a tremendous gain to him; he'd be a very Parnassan poet without them. Even if they're bad beliefs —and some were bad, some weren't, and some were terrible, of course—they made him more human and more to do with life, more to do with the times. They served him. Taking what interested him in these things gave a kind of realism and life to his poetry that it wouldn't have had otherwise.

Did you become a translator to suit your own needs or because you wanted to get certain poems, most of them not before translated, into English? Or was it a matter of both, as I suppose it usually is, and as it was for Pound?

I think both. It always seemed to me that nothing very close to the poems I've translated existed in English; and on the other hand, there was some kind of closeness, I felt a kinship. I felt some sort of closeness to Rilke and Rimbaud poems I've translated, yet they were doing things I couldn't do. They were both a continuation of my own bias and a release from myself.

How did you come to translate Propertius—in fact, how did you come to have such a great interest in Roman history and Latin literature?

At Harvard my second year I took almost entirely English courses—the easiest path. I think that could have been a disaster. But before going to Kenyon, I talked to Ford Madox Ford and Ransom, and Ransom said I had to take philosophy and logic, which I did. The other thing he suggested was classics. Ford was rather flippant about it, said, "Of course you've got to learn classics, you'll just cut yourself off from humanity if you don't." I think it's always given me some sort of yardstick for English. And then the literature was amazing, particularly the Greek; there's nothing like Greek in English at all. Our plays aren't formally like Aeschylus and Sophocles. Their whole inspiration was unbelievably different, and so different that you could hardly think of even the attempt to imitate them, great as their prestige was. That something like *Antigone* or *Oedipus* or the great Achilles moments in the *Iliad* would be at the core of a literature is incredible for anyone brought up in an English culture—Greek wildness and sophistication all different, the women different, everything. Latin's of course much closer. English is a half-Latin language, and we've done our best to absorb the Latin literature. But a Roman poet is much less intellectual than the Englishman, much less abstract. He's nearer nature somehow—somewhat what we feel about a Frenchman but more so still. And yet he's very sophisticated. He has his way of doing things, though the number of forms he explored is quite limited. The amount he could take from the Greeks and yet change is an extraordinary piece of firm discipline. Also, you take almost any really good Roman poet—Juvenal, or Vergil, or Propertius, Catullus—he's much more raw and direct than anything in English, and yet he has a block-like formality. The Roman frankness interests me. Until recently our literature hasn't been as raw as the Roman, translations had to have stars. And their history has a terrible human frankness that isn't customary with us—corrosive attacks on the Establishment, comments on politics and the decay of morals, all felt terribly strongly, by poets as well as historians. The English writer who reads the classics is working at one thing, and his eye is on something else that can't be done. We will always have the Latin and Greek classics, and they'll never be absorbed. There's something very restful about that.

But more specifically, how did Latin poetry—your study of it, your translations—affect your measure of English poetry?

My favorite English poetry was the difficult Elizabethan plays and the Metaphysicals, then the nineteenth century, which I was aquiver about and disliked but which was closer to my writing than anything else. The Latin seemed very different from either of these. I immediately saw how Shelley wasn't like Horace and Vergil or Aeschylus—and the Latin was a mature poetry, a realistic poetry, which didn't have the contortions of the Metaphysicals. What a frail, bony, electric person compared with Horace is Marvell!

What about your adaptation of Propertius?

I got him through Pound. When I read him in Latin I found a kind of Propertius you don't get in Pound at all. Pound's Propertius is a rather Ovidian figure with a great deal of Pound's fluency and humor and irony. The actual Propertius is a very excited, tense poet, rather desperate; his line is much more like parts of Marlowe's *Faustus*. And he's of all the Roman poets the most like a desperate Christian. His experiences, his love affair with Cynthia, are absolutely rending, destroying. He's like a fallen Christian.

Have you done any other translations of Latin poems?

I did a monologue that started as a translation of Vergil and then was completely rewritten, and there are buried translations in several other poems. There's a poem called "To Speak of Woe That Is in Marriage" in my last book that started as a translation of Catullus's *siqua recordanti benefacta*. I don't know what traces are left, but it couldn't have been written without Catullus.

You've translated Pasternak. Do you know Russian?

No, I have rewritten other English translations, and seldom even checked with Russian experts. I want to get a book of translations together. I read in the originals, except for Russian, but I have felt quite free to alter things, and I don't know that

Pasternak would look less close than the Italian, which I have studied closely. Before I publish, I want to check with a Russian expert.

Can I get you back to Harvard for a minute? Is it true you tried out for the Harvard Advocate, *did all the dirty work for your candidacy, and then were turned down?*

I nailed a stair carpet down. I forget who the editor was then, but he was a man who wrote on Frost. At that time people who wrote on Frost were quite different from the ones who write on him now; they tended to be conservative, out of touch. I wasn't a very good writer then, perhaps I should have been turned down. I was trying to write like William Carlos Williams, very simple free verse, imagistic poems. I had a little group I was very proud of which was set up in galleys; when I left Harvard it was turned down.

Did you know any poets at the time?

I had a friend, Harry Brown, who writes dialogue for movies and has been in Hollywood for years. He was a terribly promising poet. He came to Harvard with a long correspondence with Harriet Monroe and was much more advanced than anyone else. He could write in the style of Auden or Webster or Eliot or Crane. He'd never graduated from high school, and wasn't a student, but he was the person I felt closest to. My other friends weren't writers.

Had you met any older poets—Frost, for instance, who must have been around?

I'd gone to call on Frost with a huge epic on the First Crusade, all written out in clumsy longhand on lined paper. He read a page of that and said, "You have no compression." Then he read me a very short poem of Collins's, "How Sleep the Brave," and said, "That's not a great poem, but it has restraint." He was very kindly about it. You know his point about the voice coming into poetry: he took a very unusual example of that, the opening of "Hyperion"; the line about the Naiad, something about her pressing a cold finger to her lips, which wouldn't seem like a voice passage at all. And he said, "Now Keats comes alive here." That was a revelation to me; what had impressed me was the big Miltonic imitation in "Hyperion." I don't know what I did with that, but I recoiled and realized that I was diffuse and monotonous.

What decided you to leave Harvard and go to Kenyon?

I'd made the acquaintance of Merrill Moore, who'd been at Vanderbilt and a Fugitive. He said that I ought to study with a man who was a poet. He was very close to Ransom, and the plan was that I'd go to Vanderbilt; and I would have, but Ransom changed to Kenyon.

I understand you left much against the wishes of your family.

I was getting quite morose and solitary, and they sort of settled for this move. They'd rather have had me a genial social Harvard student, but at least I'd be working hard this way. It seemed to them a queer but orderly step.

Did it help you that you had had intellectual and literary figures in your family?

I really didn't know I'd had them till I went to the South. To my family, James Russell Lowell was the ambassador to England, not a writer. Amy seemed a bit peculiar to them. When I began writing, I think it would have been unimaginable to take either Amy or James Russell Lowell as models.

Was it through Ransom that you met Tate?

I met them at more or less the same time, but actually stayed with Tate before I knew Ransom.

And Ford Madox Ford was there at some time, wasn't he?

I met Ford at a cocktail party in Boston and went to dinner with him at the Athens Olympia. He was going to visit the Tates and said, "Come and see me down there, we're all going to

Tennessee." So I drove down. He hadn't arrived, so I got to know the Tates quite well before his appearance.

Staying in a pup tent.

It's a terrible piece of youthful callousness. They had one Negro woman who came in and helped, but Mrs. Tate was doing all the housekeeping. She had three guests and her own family, and was doing the cooking and writing a novel. And this young man arrived, quite ardent and eccentric. I think I suggested that maybe I'd stay with them. And they said, "We really haven't any room, you'd have to pitch a tent on the lawn." So I went to Sears, Roebuck and got a tent and rigged it on their lawn. The Tates were too polite to tell me that what they'd said had been just a figure of speech. I stayed three months in my tent and ate with the Tates.

And you were showing him your work all the while.

Oh, I became converted to formalism and changed my style from frail free verse, all in a few months. And everything was in rhyme, and it still wasn't any good. But that was a great incentive. I poured out poems and went to writers' conferences.

What about Ford?

I saw him out there and took dictation from him for a while. That was hell, because I didn't know how to type. I'd take the dictation down in longhand, and he rather mumbled. I'd ask him what he'd said, and he'd say, "Oh, you have no sense of prose rhythm," and mumble some more. I'd get most of his words, then I'd have to improvise on the typewriter.

So for part of Ford's opus we're indebted to you.

A handful of phrases in *The March of Literature,* on the Provençal poets.

That was the summer before you entered Kenyon; but most of the poems in Land of Unlikeness *were written after you'd graduated, weren't they?*

Yes, they were almost all written in a later year I spent with the Tates, though some of them were earlier poems rewritten. I think becoming a Catholic convert had a good deal to do with writing again. I read Catholic writers but had no intention of writing myself. But somehow, when I started again, I won't say Catholicism gave me subject matter, but it gave me some kind of form, and I could begin a poem and build it to a climax. It was quite different from what I'd been doing earlier.

Why, then, did you choose to print your work in the small liberal magazines, whose religious and political positions were very different from yours? Have you ever submitted to The New Yorker *or* The Atlantic Monthly?

I think I may have given something to *The Atlantic* on Santayana; *The New Yorker* I haven't given anything. I think *The New Yorker* does some of the best prose in the country, in many ways much more interesting than the quarterlies and little magazines. But poems are lost in it; there's no table of contents, and too much of their poetry is light verse. There's no particular continuity of excellence. There just seems no point in printing there. For a while the little magazines, whose religious-political positions *were* very different from mine, were the only magazines that would publish me, and I feel like staying with them. I like magazines like the *New Statesman, The Nation, The New Republic*—something a little bit off the great road.

Just because they are off it?

I think so. A political position I don't necessarily agree with, which is a little bit adverse, seems to me just more attractive than a time-serving, conventional position. And they tend to have good reviews, those magazines. I think you write for a small audience, an ardent critical audience. And you know Graves says that poets ought to take in each other's washing because they're the only responsible audience. There's a danger to that—you get too specialized—but I pretty much agree that's the audience you do write for. If one gets further, that's all fine.

There is, though, a certain inbred, in-group anemia to those magazines, at least to the literary quarterlies. For instance, it would have been almost inconceivable for Partisan Review, which is the best of them, I think, to give your last book a bad review or even a sharp review.

I think no magazine likes to slam one of its old contributors. *Partisan* has sometimes just not reviewed a book by someone they liked very much and their reviewer didn't. I know Shapiro has been attacked in *Partisan* and then published there, and other people have been unfavorably reviewed and made rather a point of sending them something afterward. You want to feel there's a certain degree of poorer writing that wouldn't get published in the magazine your work appears in. The good small magazine may publish a lot of rather dry stuff, but at least it's serious, and if it's bad it's not bad by trying to be popular and put something over on the public. It's a wrenched personal ineptitude that will get published rather than a public slickness. I think that has something to do with good reviews coming out in the magazine. We were talking about *Partisan*'s not slamming one of its contributors, but *Partisan* has a pretty harsh, hard standard of reviewing, and they certainly might not praise one of their contributors who'd gone to pot.

What poets among your contemporaries do you most admire?

The two I've been closest to are Elizabeth Bishop—I spoke about her earlier—and Jarrell, and they're different. Jarrell's a great man of letters, a very informed man, and the best critic of my generation, the best professional poet. He's written the best war poems, and those poems are a tremendous product of our culture, I feel. Elizabeth Bishop's poems, as I said, are more personal, more something she did herself, and she's not a critic but has her own tastes, which may be very idiosyncratic. I enjoy her poems more than anybody else's. I like some of Shapiro very much, some of Roethke and Stanley Kunitz.

What about Roethke, who tries to do just about everything you don't try to do?

We've read to each other and argued, and may be rather alike in temperament actually, but he wants a very musical poem and always would quarrel with my ear as I'd quarrel with his eye. He has love poems and childhood poems and startling surrealistic poems, rather simple experience done with a blaze of power. He rejoices in the rhetoric and the metrics, but there's something very disorderly working there. Sometimes it will smash a poem and sometimes it will make it. The things he knows about I feel I know nothing about, flowers and so on. What we share, I think, is the exultant moment, the blazing out. Whenever I've tried to do anything like his poems, I've felt helpless and realized his mastery.

You were apparently a very close friend of Delmore Schwartz's.

Yes, and I think that I've never met anyone who has somehow as much seeped into me. It's a complicated personal thing to talk about. His reading was very varied, Marx and Freud and Russell, very catholic and not from a conservative position at all. He sort of grew up knowing those things and had a wonderful penetrating humorous way of talking about them. If he met T. S. Eliot, his impressions of Eliot would be mixed up with his impressions of Freud and what he'd read about Eliot; all these things flowed back and forth in him. Most of my writer friends were more specialized and limited than Schwartz, most of them took against-the-grain positions that were also narrow. Schwartz was a revelation. He felt the poet who had experience was very much better than the poet with polish. Wordsworth would interest him more than Keats—he wanted openness to direct experience. He said that if you got people talking in a poem you could do anything. His own writing, *Coriolanus* and *Shenandoah*, is interesting for that.

Isn't this much what you were saying about your own hopes for Life Studies?

Yes, but technically I think that Delmore and I are quite different. There have been very few poets I've been able to get very much from technically. Tate has been one of the closest to me. My early poems I think grew out of my admiration of his poems.

What about poets in the past?

It's hard for me to imitate someone; I'm very self-conscious about it. That's an advantage perhaps—you don't become too imitative—but it's also a limitation. I tremble when I feel I'm being like someone else. If it's Rilke or Rimbaud or Propertius, you know the language is a big bar and that if you imitate you're doing something else. I've felt greater freedom that way. I think I've tried to write like some of the Elizabethans.

And Crane? You said you had read a good deal of Crane.

Yes, but his difficult style is one I've never been able to do much with. He can be very obscure and yet write a much more inspired poem than I could by being obscure. There's a relationship between Crane and Tate and for some reason Tate was much easier for me. I could see how Tate was done, though Tate has a rhythm that I've never been able to imitate. He's much more irregular than I am, and I don't know where the rhythm comes from, but I admire it very much. Crane said somewhere that he could write five or six good lines but Tate could write twelve that would hang together, and you'd see how the twelve were built. Tate was somehow more of a model: he had a lot of wildness and he had a lot of construction. And of course I knew him and I never knew Crane. I think Crane is the great poet of that generation. He got out more than anybody else. Not only is it the tremendous power there, but he somehow got New York City; he was at the center of things in the way that no other poet was. All the chaos of his life missed getting sidetracked the way other poets' did, and he was less limited than any other poet of his generation. There was a fullness of experience; and without that, if you just had his mannerisms, and not his rather simple writing—which if done badly would be sentimental merely—or just his obscure writing, the whole thing would be merely verbal. It isn't with Crane. The push of the whole man is there. But his style never worked for me.

But something of Crane does seem to have got into your work—or maybe it's just that sense of power thrashing about. I thought it had come from a close admiring reading of Crane.

Yes, some kind of wildness and power that appeals to me, I guess. But when I wrote difficult poems they weren't meant to be difficult, though I don't know that Crane meant his to be. I wanted to be loaded and rich, but I thought the poems were all perfectly logical. You can have a wonderful time explaining a great poem like "Voyages II," and it all can be explained, but in the end it's just a love poem with a great confusion of images that are emotionally clear; a prose paraphrase wouldn't give you any impression whatever of the poem. I couldn't do that kind of poem, I don't think; at least I've never been able to.

You said that most of the writers you've known have been against the grain. What did you mean?

When I began writing, most of our great writers were quite unpopular. They hadn't reached the universities yet, and their circulation was small. Even Eliot wasn't very popular. But life seemed to be there. It seemed to be one of those periods when the lid was still being blown. The great period of blowing the lid was the time of Schönberg and Picasso and Joyce and the early Eliot, where a power came into the arts which we perhaps haven't had since. These people were all rather traditional, yet they were stifled by what was being done, and they almost wrecked things to do their great works—even rather self-contained but very good writers such as Williams or Marianne Moore. Their kind of protest and queerness has hardly been repeated. They're wonderful writers. You won't see anyone as strange as Marianne Moore again, not for a long while. Con-servative and Jamesian as she is, it was terrible, private, and strange revolutionary poetry. There isn't the motive to do that now. Yet those were the classics, and it seems to me they were all against the grain, Marianne Moore as much as Crane. That's where life was for the small audience. It would be a tremendous subject to say whether the feelings were against the grain too, and whether they were purifying, nihilistic, or both.

Have you had much contact with Eliot?

I may have seen him a score of times in my life, and he's always been very kind. Long before he published me, he had some of my poems in his files. There's some kind of New England connection.

Has he helpfully criticized your work?

Just very general criticism. With the first book of mine Faber did, he liked this or disliked that. He said something about the last book—"These are first-rate, I mean it"—something like that that was very understated and gratifying. I feel Eliot's less tied to form than a lot of people he's influenced, and there's a freedom of the twenties in his work that I find very sympathetic. Certainly he and Frost are the great New England poets. You hardly think of Stevens as New England and puritanical. They're a continuation and a criticism of the tradition, and they're probably equally great. Frost somehow put life into a dead tradition. His kind of poetry must have seemed almost unpublishable, it was so strange and fresh when it was first written. But still it was old-fashioned poetry and really has nothing to do with modern writing—except that he is one of the greatest modern writers. Eliot was violently modern and unacceptable to the traditionalist. Now he's spoken of as a literary dictator, but he's handled his position with wonderful sharpness and grace, it seems to me. It's a narrow position and it's not one I hold particularly, but I think it's been held with extraordinary honesty and finish and development. Eliot has done what he said Shakespeare had done: all his poems are one poem, a form of continuity that has grown and snowballed with him.

I remember Jarrell in reviewing The Mills of the Kavanaughs *said that Frost had been doing narrative poems with ease for years, and that nobody else had been able to catch up.*

And what Jarrell said is true: nobody except Frost can do a sort of Chaucerian narrative poem that's organized and clear. Well, a lot of people do them, but the texture of their verse is so limp and uninspired. Frost does them with great power. Most of them were done early, in that *North of Boston* period. That was a miracle, because except for Robinson—and I think Frost is a much greater poet than Robinson—no one was doing that in England or America.

But you hadn't simply wanted to tell a story in The Mills of the Kavanaughs.

No, I was writing an obscure, rather Elizabethan, dramatic and melodramatic poem. I don't know quite how to describe this business of direct experience. With Browning, for instance, for all his gifts—and there is almost nothing Browning couldn't use—you feel there's a glaze between what he writes and what really happened, you feel the people are made up. In Frost you feel that's just what the farmers and so on were like. It has the virtue of a photograph but all the finish of art. That's an extraordinary thing; almost no other poet can do that now.

What do you suppose are the qualities that go into that ability?

I don't know. Prose writers have it much more, and quite a few prose writers have it. It's some kind of sympathy and observation of people. It's the deep, rather tragic poems that I value most. Perhaps it's been overdone with Frost, but there's an abundance and geniality about those poems that isn't tragic. With this sense of rhythm and words and composition, and getting into his lines language that is very much like the language he speaks—which is also a work of art, much better than other people's ordinary speech and yet natural to him; he has that continuity with his ordinary self and his poetic self—he's made what with anyone else would be just flat. A very good prose writer can do this and make something of it. You get it quite often in Faulkner. Though he's an Elizabethan sort of rhetorician, rather unlike Frost, he can get this amazing immediacy and simplicity. When it comes to verse, the form is so hard that all of that gets drained out. In a very conventional old-fashioned writer, or someone who's trying to be realistic but also dramatic and inspired, though he may remain a good poet, most of that directness and realism goes. It's hard for Eliot to be direct that way, though you get it in bits of *The Waste Land,* that marvelous cockney section. And he can be himself; I feel Eliot's real all through the *Quartets.* He can be very intelligent or very simple there, and *he's* there, but there are no other people in the *Quartets.*

Have many of your poems been taken from real people and real events?

I think, except when I've used myself or occasionally named actual people in poems, the characters are purely imaginary. I've tried to buttress them by putting images I've actually seen and in indirect ways getting things I've actually experienced into the poem. If I'm writing about a Canadian nun the poem may have a hundred bits of things I've looked at, but she's not remotely like anyone I've ever known. And I don't believe anybody would think my nun was a real person. She has a heart and she's alive, I hope, and she has a lot of color to her and drama, and has some things that Frost's characters don't, but she doesn't have their wonderful quality of life. His Witch of Coös is absolutely there. I've gathered from talking to him that most of the *North of Boston* poems came from actual people he knew and shuffled and put together. But then it's all-important that Frost's plots are so extraordinary, so carefully worked out, though it almost seems that they're not there. Like things in Chekhov, the art is very well hidden.

Don't you think a large part of it is getting the right details, symbolic or not, around which to wind the poem tight and tighter?

Some bit of scenery or something you've felt. Almost the whole problem of writing poetry is to bring it back to what you really feel, and that takes an awful lot of maneuvering. You may feel the doorknob more strongly than some big personal event, and the doorknob will open into something that you can use as your own. A lot of poetry seems to me very good in the tradition but just doesn't move me very much because it doesn't have personal vibrance to it. I probably exaggerate the value of it, but it's precious to me. Some little image, some detail you've noticed—you're writing about a little country shop, just describing it, and your poem ends up with an existentialist account of your experience. But it's the shop that started it off. You didn't know why it meant a lot to you. Often images and often the sense of the beginning and end of a poem are all you have— some journey to be gone through between those things; you know that, but you don't know the details. And that's marvelous; then you feel the poem will come out. It's a terrible struggle, because what you really feel hasn't got the form, it's not what you can put down in a poem. And the poem you're equipped to write concerns nothing that you care very much about or have much to say on. Then the great moment comes when there's enough resolution of your technical equipment, your way of constructing things, and what you can make a poem out of, to hit something you really want to say. You may not know you have it to say.

[1961]

A Conversation
with Ian Hamilton

IAN HAMILTON: *You have been in England for some time now. Why have you chosen to live here?*

LOWELL: Why I am in England is mostly personal and wouldn't be correct in an interview. But there are certain common reasons. I'm not here in protest against conditions in America, though here there's more leisure, less intensity, fierceness. Everyone feels that: after ten years living on so-called front lines, in New York, I'm rather glad to dull the glare.

What glare are you thinking of?

Our atmosphere sometimes bristles as if with little bits of steel in the rain when it falls. It strikes mostly in the mind, in argument, in our edginess. New York is a formidable city, though I've never known violence personally. One hears about it: friends' houses are broken into. Our break-ins are rough: one would rather not be at home, because thieves are angry for dope money. Here house-breakings are mild; thieves fear the householder.

Of course, one of the reasons why your work is so admired here is that it seems to speak out of precisely that sense of danger. In other words, the situation that you describe is the situation that feeds your work in some way. Do you fear that by leaving

America you might be leaving your subject, and that here you'll
have, well, simply less to write about?

I don't know what is lost. Last week, I read for a record—
poems since *Life Studies*; that is, from the last ten years or
twelve. I found I wrote about only four places: Harvard and
Boston, New York and Maine. These the places I lived in were
also symbols, conscious and unavoidable.

New York is our cultural city and furthest from nature;
Maine is nature, and Harvard may be somewhere between, a
university. London cannot be the culture of my blood. I suppose
if I spent summers in the Orkneys and winters in London I might
find a contrast similar to Maine and New York, but the repetition would seem distracted.

I remember that when Donald Davie left for America, one
of the things he said about why he left was that he thought he
could enjoy the luxury of expatriotism, that he wouldn't get so
involved in, or irritated by, what was going on around him. Nor
would he feel caught up in America's destiny, and so on. Perhaps
all he meant was that he'd be able to live a more peaceful life.

I wonder if he does. He wrote me when I was to teach at
Essex in his old department, saying that perhaps his reasons for
leaving England for America were mine for doing the opposite.
This must be partly true. I can't imagine being so predestined
by Wilson and Heath as by Johnson and Nixon. Davie and I are
taking vacations from our Furies.

It does seem slightly odd, though, that you should leave
America at a time when you seem to have become more overtly
concerned in your poetry with public events.

I couldn't say whether I know if it is odd for me to be in
England. I think wavering is a good feeling to achieve; all can't
be done to push a career. I've been reading more than usual in
the last months, skimming old books I loved. They grow new
for me, a difference of impression more than evaluation.

I'm older than when I first met the classics, my friends are
older and deafer (which I'm not)—I mean I'm older and still

not deaf—total character now seems nearer. I've lived as long as most of the old writers. Once fifty-four, my age, was ancient and deep in time's turnings. It's sweet to sit back with a book and ruminate changing experience. Where are the strong women of the thirties? You say I have become more overtly concerned with public events, but true public poetry must come as an inevitable accident. I grew up in anti-artist-sage days, when Eliot and Picasso worked in one surprising style for some years, then surprised with another—maturing without becoming public voices or portents. Who wants to be on call to society? Have a resonant poem for each great issue?

I remember you saying, in an earlier interview not long after the publication of Life Studies, *that you couldn't go on indefinitely writing the personal poem. Sooner or later the experience would be exhausted.*

That vein of silver gives out. Would you say that the poems in *For the Union Dead* are less personal?

No, not really, although the book does seem in many ways less intimately autobiographical than Life Studies.

I am thinking of my last four books. *Life Studies* was windfall. It was after six or seven years' ineptitude—a slack of eternity. I remember a cousin proving to someone that I was finished—at only thirty-nine! Five messy poems in five years.

These are the poems at the beginning of Life Studies?

Yes, but now heavily shaken up. Shall I say "reinspired"? The rest of *Life Studies* was written in two years, in two lunges. Plugging in the joints was more precarious than creation. After this, continuous autobiography was impossible. In *The Union Dead*, I modified the style of *Life Studies*—free-verse stanzas, each poem on its own and more ornately organized. Then came metrical poems, more plated, far from conversation, metaphysical. My subjects were still mostly realism about my life. I also wrote one long public piece, the title poem of *The Union Dead*. My next book, *Near the Ocean*, starts as public. I had turned down an invitation to an Arts Festival at the White House because of Vietnam. This brought more publicity than poems, and I felt miscast, felt burdened to write on the great theme, private though almost "global."

So one might say that the White House episode did, in a way, inaugurate your period as a public poet?

Perhaps the meter I chose, Marvell's eight-line stanza, mattered more. It hummed in my mind summer till fall. It's possible to have good meter yet bad intention or vice versa— *vers de société*, or gauche sprawl. All summer, as I say, the steady, hypnotic couplet beat followed me like a dog. I liked that. After two months, I had two poems, one a hopeless snake-skin of chimes. My last piece, my most ambitious and least public, was a "Dover Beach," an obscure marriage-poem set in our small Eastern seaboard America.

It was disconcerting for some of your admirers at that time to find you writing in tight meters. Will you go back to free verse?

Free verse leaves fewer clinging needles, but I think some of my later metrical poems are more myself, though clumsier. I didn't direct, I had to stumble. I read a book: *Prosody in Modern American Poetry*. The author praised me for once writing in Marvell's elegant baroque stanza. I remembered how twenty-five years ago I'd found it too smooth, and left it. Reading this book coincided with the White House thing. Meter and matter— I think I first tried free verse, and it slipped. My next poem, *Notebook*, is in unrhymed, loose blank-verse sonnets, a roomier stanza, less a prosodist's darling. It can say almost anything conversation or correspondence can. I use this meter again in my last book [*The Dolphin*, unpublished]. I mustn't tempt it.

In Notebook *what do you feel the fourteen lines actually did?*

Allowed me rhetoric, formal construction, and quick breaks. Much of *Life Studies* is recollection; *Notebook* mixes the day-today with the history—the lamp by a tree out this window on Redcliffe Square . . . or maybe the rain, but always the instant, sometimes changing to the lost. A flash of haiku to lighten the distant. Has this something to do with a rhymeless sonnet? One poem must lead toward the next, but is fairly complete; it can stride on stilts, or talk.

Did you find yourself falling naturally into the fourteen-line unit?

It was a stanza, as so much of my work—a measure blocked out a priori, then coaxed into form.

Having decided on the fourteen-liner, did you find it constricting, that you had poems which would have liked to spread themselves around a little more?

Yes, but that's true of any fixed form, isn't it? Take one of Milton's personal sonnets, it could have been dragged out to a *Paradise Lost* prologue. I didn't find fourteen lines a handcuff. I gained more than I gave. It would have been a worry never to have known when a section must end; variation might have been monotony. Formlessness might have crowded me toward consecutive narrative. Sometimes I did want the traditional sonnet, an organism, split near the middle, and building to break with the last line.

Often a poem didn't live until the last line cleared the lungs. That's untrue of Shakespeare's *Sonnets*, but it's true of many. True of most of Milton's. The last line shapes to complete the motion. Shakespeare, I feel, wrote the couplets to his sonnets in a single reckless afternoon. Following his inevitable music, a clang.

It has been said about Notebook *that you are less concerned with line-by-line excellence than in earlier books. Do you feel there is more of a hit-or-miss quality about it?*

I didn't think that, when writing. I wrote in end-stopped lines, and rewrote to keep a sense of line. I never wrote more, or used more ink in changes. Words came rapidly, almost four hundred sonnets in four years—a calendar of workdays. I did nothing but write; I was thinking lines even when teaching or playing tennis. Yet I had idleness, though drawn to spend more hours working than I ever had or perhaps will. Ideas sprang from the bushes, my head; five or six sonnets started or reworked in a day. As I have said, I wished to describe the immediate instant. If I saw something one day, I wrote it that day, or the next, or the next. Things I felt or saw, or read were drift in the whirlpool, the squeeze of the sonnet and the loose ravel of blank verse. I hoped in *Life Studies*—it was a limitation—that each poem might seem as open and single-surfaced as a photograph. *Notebook* is more jagged and imagined than was desirable in *Life Studies*. It's severe to be confined to rendering appearances. That seems the perfect way, what *War and Peace* is, but it flattens poetry's briefer genius . . . Sometimes free verse is like breathing naked air, and living only on it.

In certain ways, the American literary scene seems more brutally competitive than ours. Do you find this so?
I think we have a famine for greatness, and find the English lacking in this vice. We have too many rude writers who imagine they are Emerson, or Whitman or Fitzgerald—their buildings are haystacks.

Did you see the recent selection of Roethke's Letters?
Roethke fevered to be the best poet, and perhaps strained for the gift. Dylan Thomas is your equivalent, but Thomas may have more skeptically enjoyed his great revel. I dislike the law of the boxing ring for the arts; the analogy is faulty. Many run and at one time or another many win. Robert Frost had the largest ambition, but with more complication than others. He had more disguises. I loved Frost and think him as great a writer as he did, though he made no room for others. Praise *Moby Dick* to him, and he'd say "*Bartleby's* pretty good." *Bartleby* is the size of his own verse monologues. Yet Frost was infinitely civilized and possible to talk intimacy with, while Roethke, the craftsman, had the innocence and deafness of a child.

You really feel it's a peculiarly American vice, this?

You have it here, I'm sure. Our noblest example of ambition was a writer who never claimed he was the best writer alive, yet may have reached it: Melville. Whitman's boastings were saved by his shyness. Pound couldn't have attempted the *Cantos* on mere vanity. You may favor the opposite kind of writer, Edward Thomas, Philip Larkin, extreme in his ambition to be witty and solid, a mocker of the Leviathan.

It is really a meaner sort of vanity I have in mind—the relentless jockeying for applause, for awards and honors. Perhaps the fact that in America you can make a lot of money from literary success . . .

Not in poetry.

Well, one reads of James Dickey making $3,500 for a poetry reading . . .

He is another of our champions, though very talented. I suppose men vaunt and taunt to keep up their hearts. We, too, have modesty: Marianne Moore, John Crowe Ransom. But I think England and America differ. Hemingway is ours; Ivy Compton-Burnett is yours. I wouldn't want to choose particularly; a literature needs lions and foxes.

What do you make of the Black Mountain poets?

I revere Pound and Williams; I think the Black Mountain poets are their journeymen, quite powerful without being inspired or pathfinders. Pound and Williams are freer, more cultured spirits. Olson's *Maximus* is *Paterson* and the *Cantos*, though woodier. Creeley is a slender, abstract Williams; Duncan is the music of Pound without his humor or engagement. Other younger American poets, Snodgrass, Alan Dugan, and Adrienne Rich, seem more original. Of the Pound people, the most personal is Gary Snyder.

At the back of all their work there is a wish to make a distinctively American poetry. Have you ever felt the urge, or the obligation, to be more of an American poet?

I've been here only a year now, and am asked if I want to
be British. I have finished a poem, not about England, but with
an English setting, for I have to use day-to-day things. At first
I hardly dared name England, then found it hovered to me—
the tree I see from this window and people talking. Where is
America? I've had it about me for fifty remembered years; it
streams through my eyes.

*I had in mind the quarrel between Pound and Williams,
and Williams's view that* The Waste Land, *for instance, was an
act of treachery* . . .

I know their argument, and heard it at their knees. I'd like to
state Williams differently. What's good about him that Pound
doesn't have is that he worked in his locale. On my next-to-last
visit to him, he had recovered from a stroke. When he came out
on Sunday, he didn't go to church but walked through the streets,
and everyone said, "Dr. Williams, we are glad you are better."
He knew things not on the Sunday walk, how his patients talked,
what happened in their marriages. His hand was on the car
wheel, as Pound's could never have been in Rapallo. Williams is
more certain of image and idiom than Pound, less magnificent.
I don't think *The Waste Land* would have been more authentic
if Eliot had never left Boston. Williams's nationalist counterpart
is Philip Larkin.

Williams would never write a sonnet.

Nor would Eliot or Pound. Both had boldness, modernity,
and formal imagination. With Pound—I think of the *Pisan
Cantos*—a hard, angular, in some ways shrill and artificial man
by courage let the heart break through the iron rib . . . more
heart than any poet since Hardy.

*To go back for a moment to the current American scene,
I wonder what you think of* The New York Review of Books—
its increasing neglect of the arts, and of poetry in particular.

I don't want to say very much about it. My wife is consulting editor and I know Robert Silvers, the editor, very well. I know Barbara Epstein very well. I'm deeply in it, in a personal sense. It never was primarily interested in the arts, nor pretended to be. It's a review for commentator and politician, an epic *New Statesman* . . . Poetry reviews are more in the whirl here than with us. I wouldn't assert the quality is finer. The true review, that sinks into the reviewed's mind, causing change and discovery, can never be anticipated anywhere. We assign too many reporters and popularizers to judging poetry; you save them for plays.

You once said that the last critic you found useful was Randall Jarrell. Is it the case that poetry criticism in America is less concerned than it is here with questions of evaluation?

Jarrell's evaluations were often more imaginative than his authors'. We both began in the age of the New Critics. They are a little maligned, I think, though we both grew too roughed to remain disciples. The first had artistic genius; Winters, Blackmur, Kenneth Burke, Allen Tate . . . even Hart Crane wrote thoughtful New Criticism in letters. That age has passed; its last spirit was Randall. Of the younger English critics, I read A. Alvarez and Donald Davie. The king of the critics is William Empson. He's not a messiah for the young; I don't believe he has written on anyone younger than Orwell and Dylan Thomas. But even his shortest notes change the mind. Then Leavis, the fire-blackened oak . . .

Do you read novels much?
I reread.

You've never thought of writing a novel?
I couldn't. I don't have that re-creation. I like to put what I see and hear into poems, but to write a whole book, pages consisting of nothing but story . . . I haven't the wind of dialogue.

Do you think the novel is a promising chance now? Most have the same plot with changed decor. It seems the age of shadow novels, compared to the twenties or thirties, or compared to the last century's great Russian, French, and English. The forest is growing bald.

Was there any sort of novelistic intention behind Note-book? *In parts it does read like a novel.*

I hope so. I hoped to steal from the novel—even from our new novel—because I think poetry must escape from abstractives. It might be better for a long poem to be drawn from *Madame Bovary* than the *Cantos*. The *Cantos* did this; after Tennyson's *Idylls* or *The Ring and the Book*, they look for a transcendence in the day's abundance. The novel is the great form . . . though little since Mann and Faulkner.

I'd like to go back a bit now and ask you about your own career. The most obvious first question, I suppose, is to do with being a Lowell. How important has that been to you?

I never knew I was a Lowell till I was twenty. The ancestors known to my family were James Russell Lowell, a poet pedestaled for oblivion, and no asset to his grandnephew among the rich athletes at boarding school. Another, my great-grandfather, James Russell's brother, had been headmaster of my boarding school, and left a memory of scholarly aloofness. He wrote an ironic Trollopian *roman à clef* about the school. There was Amy Lowell, big and a scandal, as if Mae West were a cousin. And there were rich Lowells, but none as rich as my classmates' grand-fathers in New York. Of course, the Lowells were flesh-and-blood, but I am talking down rumors of grandeur. My immediate family, if you have an English equivalent, would be the Duke of Something's sixth cousins. We gave no feeling of swagger. Later I felt a blood kinship with James Russell's savage vernacular anti-Mexican War and pro-Civil War *Bigelow Papers*—they were not for the thirties. Was Amy a rebel artist or an entrepre-neur? Ours was an old family. It stood—just. Its last eminence was Lawrence, Amy's brother, and president of Harvard, for millennia a grand *fin de siècle* president, a species long dead in America. He was cultured in the culture of 1900—very deaf, very sprightly, in his eighties. He was unique in our family for being able to read certain kinds of good poetry. I used to spend evenings with him, and go home to college at four in the morning.

How did it happen that you became a Catholic? Torment, I hope?

I don't know. I am not a Catholic, and yet I was. It came from despair and the exuberance of learning a religion, the despair at my circumstances, a character problem—I was just married and couldn't get a job. I was too tense to converse, a creature of spiritual perversity. Christianity was a welcome. I kept swallowing more and more for a number of years, though now it seems unbelievable. When I meet knowing Catholics, I go along with them and feel I have somewhat of their geography. I don't believe, but I am sort of a gospeler, I like to read Christ's words.

It is often said that the technique of your early poems—the poems of Lord Weary's Castle, Land of Unlikeness—*enacts a quarrel between your Calvinist background and your adopted Catholicism. Do you see it this way?*

I was born a nonbelieving Protestant New Englander; my parents and everyone I saw were nonbelieving Protestant New Englanders. They went to church, but faith was absurd. In college, I began reading Hawthorne, Jonathan Edwards, English seventeenth-century preachers, Calvin himself, Gilson, and others, some of them Catholics—Catholics and Calvinists I don't think opposites; they are rather alike compared to us in our secular sprawl. From zealous, atheist Calvinist to a believing Catholic is no great leap. We overhammer the debating points. Yet Calvinism is a too-conceived abstract-expressionist Church of Rome.

Did your contact with the Southern school of poets have anything to do with all this?

It probably mostly came through Allen Tate. I think it connects with the New Criticism. Tate and Ransom, poets and critics, were Southerners and the line they took was that Southerners looked at the whole thing, and not just at intellect like a Yankee. If Ransom writes a poem about a man and woman, the man is a Calvinist and the woman a Southerner who knows flowers, the flesh, beauty, and children. One might say that Catholicism notices things, the particular, while Calvinism studies the attenuated ideal. I was too deep in that dogfight to ever get out. Allen Tate would have said, and did say when I was a young man and he was about forty, that I was an idealist New Englander, a Puritan, and so forth; yet Allen's wife would have said he couldn't name the trees in his path. Man is always Puritan.

It was presumably the presence of people like Tate and Ransom that attracted you to the South in the first place.

They—but not at that time their positions. They seemed the best men who wrote poetry and taught. I liked Pound and Williams and Eliot and Hart Crane and Proust and Milton, but I hadn't read Tate and Ransom. I did my cramming on the train before we met.

Was Blackmur around at that time?

I knew him quite well but only painfully and later. He was more of New England than anyone, and had a genius. In his prose, every sentence struggles to be poetry, form ringing on rock. He was a good poet, weird, tortured, derivative, original—and more a poet in his criticism. A side of him wanted to write novels, because he remembered everything and felt things most critics can't—people. He was more industrious than other critics with style, wrote heavily and yet with a grace; had anarchy and discipline—perhaps he overcherished both . . . the type of the sincere.

Who, out of that group, was the most important to you as a poet?

I think the best poems were written by Ransom. Winters, a humanist, our Malherbes, maybe wrote the clearest criticism . . . intuitive, authoritative, willful. My own poetry was closest to Tate's. I couldn't write a Ransom poem. Ransom is a graceful, smoother, and smaller Hardy. I think he is perfect, at times, that is, impossible to improve on. He would say to me, "You're a forceful poet but your poems are weighty," and I knew my poems would always be weighty next to his.

You first published in the South, I believe.
As a college junior, I published in Ransom's *Kenyon Review*, then nothing more for four years. I had grown too grave for print. Then, after a year with Tate and his wife, I wrote my first rude Christian stanzas. They didn't meet universal approval, and were published.

That "year and a day" you were sentenced to jail as a conscientious objector—what was that like?
I corrected proofs. I was quite scared going in, but only spent five and a half months in jail, then six and a half on parole in a Catholic cadet nurses' dormitory, mopping corridors and toilets. It was filthier work than jail, but I was free and with my wife [Jean Stafford]. Jail was monotonous and weak on incident. I queued for hours for cigarettes and chocolate bars, and did slow make-work like wheeling wheelbarrows of cinders. I found life lulling. I slept among eighty men, a foot apart, and grew congenial with other idealist felons, who had homemade faiths. I was thankful to find jail gentler than boarding school or college—an adult fraternity. I read—*Erewhon* and *The Way of All Flesh* . . . and God knows what now . . . a thousand pages of Proust. I left jail more educated—not as they wished *re-*educated.

You'd recommend it?
No; it did. Luckily I couldn't write. When I started to think again, I had a more Southern wholeness. The luck was not writing.

How much hesitation did you feel about becoming a conscientious objector? You hadn't always been one, had you?

No, I didn't feel that way at the beginning of the war. I became an objector after the saturation bombing of Hamburg and the proclamation of unconditional surrender. I feared, too, the Russians would control China and half of Europe, a less dangerous possibility today. The communists' dull, humdrum, tyrannical bureaucracies are more of a disappointment and yet less a terror. All nations are now fiercer than we feared.

I believe you had volunteered for the Navy some time before?

Yes, I did volunteer. Later in 1943, when we'd conquered Sicily, and won the war, in a sense, I refused to report to the Army, and sent a rather humorless bombastic statement to President Roosevelt.* I still stand on it.

And you'd take a similar position now, on Vietnam?

I would on Vietnam. But if I were young now, what would I do? It's unimaginable—if I were eighteen and coming up for the draft. I pray that I'd take the position of the draft evader, not leave the country but go to jail.

Do you feel you have much of a response among the young in America?

No one meets the young. The individuals I know are about your age, late twenties, early thirties, graduates. They are people I often get along with professionally. Undergraduates seem to have characters still to come. I judge from a point of disadvantage. This is another young generation and it's always good to be young—they live on. I don't find *all* youth sympathetic—maybe ours are slightly more so because of the way they dress and slop. This generation, like ours once, is hope. I hate to ape their anti-

* See page 367.

liberalism, but the liberal blueprints were too pure, too idealistic. My heart never beat with Roosevelt's, now the young don't salute him. Liberal heroes tarnish; but is this progress? Pollution disgusts me; dope doesn't send me. I am against violence; if I were still Calvinist, I would call it hellfire.

What about their literary taste?

I don't think the young read anything, except for a few with literary concern. Later maybe they become readers or writers. Their taste? Suppose some writer wrote poems about violence as the essential experience—I haven't, but I have written splintery things—he shouldn't be flattered if crowds of twenty-year-olds say violence is *the* essential experience, and then, without light or passion, begin chanting, "Guns are beautiful." I would be bored and horrified. I have a schoolteacher's conceit that I know more than my students. I really must. I've had the time. Most students, now and always, are the philistines, old fraternity brothers. In our society, culture, I fear, must be *elite*; the bulk and brawn of any generation, new or past, can't tell the *Sentimental Education* from education.

You were involved for a time in Eugene McCarthy's campaign for the Presidential nomination. That must have been strange.

Senator McCarthy was a strange candidate. He was interested in ending the war in Vietnam, and finding power that could do something. McCarthy was one of various senators I went with my wife to see in Washington—she was going to write an article and I tagged along. Some people suggested to us weren't there and I think somewhat at the last minute McCarthy's name was given. We met McCarthy and Fulbright. Fulbright was an impressive nineteenth-century Southern senator, rather like one of my older Southern writer friends. McCarthy was interested in and liked writers, knew them, was one. We talked and told stories.

Did you find the atmosphere of power, of big-time politics, exciting?

I dare not admit it. I liked to talk to McCarthy, and he liked to talk to me and blow off his tension. He didn't actually talk heavy politics—more, points made by agricultural parables, deadpan sketches of politicians; he made Bobby Kennedy act like a character in Ring Lardner. It was like listening to a baseball player while watching his game.

So you didn't feel that here was a unique joining together of politics and poetry, or anything of that sort?

I doubt if McCarthy was exactly politics; it was his profession but he was a lost-cause man, and ironical. He had to face terrible things: the headless crowds, the reflex applause, the ghost-written speech, the boiled eulogy. He wasn't much interested in the vote-getting boasts, which probably someone else had written for him; such things are always written by someone else, and for someone else. If he had been elected, one would have felt a human being was in the White House—with flaws and flair, but someone. He was something for affection, unlike most of the others. If an effect must be proportioned to its cause, as the Thomists say, how can ghosted political shoptalk turn a stump into a rider? It didn't strike me that McCarthy would be President. I was surprised when he carried Oregon and northern California against Bobby Kennedy. I could feel the excitement of that, and maybe thought we were riding high tide. I wrote a poem to him that midsummer . . . "Coldly willing to smash the ball past those who bought the park." There was allure in having a friend whose shadow had fallen like a hand on the handle of the grindstone.

It was not, then, an episode that changed anything for you, for you personally?

I mustn't overplay what happened. In a way, it was sightseeing a new country. I spent a month and a half traveling. It was like my going to Italy for the first time, as serious maybe as that, more hurried and hard. I have never known how Italy changed me.

What did you make of Norman Mailer's portrait of you in The Armies of the Night?

I didn't know him too well—that comes out in his book— and he didn't know me very well. We'd met before. We've since grown closer. I think maybe the form of his book came from me. Not from anything I said but from contrasting me dramatically with himself. That's very heavily emphasized in his beginning. The picture of me . . . it isn't quite true. I am made more a goy, New England, aristocratical, and various things, a Quixote in the retinue of Sancho Panza. I think it's the best, almost only thing written about me as a living person. Later, I wrote him I hoped we'd remain as good friends in life as we were in fiction.

And yet it was a fairly hostile portrait, wasn't it?

It starts that way, in the first thirty pages or so, and then I think it's not. I had no idea he saw plots to put him down in things I said lightly. Also, I didn't realize he saw everything. Moments when he didn't seem to be attending anything, not even himself. In everything I saw and could test, I felt he was as accurate as memory should be. His story is actually, not literally, true. Accuracy isn't measuring faces through the eye of a needle. I am flattered I didn't step on Mailer's corns more; I was treated with kindness. Is the frame of a portrait a coffin?

Do you have any clear sense of an audience?

I don't meet it intimately. I sit here in my room, I have my life. I have my personal hopes and difficulties and interests. An audience cannot come in and talk; its conglomerate voice isn't English. I can at least *read* my reviewers; but most are assertions. Fame? Occasionally someone sends me his poems, and writes: "You're the greatest poet, and would you annotate my manuscript?" I must put it aside, I don't send it back, I don't have a large enough envelope. In a while maybe, a second letter comes reversing the praise, threatening to sue me for postage.

What about readings, though?

In America a poet can make a living and shorten his life expectancy by readings. He can make from five hundred to a thousand dollars a shot. Here it pays train fare. I fear the performance. I expand on stage and feel grand. One goes to Birmingham, anywhere, and takes two and a half hours to get there, and meets—I've never been to Birmingham—I meet Dr. So-and-so, I give my reading, I am promised twenty pounds, which about pays for two days—if anything can. And I have exported my poems. Some readings are delightful, a change of air.

You don't find anything tempting in the availability of all that cash and applause?

Never quite, because it is absolutely exhausting . . . due perhaps to my imprudent habits. No one shuns audiences and cash. It would be hypocritical to say I do. I hate getting to the spot, making talk in the Green Room, going on. I like answering questions better than reading poems, but my audiences don't . . . Then the lonely, distracted ride home! I prefer teaching.

You have said, though, that poetry readings helped you to find the style of Life Studies.

At that time, poetry reading was sublimated by the practice of Allen Ginsberg. I was still reading my old New Criticism religious, symbolic poems, many published during the war. I found—it's no criticism—that audiences just didn't understand, and I didn't always understand myself while reading. Much good poetry is unsuited to audience performance; mine was incomprehensible. Even Dylan Thomas came over as sound. I didn't want to be Ginsberg; I hoped to write poems as pliant as conversation, so clear a listener might get every word, and I would. Shall I confess that I can seldom follow a voice without seeing the text? *Life Studies* is heightened conversation, not a concert.

You take a rather skeptical view of your audience, whoever they may be. I wonder, what do you think literature can do—anything or nothing?

Auden says poetry makes nothing happen. In the teeth of this, Flaubert wrote that his *Education Sentimentale* might, if read, have prevented the bloodshed of the Paris Commune. I do think being in something makes a difference. Take Flaubert, who led a life even Henry James called flat—a single long love affair, a trip on the Nile, fifty years with his mother, writing, looking out on the provincial Seine at Rouen from his study. I feel he was ferociously in it, in his misses as well as his successes . . . He believed in form, a form not like the Goncourts' and Maupassant's, but irregular and heart-stained—the grace of anonymity, the coarseness of one person. I would grope up all I knew in this search . . . The best new poems I've read in the last fifteen months are by Heine, written in Paris, when his spine was melting, and he thought he was going to die in a month or two. He wrote a poetry beyond his power. Some of the most touching are to his wife, a simple soul, his child almost. He even fell in love with another woman at this time, even wished he could sleep with her. The first poems are almost the tenderest ones anyone has ever written to a wife; the second are spiritual, because the other woman was intellectual, read Hegel and Goethe, etc. One inspiration worked as well as the other; Heine never thought to harmonize the contradiction. The meter he took was his old rhymed quatrains—he felt no need of a new technique. I feel he was man absolutely facing reality, facing it with his old style of wit and ballad, Jewish jokes and German Romanticism, spending all of his terrible experience. The last thing he wanted was to die, even though opium and morphine no longer killed his pain. He said he'd written a poetry no other German had written, only because no other German had been in his physical misery.

How do you feel about the often rather melodramatic characterizations of you as a "poet of extremity"?

I don't deserve the eulogy. I think I've lived a life more than the average poet, but other people have lived their lives much more than I have. In *Life Studies*, I caught real memories in a fairly gentle style. It's not meant to be extremity. I agree with the critics who say it is artificially composed. I have been through mania and depression; *Life Studies* is about neither. Mania is sickness for one's friends, depression for one's self. Both are chemical. In depression, one wakes, is happy for about two minutes, probably less, and fades into dread of the day. Nothing will happen, but you know twelve hours will pass before you are back in bed and sheltering your consciousness in dreams, or nothing. It isn't danger; it's not an accomplishment. I don't think it a visitation of the angels but a weakening in the blood. In *Life Studies*, I wrote about my marriage and parents; I didn't see them as desperate—though life must be askew. When I wrote, most good American poetry was a symbol hanging like a gun in an armory. Many felt this.

Whom do you have in mind?

There was Snodgrass. The Beats were a breakthrough. They had little interest, most of them, in experience but had a great interest in stirring utterance. *Howl* doesn't seem to have much to do with the stir of life but it is a stirring sermon.

Before Life Studies *you presumably felt that your own style had become mechanical. It can never be easy to know just when a manner one has perfected becomes played out.*

Most of us seek our standard style: an average Browning poem, an average Auden poem, where the poet's mannerisms do much of the invention. Sometimes a blessed knock comes and extends mannerism to inspiration. I've sometimes, in reading at least, known this. I had a mechanical, gristly, alliterative style that did not charm much, unless . . . something slipped.

During these periods of depression that you've described, do you carry on writing, or does poetry come to seem meaningless?

Depression's no gift from the Muse. At worst, I do nothing. But often I've written, and wrote one whole book—*For the Union Dead*—about witheredness. It wasn't acute depression, and I felt quite able to work for hours, write and rewrite. Most of the best poems, the most personal, are gathered crumbs from the lost cake. I had better moods, but the book is lemony, soured, and dry, the drought I had touched with my own hands. That, too, may be poetry—on sufferance.

You have quite a few imitators—indeed, there was supposed to be something called a Confessional School. How do you feel about them, about a poet like, say, Anne Sexton?

I don't read on far with many. But Anne Sexton I know well. It would be a test to say what I thought of her. She is Edna Millay after Snodgrass. She has her bite. She is a popular poet, very first-person, almost first on personality. I had a mortifying revelation. I was reading an anthology and imagined I was reading another poet I often prefer to Sexton. It was marvelous, "much X's best poem." I thought X had become unmuddy and personal at last; but the poem was by Anne. Then the poem sank a little, I'm afraid. I knew Anne could be personal. I read her with bias.

What about Sylvia Plath?

I glory in her powers. I don't know whether she writes like me. In an extreme life-and-death style, she is as good as Sir Walter Raleigh; no, she's not as good, but no poetry has a more acid sting. Few women write major poetry. Can I make this generalization? Only four stand with our best men: Emily Dickinson, Marianne Moore, Elizabeth Bishop, and Sylvia Plath. It's a rough road. Sylvia is not the most consoling, she's perhaps my least favorite, but she belongs to the group, and has her half-dozen supreme, extreme poems. Years ago, Sylvia and Anne Sexton audited my poetry class. Anne was more herself, and knew less. I thought they might rub off on each other. Sylvia learned from Anne.

*What about English poetry? Do you take much interest
in what is going on here?*

I like more dead English poets than I can remember; I
like mostly the living ones I liked before I came here. Of the
older: Auden, Robert Graves, Empson, David Jones, Mc-
Diarmuid, Larkin, and Hughes in poems like "Pike" and "Pig."
That's the top of it. I like Stevie Smith, Spender, and Betjeman.
There are many good poets; these are the ones I am wild about.
There would be about the same number in America . . . and
rather more, I pray.

*Do you take any interest in so-called popular culture? Do
you take any of it seriously?*

You mean the Beatles? I was teaching my students Stevens,
I think it was, and I said to them, "What do you really like?" and
they said the Beatles and Rod McKuen. So we read pop for a
month. The Beatles are a cross between Noel Coward and
Gilbert, more polished and idiomatic than most poets. McKuen
I get nothing out of. Bob Dylan is alloy; he is true folk and fake
folk, and has a Caruso voice. He has lines, but I doubt if he has
written whole poems. He leans on the crutch of his guitar.

I'd like to ask you something about the theater . . .
I wish I could be as breezy on that as I was on pop culture.

Do you think there's any future for the verse drama?

I think there's little in this century except *Sweeney Agonistes*
and the last short plays of Yeats. Brecht, I suppose, is the strongest modern dramatist; he is a poet even though he writes in
prose—as good as verse.

*Do you see this as something you yourself are going to do
much more of?*

I am gun-shy of the theater. I've had brilliant directors,
Jonathan Miller, and good, even star actors. I can't love the
game. I know this is slightly paranoid, but I can't feel acted
plays are literature. I'm not happy with my own, read or acted.

We've never had *the* American playwright, our nearest is O'Neill.
Many things are fun, Williams, Albee, many more Off-Broadway;
they do not breathe the same air as Faulkner or Eliot. I think it's
a trapped and thwarted art—that's the challenge. And isn't it a
backache to sit through a whole play? Much the best English
or American writer is Shakespeare and he wrote plays and they
are meant to be acted, they're not meant to be read in an armchair. Yet plays perform worse than opera; *Othello* is inferior to
Verdi's inferior *Otello*.

What do you feel about your own plays?

I wrote one play which I think well enough of, *Benito
Cereno*; I'm not sure whether it is mine or Melville. Two American history plays I wrote to go with it, I find have good spots.
Are they mine or Hawthorne? They were speedy to write, and
took me less time than verse translation. I think of *Benito* as
prose, my best.

You did deviate somewhat from the original, didn't you?

I had to put the whole thing in dialogue; most of Melville's
novella is reverie and description. Somehow the main character,
the American captain, is different. Some think I've added, others
see caricature. My hero is a State Department autocrat, Melville's is an innocent abroad. My man is imperial, his is poignant.
Mine knows everything, so steers for disaster. Some critics wish
I hadn't hardened and politicized. I'm sure my play's genius is
Melville.

*When you look back over your career as a poet, do you see a
high point anywhere, or do you feel that there has been a steady
development and improvement?*

When I look back on my career, I remember high points—
high in their moment. Later, they lost stature. I cannot calculate
this or that was a mountain. I am always looking backward when
idle, and upward when revising—revision is inspiration, no reading of the finished work as exciting as writing in the last changes.
My art, like many others, fails. The failure is uncertain. Months

of false casts, then a day of strikes—something happier than anything done by me before. I mustn't assert too bravely—Leavis reading over all his essays, finding the least limiting, and saying, "I was a genius when I wrote *George Eliot*." I don't read my earliest books with full sympathy. Those I like best are *Life Studies* and my last two. The last, *The Dolphin*, is unpublished. So I've a happy ending.

[1971]

Antebellum Boston

I, too, was born under the shadow of the Boston State House, and under Pisces, the Fish, on the first of March 1917. America was entering the First World War and was about to play her part in the downfall of four empires. At this moment, the sons of most of the old, aristocratic, Republican Boston families were waiting on their doorsteps like spent hounds. They were, these families and sons, waiting and hoping for a second wind. James Michael Curley was out of jail and waiting for a mandate from the people to begin the first of his many terms as Mayor of Boston. Nothing from now on was to go quite as expected—even downhill.

My Grandfather Winslow had chosen to live at 18 Chestnut Street, high on Beacon Hill. In his doorway were two loutish, brownstone pillars copied from the Temple of the Kings at Memphis. Here, each afternoon, my grandfather would pause for a few minutes at four o'clock and finger his cane, inscribed with the names and altitudes of mountains in Norway which he had climbed. Looking about, he took satisfaction in seeing himself surrounded by neighbors whose reputations had made state, if not universal, history. When these people died, their houses, resting on the solid brick of their names, were starred in the guidebooks. Across the street Edwin Booth had lived; across the street Julia Ward Howe still lived; across the street Ralph Adams Cram had lately settled. Edwin Booth had been so famous one could forget he was an actor; Julia Ward Howe was so old and so distinguished one could forget she was only a woman; Cram, he decided, went rather fatiguingly far afield in his search for old ways of building new churches. Grandfather was not content with Cram, yet he kept Cram drawings scattered over the wormy desk he had brought home from Palermo, thus enjoying the exalted ceremonial of seeing his own just derision continually defeated by his good nature. Twenty houses down Chestnut Street stood the house that had belonged to Francis Parkman, and nearby was the house in which Oliver Wendell Holmes had lately died, another in which Percival Lowell had also lately died. Grandfather was a Boston boy who had made good as a mining engineer in Colorado. He was proud of being self-made. He was proud, too, of his descent from New England Winslows who had supported George III in the eighteenth century, just as furiously as they had supported Cromwell a century earlier. These Winslows had been ruined and even, temporarily, exiled to Canada during the American Revolution. My grandfather wanted everyone to be pre-revolutionary and self-made. In the mornings he would declare that everyone in Boston was an opportunist and a *parvenu*; in the evenings he would glumly suggest that his neighbors were decadents who lived on their mere names. In 1917 my grandfather was well satisfied. Yet, from time to time, something of the poison of his later agony would show; his vitals burned and he looked out with a pale, aching eye.

From my mother's scrapbooks and from her reminiscences, I can imagine scenes that took place in 1915. Perhaps it is fraudulent for me to describe recollections of things I did not see. Nevertheless, the two years before my birth are more real to me than the two years which followed. America entered the war and my mother entered marriage in the two years after 1915. I was often glad I could not be blamed for anything that happened during the months when I was becoming alive.

When I was three or four years old I first began to think about the time before I was born. Until then, Mother had been everything; at three or four, she began abruptly and gratingly to change into a human being. I wanted to recapture the mother I remembered and so I began to fabricate. In my memory she was a lady preserved in silhouettes, outlines, and photographs; she sat on a blue bench; she wore a blue serge dress; she smiled at my father, a U.S. Navy lieutenant in a collarless blue uniform. Blue meant the sea, the Navy, and manhood. Blue was the ideal defining color Mother had described to Father as his "Wagnerian theme," the absolute he was required to live up to. I was a little doll in a white sailor suit with blue anchors on the pockets, a doll who smiled impartially upon his mother and father and in his approbation thus made them husband and wife. But when I was at last three years old all that began to change. I could no longer see Mother as that rarely present, transfigured, Sunday-best version of my nurse. I saw her as my mother, as a rod, or a scolding, rusty hinge—as a human being. More and more I began to try to imagine Mother when she was happier, when she had been merely her father's favorite daughter, when she was engaged and unmarried. Perhaps I had been happiest then, too, because I hadn't existed and lived only as an imagined future.

I found that all I had to do was to hold my breath when Mother talked about her girlhood and then it all came vividly to me. The large houses, the staff of servants, the immense house parties, the future—I was there, living it all. One day I held my breath longer and longer and more perfectly than ever before. I found myself breathing with ponderous, earthy effort. I found I was ill with croup. I could, in reality, hardly breathe. I lay staring at my black fingernails outlined against the white sheet. "You are a design for mourning," Mother said. "If you try to clean your fingernails, you'll have to dig in up to your elbows. You'll come out on the other side of the earth, in China."

For three long breathless nights I lay awake, blowing on the flame of my croup kettle to keep it burning. I breathed the deadening, aromatic benzoin and felt it was the myrrh of the Magi. Traditionally, they came at first with lambs and camels, but later my delirious visitors brought me bizarre, comforting, unorthodox creatures: flying squirrels, jumping mice, a duckbilled platypus. My animal sights danced about the benzoin flame all night long in a command performance, and it pleased me to believe that they chose me to visit rather than President Coolidge, whose son had just died. Mother sat by me on the same blue bench. She remained as long as I could keep my eyes open, which was for three days and nights. I watched the planes, gyres, and pyramids of her amazingly abundant brown hair and tried to explain to her that flying squirrels were whirling joyously over her head, going on tirelessly like children on the swings of an all-day recess; and the jumping mice were burying glittering trinkets in the loops of her hair; the platypus was imitating a clipped-wing duck by flapping his paws like wings and making nutcracker sounds. Then, the scene changing, I would pass away the sick hours looking at Raphael's Portinari and the Madonnas of Carlo Dolce in Mother's scrapbook. There was Mother with her brother and sisters, arranged in various photographs taken of the family from time to time. There were snapshots from house parties; five colored postcard poses of Sarah Bernhardt as L'Aiglon. I wondered why the picture pasting had left off when the book was only half full. One of the last pictures showed my mother and grandfather together. Grandfather had written their initials in white ink on the black paper: A.W. *and* C.W., 1915.

I can still see Mother as she was in that picture, posed before the brownstone pillars of 18 Chestnut Street. I see her strong, firmly modeled chin, her pulled-in, tiny waist, her flounces, her beaver muff, and her neck, which was like a swan's neck crowned with an armful of pyramidal hair and an ostrich feather. She seemed a lady out of Edith Wharton's *Age of Innocence*. The time covered in the novel would have been at least a decade earlier, but Boston and my grandfather proudly worked at lagging behind the fashions, a precise and mysterious degree of lagging, just as difficult to comprehend as the latest fashion itself. In the photograph of Mother snapped in front of the Chestnut Street house, Grandfather stood behind her in the doorway. He wore a round fur cap which made him look like a Cossack and he was smiling; to my curious eye he seemed not so much a person as a fascinating, ever-new face with a grin, and a lasso of fur about him.

I imagined Mother waiting to be handed into her touring car, a frail, ailing, indestructible, thirty-foot, carriage-like affair which already had the distinguished and obsolete air of a museum piece or a prop in a silent movie. Mother, her strong chin unprotected and chilled in the helpless autumn, seemed to me the young Alexander, all gleam and panache, Alexander, as in her copy of Plutarch, conferring with his aide-de-camp before the battle of Granicus. Mother, also, was a sort of commander in chief of her virgin battlefield. Steaming up out of my croupy delirium, I saw horses, wondrously tall, stepping up Chestnut Street—horse-chestnut street where the stables were even then being altered into garages. The horses looked down their bald, bleached Norman noses at me, and shook awkward silver bells that turned out to be my christening cups, which Mother had sold because she wanted to clear her shelves. My horses reached their noses into the upper foliage of trees and pulled down bushels of green-and-gold leaves; they nibbled grotesquely and dribbled out of the sides of their mouths a landslide of green slates that were slipping from the stable roof. A flight of green umbrellas drifted through the air, upside down. On another page of Mother's scrapbook I saw crowds in London, Brussels, and Paris; the people grimaced under their shiny, rained-on umbrellas. They had the look of spectators at a gladiatorial show. They were listening to the declaration of World War I.

If you looked quickly at the snapshot I have mentioned, you first noticed only my mother and grandfather. It took a second glance to reveal that my father was also "in the picture" —and this recessiveness, within the family portrait, was not, alas, an accidental aspect of a single photograph but the genuine and enduring placement at all times. Even Father's four disturbingly evident initials (R.T.S.L.) retreated into corners of the album. He was a young man in a collarless blue lieutenant's uniform, always slightly out of place, with even his scrupulous neatness appearing somewhat impersonal, not really his, but as if he and his clothes were each morning hastily cleaned and pressed after a night of neglect. He smiled and smiled in his photographs, just as he smiled and smiled in life. He would look into the faces of others as if he expected to find himself reflected in their eyes. He was a man who treated even himself with the caution and uncertainty of one who has forgotten a name, in this case his own. Father was not to straightforward, nor too backward, neither too slack nor too hard; the refusal of over-statement was the pillar he leaned on, the inclining Tower of Pisa which was his pose, his definition, his color, and his sup-port. In the photograph, Father was self-consciously holding a leash which had on its end a tobacco-colored, senile Sealyham. Old as the creature was, it nevertheless suggested that my father was its slave, rather embarrassingly serving as attendant on walks. In the picture, Mother seemed to be caught on an exciting and fated young day, as if at this moment she had found the courage to say to my grandfather, "Papa, Lieutenant Lowell and I want to be engaged," and daring to add, or at least to think, "And Bob hasn't a mean or an extraordinary bone in his body."

Mother's conception of her father was very different from her notion of her Lieutenant Lowell. Even her military notions were reserved for her father, who was a great conquering em-peror in her mind. Six years before, she had read the Duchess d'Abrantès's *Memoirs of Napoleon*:

> In short, when I recollect Napoleon entering the court-yard of the Hôtel de la Tranquillité in 1793, with a shabby round hat drawn over his forehead, and his ill-powdered hair hanging over the collar of his grey great-coat, which afterwards became as celebrated as the white plume of Henry IV, without gloves, because he used to say they were a useless luxury, with boots ill-made and ill-blackened, with his thinness and his sallow complexion . . .

Yes, he was "a sloven," but Mother with her intense and extraordinary neatness could love this personage she wished to tidy, could imagine herself as a tidying, organizing hand to greatness. She began to bolt her food, and for a time slept on an Army cot and took cold dips in the morning. In all this she could be Napoleon made over in my grandfather's Prussian image. It was always my grandfather she admired, even if she called him Napoleon. She might run into her father's library and say, "I wish you were puny and green in the face with genius, and not six feet tall with a red and brown face." She had learned how to lead her father: she only pretended to let him dominate.

My grandfather's behavior inclined strongly toward exaggeration. When Mother's suitors came, he acted with a bossy, tense attentiveness that was absurd even in that era of protective patriarchs. Mother and the young man would sit down in the "Louis Seize" room at Chestnut Street. My grandmother and grandfather sat in the next room only a few feet away. They were partially visible and utterly audible. But, with the plea that they were thinking of Mother's privacy, they would stubbornly refuse to be introduced and said there was no need for the young people to be mindful of their presence, a forgetfulness no one ever experienced, however.

In the war years there was much talk about the Prussians and the Austrians. My Grandmother Winslow came from Raleigh, North Carolina. She was too joyful, quick, and amused to blame Grandfather for the Civil War, although in her heart she may have decided that "his kind" was at fault. She couldn't imagine ranting about family, or pretending to discontent with the wealth my grandfather had won for her. Still, she could never quite swallow New England. It was a place peculiarly designed to irritate. She did not feel that New England had formed my grandfather so much as that his strictness had somehow chosen New England for its proper setting. When Austria came up in conversation, Grandmother would grow excited with critical feeling; she would say, "If only those humorless, crop-haired Prussians would stay in their own country." She would grunt and condemn and mix up von Moltke, General Sherman, Rutherford B. Hayes, and Prince Hohenlohe. My grandfather would immediately and violently take offense. He would repeat that he had spent two years studying in Stuttgart, and to good effect; he would insist that northern climes were the nurses of character. As he talked, his bulletins from the English Speaking Union would slide from the table and he would brush aside the cuttings from the *National Geographic* he had fastened together with paper clips and which he meant to mail to some country relative. In argument he grew heated and sometimes even stamped the floor. Whenever one of Mother's utterly subdued young men said something Grandfather disapproved of, he would cough. No one ever coughed back. Before he could propose to Mother, Father had to break through all these coughs, disapprovals, impediments.

The wedding took place. Photographs of the bride and her bridesmaids remained, yellowing on the mantels; there also remained the tale of a gold-and-platinum watch-chain given to Father by his shipmates. Never before had there been a chain fashioned with such an abundance of precious material. It was interestingly costly and pronounced scandalous in the tastelessness of its design. Mother somehow managed to dispose of this chain—she was not one whose hand was stayed from destruction by sentiment. Because it had been so outlawed, and yet strangely unkillable at least as a topic of conversation, I used even years later to wish that I might see the heavy, hopeless chain for myself. Mother never liked the presents she received; she either exchanged the gift or had it in some vaguely accusing fashion remodeled. If you gave her a silver belt buckle, she would have one half made into a pin for her coat; if you gave her a traveling case, she would say with a sigh that she never hoped to see another train or boat as long as she lived.

For their honeymoon my parents took a two-week journey to the Grand Canyon. The choice was so heroic and unoriginal that it left them forever after with a feeling of gaping vacuity: the whole thing was also inexplicable because my parents, in great moments at least, fell in with what was fashionable and accepted: coming-out parties, grand tours, good hotels, photographs by Bachrach, dresses by Worth. Striking the common, humble, young honeymooners' note in the Grand Canyon was for them a peculiar dissonance, always a bit jarring. I have never thought our lives determined by the stars, and yet at idle moments I could imagine myself stamped with the mark of the Grand Canyon, as if it were a sticker on an automobile. The canyon's yawning hugeness was a sort of bad start for us all. I have never seen it; it is, indeed, too familiar to be seen.

Immediately after their marriage, Mother went to Jamestown, or rather she was taken there or *sent* there. My father was stationed at this inexpensive little haven near Newport. Father had often to be away for weeks at sea, but Jamestown had the grandeur of its nearness to Newport, some society, and a great deal of solitude to offer my mother. She made a great point of liking it all. As a very green and reckless housekeeper, for a whole week she ordered three quarts of cream a day under the impression it was only Grade A milk. Her new husband had no complaints to offer; he did not presume to advise and direct. Mother sighed for her father, whose urgent domination she had long been accustomed to and been sustained by.

Winter came and my father went off to Guantanamo. Mother was then sent to Staten Island, across the bay from New York City, to stay with Grandmother Lowell and Great-grandmother Myers, Father's mother and grandmother. To Mother's unhappy eyes, Grandmother Lowell appeared to be sapless, resigned, depressed, dependent, and contented. She had lovely, soft white hair which she wore in braids; her husband, my father's father, had died in the fifth month of their marriage, five months before my father was born.

This terrible, early bereavement bewildered Grandmother Lowell. She remained a young girl, chaste, tender, sentimental, and sad. She adored her son and looked forward with girlish delight to the hope that my mother would bring something fresh and gay into her life. But Mother felt mislaid and lost in a household without brothers and sisters, men, arguments, explosions. She didn't enjoy Grandmother Lowell and Great-grandmother Myers at all; she was miserable with them. The only thing she enjoyed was taking brisk walks and grieving over the fact that she was pregnant. She took pride in looking into the great Atlantic Ocean and saying, without a trace of fear or illusion, "I wish I could die." On her insistence, and certainly contrary to my father's wishes, we made our first of those many intense moves back to Boston, from where my father's life and work had sent us. My mother's true lover was Boston, or living in Boston, or perhaps *not* living away from Boston; she died during the separations. I was born at Grandfather Winslow's, on the first of March 1917.

What I know of my parents' engagement, marriage, and honeymoon comes from what I was told later and from what I can imagine out of my knowledge of my parents' lives and characters. Of the first years of my life I remember quite a bit —in my mind, white sunlight on white sand stays with a brute, unlocked, dumb insistence—and of course much was told to me.

On the top floor of our house, in a room that was dark but always germ-free because the windows were open, I used to lie on my back, hold my knees, and vibrate. "*Stop rocking,*" my nurse or Mother would say. I remember this trembling fury, but I do not know its reason. Remembering, I seem to see water dropping from the ceiling, down on the wallpaper, but that happened later, when we rented our house to people who were "irresponsible vandals." I can see sunlight striking our gray carpet, the rays falling on the sideboard and the marmalade jar in our Brimmer Street house. The house was the first my parents owned in Boston as newlyweds. It was a financial miracle. Mother hadn't paid a penny for it. Grandfather Winslow had first taken a mortgage and then a second mortgage to pay the first; then he took out a loan of some kind in order to pay the second mortgage; then he gave Mother a Christmas present to pay the interest on the loan. Perhaps there were other steps in these exciting negotiations, maybe even third and fourth mortgages, all taken by Grandfather, who was reputed to be a wizard in such affairs and who had plenty of time on his hands to execute his amazing financial schemes.

When Mother finally sold the house on Brimmer Street, she paid off all the debts on it and cleared a thousand dollars. The room where I had held my knees and trembled with stubbornness has faded; more alive, more vivid long after is the sensation of the resentment occasioned by the fact that my father's naval duties forced us to move from Boston. Mother, despising the demands the Navy made upon her, would say mysteriously that she needed character and courage to prevent my father from allowing things simply to take their quiet course and, thereby, ruin us.

From the period of the Brimmer Street house a scene remains, a childish drama embarrassingly heavy with religious symbolism and black magic. When real events are so starkly allegorical, the accidental nature of such happenings is blackly underscored. When I was two years old I had a young nurse who herself was only eighteen or so years old and had come to Boston from Ireland. She was always spoken of as a beautiful girl, firmly conforming to her national pattern: she had raven hair which was soft and wavy, sky-blue eyes, fair skin, and an exquisite brogue. She was pious, irreverent, and loose-limbed—the pretty possessor of what Grandfather Winslow described as a "loosely laced mind." Her name was Katherine. Katherine's rosary was a memorable work of religious mass production. It was designed with a Celtic exaggeration and the beads were made of some material which had the appearance and texture of rock candy. These beads were so hard, cold, and precious and of such fascination that immediately the fat, warm, wooden beads which decorated my crib lost all their appeal to me. But what I loved more than the beads of Katherine's rosary was the silver crucifix. It was heavy, intricate, and important, as I could see from Katherine's awed and loving glance upon it. Katherine told me about Jesus and I regret to recall that my feelings were highly egocentric: I saw, with despair, that I was second fiddle even in my nurse's affections. And then suddenly the rosary disappeared and the house was disturbed by the mystery. I was questioned, but

I merely gaped sweetly and presented myself as a figure of innocence, all sunlight and brown curls. I smiled and smiled and
smiled, very much in the perplexing way my father smiled and
smiled and smiled. A day or so later the rosary was found, hidden under the corner of the rug, where it had slipped by mistake
according to the decision taken by the household. However, it
was noted that the Christus was missing, and also, with embarrassment, that the chain of the rosary had been chewed. I
returned to my denying smile, but later Mother saw me pushing
strips of paper down the register. "You will burn up the house,"
she said. But two days later she again saw me pushing a whole
handful of paper strips down the register. "You are setting the
furnace on fire," she said. I smiled and smiled, to her intense
displeasure. "Yes, I know," I said. "That's where Jesus is."

My father was sent to Philadelphia and so we were to be
packed up and sent there, too, for my third and fourth winters.
These years were unhappy, or so they were always described by
my mother, who did not want to go to Philadelphia or anyplace
else. The theme of her early married life was clear and constant
and alarming: *I want to live in Boston.* I can still feel the bite of
those two Philadelphia winters and the dismal chill of the scene,
a clammy, snowless, sooty, sunless prospect of an insupportably
long street bordered by indistinguishable residences. Now, looking back, I can wonder why Mother pronounced Philadelphia
"absolutely unbearable." Wasn't it, after all, just a bigger,
warmer Boston?

Philadelphia—our winters there leave an unpleasant trace
in my history, like a metallic taste in the mouth. This, I suppose,
came from Mother's utter detestation of this period, because I
could not have cared one way or another. I remember our train
journey, very snug and very serious. I felt I was setting sail for
Europe or another age, and that it was only my steady courage
and enduring patience which made the arrival possible. Mother
undertook the trip with all the bravado of unpleasant duty,
which seemed to say that if she was wrong in not wishing to go
she was at least triumphantly admirable in going anyway. Her
dress, her proud walk, her dramatic tension which made her

assume in moments of stress an abnormally casual and indifferent air! I discovered at this time that adults enjoyed drama, even painful drama, for only then when they were boiling and raging inside could they act calmly, with a sense of importance and control.

We did, at last, solemnly and importantly and dutifully arrive in Philadelphia. We had taken an apartment which had a certain number of distinct rooms but was, nevertheless, quite small. The windows ran from floor to ceiling and admitted little sunlight, but much electric glare, dust, and drafty air; the windowpanes were blue-gray and framed in iron—all of our glassy view of the outside and inside world was a little shadowed and askew, like the decor for a German Expressionist film. The apartment's bedrooms, servant's room, dining room, nursery, and parlor were a Lilliputian annex to a kitchen, whose floor was covered with a peeling black-and-white linoleum. When we finally arrived, my parents spent hours screwing in light bulbs, while I sat serenely crackling the paper in a box of Fig Newtons. The confusion of the move, the disappointment of the apartment threw everything out of balance and accounted for the unprecedented availability of the Fig Newton box and even for the cookie itself, a rich, exotic mixture usually disapproved of, unlike the salutary graham cracker.

Philadelphia: one afternoon at about four o'clock, when winter and coal smoke had already made the sky impenetrably black, I wandered out of our long kitchen and to my horror saw Father lying in his brown, monkish wrapper on a sofa that had been moved into the hall. He was ill with flu; his temperature was 103, and he lay back, sack-like, and smiling still. Father looked cold and waxen and I thought his cheap Chinese slippers very much like little snowshoes. On the hard chair at his elbow lay his shirt and underwear—he seemed somehow on the alert. Father, in his illness, had removed himself from the bedroom he shared with Mother, so that the room might remain healthy and germ-free and spared the disorder of his convalescing presence. In his quiet, smiling, feverish banishment, he meant to be an ideal husband whose demands were infinitesimal. But, nevertheless, with every move we stumbled gracelessly upon the un-selfish invalid. The strain brought about by his effort to make himself heroically nonexistent was extreme; all was hushed, vexed, and ajar. Still, after a day of such exposure and boldness, Father was cured. It did not pay to be sick in this way and it seemed to me that the cure had come from some glorious modesty and self-sacrifice on Father's part. His object, however, was defeated, because Mother caught flu and was sick for a week. She lay in warmth and splendor in her bedroom, supported by hot-water bottles, gardenias, doctors, and trays with pink napkins on them. In her self-indulgent illness, nothing was set at odds in the household; instead, everything was more smooth than ever, as if music were playing and we were all living in a floating palace.

This Philadelphia illness was my first experience with the strange contraries of hardiness and sickness which were always a great part of our family life. At this time I, too, came down with flu, which mysteriously lasted for three weeks. I felt very close to Mother because she took joy in giving me every comfort and care. I was even allowed to feel that the very act of being sick for three long weeks was an extraordinary accomplishment. This feat gave much trouble and expense and yet it was the kind of trouble that one need not be ashamed of. Here was a difficulty Mother could rise to. She made sickness something of a pleasure and a privilege and surrounded it with good sense, humor, and ease. Yet, mentally or verbally, it was hardiness which was always praised. When, later, I simply would not be sick, hardiness was fine and yet somehow associated in my mind with perverse stubbornness, with an assertion of my will against my mother's. Hardiness could be hardness of heart, self-love, whereas a few convenient light illnesses were an announcement of one's tender-ness, tolerance, and family spirit.

On the matter of illness, Mother was perplexed, and theory and practice were not always united. She believed desperately in hardiness and always said firmly, "I am never ill," but mean-while she spent several days every month in bed for one reason or another. When the men of her household were sick, her duties were definite, domesticity soared in importance, and the stubborn wills around her were pleasantly resting and recuperating. Sickness was at once the supreme proof of masculine recklessness and absurdity and a penalty which strangely eased domestic tensions. If one was sick he was culpable and unworthy, but on the other hand his behavior was better, more considerate: an ill man won't be late to dinner. A passive, emergency object could be dealt with in prescribed terms, and the emergency itself gave a pleasant drama to the routine days.

When I was convalescing from flu, Christmas holidays arrived and I associated in my mind the lazy, indulgent recovering days with actual calendar holidays. Father was away at sea and Grandfather Winslow made us a surprise visit from Boston. My father sent me a big bundle of toys and in my self-concentration I thought I had the toys only because Father was away, and so his absence seemed delightful. When he returned, I ran up to him with tears in my eyes and said, "Daddy, I love you, but please go away again so that Santa can mail us a wagon-load of toys." Father seemed rather queasy in the face of this demonstration from his son.

The toys had been chosen with the notion of impressing upon me the glamour of Father's naval career by comparison with mere civilian life and parenthood. Someone in the Philadelphia Yard had ordered naval toys wholesale from Japan and was selling them at a discount to men in the service. Among my gifts was a grim, gray wooden model of a German U-boat. By pressing a button, I could snap a trap-like spring inside the U-boat which made its gear collapse on the carpet, as though the thing had been hit by a depth bomb. This device was meant to teach children that wars meant business and, further, it was the very magic of the toy itself. I was dismayed when Mother snatched my prize from me, disemboweled it of its spring, and then returned it, a miserable, weightless, warped wreck of its former war-like self. The intricate and banned U-boat gave a fascination to the German character which had produced it. I thought they must be amazing people with their model boats and guns and torpedoes; I imagined they were the sort to hide stones in snow-balls and put barbs back on fishhooks. When my father came home he told me my toy submarine was skippered by a six-foot blond boy from Stuttgart, a creature named Fritz Shoemaker, who was drowned whenever the spring was snapped. For a few nights I had nightmares in which I saw poor Fritz's cold, stiff, lifeless German body.

I was partially consoled for the loss of my U-boat by another gift, a set of six hand-painted French sailors, with red tufts on the top of their sailor hats. All through Christmas morning I kept wretchedly fumbling about in the heavy sheets of brown paper in which the sailors had been wrapped. Concealed in the heavy paper, I had been told, was a seventh sailor. I wanted the other sailor and when I couldn't find him I had the desperate feeling that my method of looking for him was wrong, that somewhere in the paper he lay and that it was only my clumsiness and headlong, impatient ways which prevented him from being instantly revealed. Grandfather Winslow walked up and down in front of the fireplace, snapping his gold matchbox open and shut. Mother jokingly said the sailor was in the matchbox, but I looked and saw only a green-black musty darkness. This looking for the sailor was filled with anguish, self-hatred for my ineptness, genuine despair. I felt shaken and believed I had actually experienced the finding of the sailor, that I had mastered the mystery of the folded paper, but had somehow mysteriously lost my knowledge. The joy of hunting, my tireless and awkward persistence, which had in it a certain measure of satisfaction, went along with my grief and anxiety. Now I cannot decide whether there had ever truly been a seventh sailor in a seventh hat with a red tassel on it.

Philadelphia was a watery dinginess, like the black cement floor of its own principal railroad station. The ice floes of white enamel in our long kitchen shivered and shimmered; soot floated calmly in the air and the windows glared steel-blue. In the newness of our life, the unfamiliarity, the fact that we wouldn't stay long enough ever to be really of the city, all of this meant that about us people existed, lived, gossiped, and accepted their lives, but we did not exist. We seemed to be treading water all day, getting nowhere. Mother felt Philadelphia society was a bit limp and peripheral, an oversized and ersatz Boston. Some natives of the city called upon us. The visits passed with tenderness and mutual respect, but my mother thought these lone ladies and dignified couples peculiarly lacking in gaiety and eccentricity. They were, in character at least, Quakerish, serenely accustomed to the bromidic flow of life.

One day a person named Martha Bent came to call. She had a nose like an acorn and her penitential purple hat threw a friendly shadow over her eyes. Around her neck she wore a plain black cord upon which she had attached a cracked ivory elephant, the color of jaundice and no bigger than a man's molar. Mother could not prevent Martha from "theeing and thouing" Father and calling him "Cousin Bob." She also had an unfortunate, showy way of giggling every time he spoke to her or talked naval shop in an urgent voice. As the weeks passed, Martha Bent became what is called "a fixture about the house." She was, indeed, a piece of machinery, always making its own characteristic noise as it worked away. She adored children and liked to drop in on me once a day; the time she chose was nearly always around teatime when Father would be getting back from the Yard. Martha was what my father liked to call "a regular fella" and he didn't waver from this sturdy opinion even when my mother said she was dreary and a flirt. On the subject of Martha Bent I was torn in two, accepting painfully the attitudes of my parents as correct and finding myself left with a person who was both to be wooed and to be rejected, an object as mixed and bewildering as Philadelphia itself. I already felt the stirrings of revolt against my mother's judgment; I already felt an attraction to what she rebuked or condemned; in her enemies, or at least in her castoffs, I always saw a possible ally of my own. In my grim self-adoration I devised a way to try Martha Bent's patience, to prove her goodness, test her loyalty. She must give me her ivory elephant! I wanted the elephant not only as proof of devotion but greedily for itself, because it was small, heavy, precious, useless—the heart that Martha wore on her sleeve as well as the absurd animal around her neck. Then somehow I had been "given" the elephant: I lay back in my bed, looking at the dusty, gray sunlight which filtered through the window shade I had drawn in order to enjoy my treasure unseen, in near darkness. I tapped the ivory on my teeth as though it were a piece of rock candy. And then it went down. Doctors came. Mother kept saying with Gargantuan suavity, "Bobby has swallowed an elephant." Then it was unmentionably ascertained that the ivory elephant had come out in my chamber pot. I was told it was broken into three pieces so that I couldn't see it again. And that was the sly, stupid end of a little trinket cherished by a foolish woman and by me.

[1957]

91 Revere Street

The account of him is platitudinous, worldly, and fond, but he has no Christian name and is entitled merely Major M. Myers in my Cousin Cassie Mason-Myers Julian-James's privately printed *Biographical Sketches: A Key to a Cabinet of Heirlooms in the Smithsonian Museum.* The nameplate under his portrait used to spell out his name bravely enough: he was Mordecai Myers. The artist painted Major Myers in his sanguine War of 1812 uniform with epaulets, white breeches, and a scarlet frogged waistcoat. His right hand played with the sword "now to be seen in the Smithsonian cabinet of heirlooms." The pose was routine and gallant. The full-lipped smile was good-humoredly pompous and embarrassed.

Mordecai's father, given neither name nor initial, is described with an air of hurried self-congratulation by Cousin Cassie as "a friend of the Reverend Ezra Styles, afterward President of Yale College." As a very young man the son, Mordecai, studied military tactics under a French émigré, "the Bourbons' celebrated Colonel De la Croix." Later he was "matured" by six years' practical experience in a New York militia regiment organized by Colonel Martin Van Buren. After "the successful engagement against the British at Chrysler's Field, thirty shrapnel splinters were extracted from his shoulder." During convalescence, he wooed and won Miss Charlotte Bailey, "thus proving himself a better man than his rivals, the united forces of Plattsburg." He fathered ten children, sponsored an enlightened law exempting Quakers from military service in New York State, and died in 1870 at the age of ninety-four, "a Grand Old Man, who impressed strangers with the poise of his old-time manners."

Undoubtedly Major Mordecai had lived in a more ritualistic, gaudy, and animal world than twentieth-century Boston. There was something undecided, Mediterranean, versatile, almost double-faced about his bearing which suggested that, even to his contemporaries, he must have seemed gratuitously both *ci-devant* and *parvenu*. He was a dark man, a German Jew—no downright Yankee, but maybe such a fellow as Napoleon's mad, pomaded son-of-an-innkeeper-general, Junot, Duc D'Abrantes; a man like mad George III's pomaded, disreputable son, "Prinny," the Prince Regent. Or he was one of those Moorish-looking dons painted by his contemporary, Goya—some leader of Spanish guerrillas against Bonaparte's occupation, who fled to South America. Our Major's suffering almond eye rested on his luxurious dawn-colored fingers ruffling an off-white glove.

Bailey-Mason-Myers! Easygoing, Empire State patricians, these relatives of my Grandmother Lowell seemed to have given my father his character. For he likewise lacked that granite *back-countriness* which Grandfather Arthur Winslow attributed to his own ancestors, the iconoclastic, mulish Dunbarton New Hampshire Starks. On the joint Mason-Myers bookplate, there are two merry and naked mermaids—lovely marshmallowy, boneless, Rubensesque butterballs, all burlesque-show bosoms and Flemish smiles. Their motto, *malo frangere quam flectere*, reads: "I prefer to bend than to break."

Mordecai Myers was my Grandmother Lowell's grandfather. His life was tame and honorable. He was a leisured squire and merchant, a member of the state legislature, a mayor of Schenectady, a "president" of Kinderhook village. Disappointingly, his famous "blazing brown eye" seems in all things to have shunned the outrageous. After his death he was remembered soberly as a New York State gentleman, the friend and host of worldly men and politicians with Dutch names: De Witt Clinton, Vanderpoel, Hoes, and Schuyler. My mother was roused to warmth by the Major's scarlet vest and exotic eye. She always insisted that he was the one properly dressed and dieted ancestor in the lot we had inherited from my father's Cousin Cassie. Great-great-grandfather Mordecai! Poor sheepdog in wolf's clothing! In the anarchy of my adolescent war on my parents, I tried to make him a true wolf, the wandering Jew! *Homo lupus homini!*

Major Mordecai Myers's portrait has been mislaid past finding, but out of my memories I often come on it in the setting of our Revere Street house, a setting now fixed in the mind, where it survives all the distortions of fantasy, all the blank befogging of forgetfulness. There, the vast number of remembered *things* remains rock-like. Each is in its place, each has its function, its history, its drama. There, all is preserved by that motherly care that one either ignored or resented in his youth. The things and their owners come back urgent with life and meaning—because finished, they are endurable and perfect.

Cousin Cassie only became a close relation in 1922. In that year she died. After some unpleasantness between Mother and a co-heiress, Helen Bailey, the estate was divided. Mother used to return frozen and thrilled from her property disputes, and I, knowing nothing of the rights and wrongs, would half-perversely confuse Helen Bailey with Helen of Troy and harden my mind against the monotonous *parti pris* of Mother's voice. Shortly after our move to Boston in 1924, a score of unwanted Myers portraits was delivered to our new house on Revere Street. These were later followed by "their dowry"—four moving vans groaning with heavy Edwardian furniture. My father began to receive his first quarterly payments from the Mason-Myers Julian-James Trust Fund, sums "not grand enough to corrupt us," Mother explained, "but sufficient to prevent Daddy from being entirely at the mercy of his salary." The Trust sufficed: our lives became tantalized with possibilities, and my father felt encouraged to take the risk—a small one in those boom years—of resigning from the Navy on the gamble of doubling his income in business.

I was in the third grade and for the first time becoming a little more popular at school. I was afraid Father's leaving the Navy would destroy my standing. I was a churlish, disloyal, romantic boy, and quite without hero worship for my father, whose actuality seemed so inferior to the photographs in uniform he once mailed to us from the Golden Gate. My real *love*, as Mother used to insist to all new visitors, was toy soldiers. For a few months at the flood tide of this infatuation, people were ciphers to me—valueless except as chances for increasing my armies of soldiers. Roger Crosby, a child in the second grade of my Brimmer Street School, had thousands—not mass-produced American stereotypes, but hand-painted solid lead soldiers made to order in Dijon, France. Roger's father had a still more artistic and adult collection; its ranks—each man at least six inches tall —marched in glass cases under the eyes of recognizable replicas of mounted Napoleonic captains: Kleber, Marshal Ney, Murat, King of Naples. One delirious afternoon Mr. Crosby showed me his toys and was perhaps the first grownup to talk to me not as a child but as an equal when he discovered how feverishly I followed his anecdotes on uniforms and the evolution of tactical surprise. Afterward, full of high thoughts, I ran up to Roger's playroom and hoodwinked him into believing that his own soldiers were "ballast turned out by Central European sweatshops." He agreed I was being sweetly generous when I traded twenty-four worthless Jordan Marsh papier-mâché doughboys for whole companies of his gorgeous, imported Old Guards, Second Empire "redlegs," and modern *chasseurs d'Alpine* with sky-blue berets. The haul was so huge that I had to take a child's wheelbarrow to Roger's house at the top of Pinckney Street. When I reached home with my last load, Mr. Crosby was talking with my father on our front steps. Roger's soldiers were all returned; I had only the presence of mind to hide a single soldier, a peely-nosed black sepoy wearing a Shriner's fez.

Nothing consoled me for my loss, but I enjoyed being allowed to draw Father's blunt dress sword, and I was proud of our Major Mordecai. I used to stand dangerously out in the middle of Revere Street in order to see through our windows and gloat on this portrait's scarlet waistcoat blazing in the bare, Spartan whiteness of our den-parlor. Mordecai Myers lost his glory when I learned from my father that he was only a "major *pro tem.*" On a civilian, even a civilian soldier, the flamboyant waistcoat was stuffy and no more martial than officers' costumes in our elementary-school musicals.

In 1924 people still lived in cities. Late that summer, we bought the 91 Revere Street house, looking out on an unbuttoned part of Beacon Hill bounded by the North End slums, though reassuringly only four blocks away from my Grandfather Winslow's brown pillared house at 18 Chestnut Street. In the decades preceding and following the First World War, old Yankee families had upset expectation by regaining this section of the Hill from the vanguards of the lace-curtain Irish. This was bracing news for my parents in that topsy-turvy era when the Republican Party and what were called "people of the right sort" were no longer dominant in city elections. Still, even in the palmy, laissez-faire twenties, Revere Street refused to be a straightforward, immutable residential fact. From one end to the other, houses kept being sanded down, repainted, or abandoned to the flaking of decay. Houses, changing hands, changed their language and nationality. A few doors to our south the householders spoke "Beacon Hill British" or the flat *nay nay* of the Boston Brahmin. The parents of the children a few doors north spoke mostly in Italian.

My mother felt a horrified giddiness about the adventure of our address. She once said, "We are barely perched on the outer rim of the hub of decency." We were less than fifty yards from Louisburg Square, the cynosure of old historic Boston's plain-spoken, cold roast elite—the Hub of the Hub of the Universe. Fifty yards!

As a naval ensign, Father had done postgraduate work at Harvard. He had also done postgraduate work at M.I.T., preferred the purely scientific college, and condescended to both.

In 1924, however, his tone began to change; he now began to speak warmly of Harvard as his second alma mater. We went to football games at the Harvard Stadium, and one had the feeling that our lives were now being lived in the brutal, fashionable expectancy of the stadium: we had so many downs, so many minutes, and so many yards to go for a winning touchdown. It was just a winning financial and social advance that my parents promised themselves would follow Father's resignation from the Navy and his acceptance of a sensible job offered him at the Cambridge branch of Lever Brothers' Soap.

The advance was never to come. Father resigned from the service in 1927, but he never had a civilian *career*; he instead had merely twenty-two years of the civilian *life*. Almost immediately he bought a larger and more stylish house; he sold his ascetic, stove-black Hudson and bought a plump brown Buick; later the Buick was exchanged for a high-toned, as-good-as-new Packard with a custom-designed royal blue and mahogany body. Without drama, his earnings more or less decreased from year to year.

But so long as we were on Revere Street, Father tried to come to terms with it and must have often wondered whether he on the whole liked or disliked the neighborhood's lack of side. He was still at this time rather truculently democratic in what might be described as an upper-middle-class, naval, and Masonic fashion. He was a mumbler. His opinions were almost morbidly hesitant, but he considered himself a matter-of-fact man of science and had an unspoiled faith in the superior efficiency of northern nations. He modeled his allegiances and humor on the cockney imperialism of Rudyard Kipling's swearing Tommies, who did their job. Autochthonous Boston snobs, such as the Winslows or members of Mother's reading club, were alarmed by the brassy callousness of our naval visitors, who labeled the Italians they met on Revere Street as "grade-A" and "grade-B wops." The Revere Street "grade-B's" were Sicilian Catholics and peddled crummy second-hand furniture on Cambridge Street, not far from the site of Great-great-grandfather Charles Lowell's disused West Church, praised in an old family folder as "a haven from the Sodom and Gomorrah of Trinitarian orthodoxy and the tyranny of the letter." Revere Street "grade-A's," good North Italians, sold fancy groceries and colonial heirlooms in their shops near the Public Garden. Still other Italians were Father's familiars; they sold him bootleg Scotch and *vino rosso* in teacups.

The outside of our Revere Street house was a flat red brick surface unvaried by the slightest suggestion of purple panes, delicate bay, or triangular window cornice—a sheer wall formed by the seamless conjunction of four inseparable façades, all of the same commercial and purgatorial design. Though placed in the heart of Old Boston, it was ageless and artless, an epitome of those "leveler" qualities Mother found most grueling about the naval service. 91 Revere Street was mass-produced, *regulation-issue*, and yet struck Boston society as stupidly out of the ordinary, like those white elephants—a mother-of-pearl scout knife or a tea-kettle barometer—which my father used to pick up on sale at an Army-Navy store.

The walls of Father's minute Revere Street den-parlor were bare and white. His bookshelves were bare and white. The den's one adornment was a ten-tube home-assembled battery-radio set, whose loudspeaker had the shape and color of a Mexican sombrero. The radio's specialty was getting programs from Australia and New Zealand in the early hours of the morning.

My father's favorite piece of den furniture was his oak and "rhinocerous hide" armchair. It was ostentatiously a masculine, or rather a bachelor's, chair. It had a notched, adjustable back; it was black, cracked, hacked, scratched, splintered, gouged, initialed, gunpowder-charred, and tumbler-ringed. It looked like pale tobacco leaves laid on dark tobacco leaves. I doubt if Father, a considerate man, was responsible for any of the marring. The chair dated from his plebe days at the Naval Academy, and had been bought from a shady, shadowy, roaring character, midshipman "Beauty" Burford. Father loved each disfigured inch.

My father had been born five months after his own father's death. At each stage of his life, he was to be forlornly fatherless.

He was a deep boy brought up entirely by a mild widowed mother and an intense widowed grandmother. When he was fourteen and a half, he became a deep young midshipman. By the time he graduated from Annapolis, he had a high sense of abstract form, which he beclouded with his humor. He had reached, perhaps, his final mental possibilities. He was deep—not with profundity, but with the dumb depth of one who trusted in statistics and was dubious of personal experience. In his forties, Father's soul went underground: as a civilian he kept his high sense of form, his humor, his accuracy, but this accuracy was henceforth unimportant, recreational, *hors de combat*. His debunking grew myopic; his shyness grew evasive; he argued with a fumbling languor. In the twenty-two years Father lived after he resigned from the Navy, he never again deserted Boston and never became Bostonian. He survived to drift from job to job, to be displaced, to be grimly and literally that old cliché, a fish out of water. He gasped and wheezed with impotent optimism, took on new ideals with each new job, never ingeniously enjoyed his leisure, never even hid his head in the sand.

Mother hated the Navy, hated naval society, naval pay, and the trip-hammer rote of settling and unsettling a house every other year when Father was transferred to a new station or ship. She had been married nine or ten years and still suspected that her husband was savorless, unmasterful, merely considerate. Unmasterful—Father's specialized efficiency lacked utterly the flattering bossiness she so counted on from her father, my Grandfather Winslow. It was not Father's absence on sea duty that mattered; it was the eroding necessity of moving *with* him, of keeping in step. When he was far away on the Pacific, she had her friends, her parents, a house to herself—Boston! Fully conscious of her uniqueness and normality, she basked in the refreshing stimulation of dreams in which she imagined Father as suitably sublimed. She used to describe such a sublime man to me over tea and English muffins. He was Siegfried carried lifeless through the shining air by Brunhilde to Valhalla, and accompanied by the throb of my Great-aunt Sarah playing his leitmotif in the released manner taught her by the Abbé Liszt. Or Mother's hero dove through the grottoes of the Rhine and slaughtered the homicidal and vulgar dragon coiled about the golden hoard. Mother seemed almost light-headed when she retold the romance of Sarah Bernhardt in *L'Aiglon*, the Eaglet, the weakling! She would speak the word *weakling* with such amused vehemence that I formed a grandiose and false image of L'Aiglon's father, the *big* Napoleon: he was a strong man who scratched under his paunchy little white vest a torso all hair, muscle, and manliness. Instead of the dreams, Mother now had the insipid fatigue of keeping house. Instead of the Eagle, she had a twentieth-century naval commander interested in steam, radio, and "the fellows." To avoid naval yards, steam, and "the fellows," Mother had impulsively bought the squalid, impractical Revere Street house. Her marriage daily forced her to squander her subconsciously hoarded energies.

"*Weelawaugh, we-ee-eelawaugh, weelawaugh,*" shrilled Mother's high voice. "*But-and, but-and, but-and!*" Father's low mumble would drone in answer. Though I couldn't be sure that I had caught the meaning of the words, I followed the sounds as though they were a movie. I felt drenched in my parents' passions.

91 Revere Street was the setting for those arthritic spiritual pains that troubled us for the two years my mother spent in trying to argue my father into resigning from the Navy. When the majestic, hollow boredom of the second year's autumn dwindled to the mean boredom of a second winter, I grew less willing to open my mouth. I bored my parents, they bored me.

"Weelawaugh, we-ee-eelawaugh, weelawaugh!" "But-and, but-and, but-and!"

During the weekends I was at home much of the time. All day I used to look forward to the nights when my bedroom walls would once again vibrate, when I would awake with rapture to the rhythm of my parents arguing, arguing one another to exhaustion. Sometimes, without bathrobe or slippers, I would wiggle out into the cold hall on my belly and ambuscade myself behind the banister. I could often hear actual words. "Yes, yes,

yes," Father would mumble. He was "backsliding" and "living in the fool's paradise of habitual retarding and retarded do-nothing inertia." Mother had violently set her heart on the resignation. She was hysterical even in her calm, but like a patient and forbearing strategist, she tried to pretend her neutrality. One night she said with murderous coolness, "Bobby and I are leaving for Papá's." This was an ultimatum to force Father to sign a deed placing the Revere Street house in Mother's name.

I writhed with disappointment on the nights when Mother and Father only lowed harmoniously together like cows, as they criticized Helen Bailey or Admiral De Stahl. Once I heard my mother say, "A *man* must make up his *own* mind. Oh, Bob, if you are going to resign, do it *now* so I can at least plan for your son's *survival* and education on a single continent."

About this time I was being sent for my *survival* to Dr. Dane, a Quaker chiropractor with an office on Marlborough Street. Dr. Dane wore an old-fashioned light tan druggist's smock; he smelled like a healthy old-fashioned drugstore. His laboratory was free of intimidating technical equipment, and had only the conservative lay roughness and toughness that was so familiar and disarming to us in my Grandfather Winslow's country study or bedroom. Dr. Dane's rosy hands wrenched my shoulders with tremendous éclat and made me feel a hero; I felt unspeakable joy whenever an awry muscle fell back into serenity. My mother, who had no curiosity or imagination for cranky occultism, trusted Dr. Dane's clean, undrugged manliness —so like home. She believed that chiropractice had cured me of my undiagnosed asthma, which had defeated the expensive specialists.

"A penny for your thoughts, Schopenhauer," my mother would say.

"I am thinking about pennies," I'd answer.

"When *I* was a child I used to love telling Mamá everything I had done," Mother would say.

"But you're not a child," I would answer.

I used to enjoy dawdling and humming "Anchors Aweigh" up Revere Street after a day at school. "Anchors Aweigh," the official Navy song, had originally been the song composed for my father's class. And yet my mind always blanked and seemed to fill with a clammy hollowness when Mother asked prying questions. Like other tongue-tied, difficult children, I dreamed I was master of cool, stoical repartee. "What have you been doing, Bobby?" Mother would ask. "I haven't," I'd answer. At home I thus saved myself from emotional exhaustion.

At school, however, I was extreme only in my conventional mediocrity, my colorless, distracted manner, which came from restless dreams of being admired. My closest friend was Eric Burckhard, the son of a professor of architecture at Harvard. The Burckhards came from Zurich and were very German, not like Ludendorff, but in the kindly, comical, nineteenth-century manner of Jo's German husband in *Little Men*, or in the manner of the crusading *Sturm und Drang* liberal scholars in second-year-German novels. "Eric's mother and father are *both* called Dr. Burckhard," my mother once said, and indeed there was something endearingly repellent about Mrs. Burckhard with her doctor's degree, her long, unstylish skirts, and her dramatic, dulling blond braids. Strangely, the Burckhards' sober Continental bourgeois house was without golden mean—everything was either hilariously old Swiss or madly modern. The Frau Doctor Burckhard used to serve midmorning hot chocolate with rosettes of whipped cream, and receive her friends in a long, uncarpeted hall–drawing room with lethal ferns and a yellow beeswaxed hardwood floor shining under a central skylight. On the wall there were large expert photographs of what at a distance appeared to be Mont Blanc—they were in reality views of Frank Lloyd Wright's Japanese hotel.

I admired the Burckhards and felt at home in their house, and these feelings were only intensified when I discovered that my mother was always ill at ease with them. The heartiness, the enlightenment, and the bright, ferny greenhouse atmosphere were too much for her.

Eric and I were too young to care for books or athletics.

Neither of our houses had absorbing toys or an elevator to go up and down in. We were inseparable, but I cannot imagine what we talked about. I loved Eric because he was more popular than I and yet absolutely *sui generis* at the Brimmer School. He had a chalk-white face and limp, fine, white-blond hair. He was frail, elbowy, started talking with an enthusiastic Mont Blanc chirp, and would flush with bewilderment if interrupted. All the other boys at Brimmer wore little tweed golf suits with knicker-bockers, but Eric always arrived in a black suit coat, a Byronic collar, and cuffless gray-flannel trousers that almost hid his shoes. The long trousers were replaced on warm days by gray-flannel shorts, such as were worn by children still in kindergarten. Eric's unenviable and freakish costumes were too old or too young. He accepted the whims of his parents with a buoyant tranquillity that I found unnatural.

My first and terminating quarrel with Eric was my fault. Eventually almost our whole class at Brimmer had whooping cough, but Eric's seizure was like his long trousers—untimely: he was sick a month too early. For a whole month he was in quarantine and forced to play by himself in a removed corner of the Public Garden. He was certainly conspicuous as he skip-roped with his Swiss nurse under the out-of-the-way Ether Me-morial Fountain far from the pond and the swan boats. His parents had decided that this was an excellent opportunity for Eric to brush up on his German, and so the absoluteness of his quarantine was monstrously exaggerated by the fact that child and nurse spoke no English but only a guttural, British-sounding Swiss German. Round and round and round the fountain, he played intensely, frailly, obediently, until I began to tease him. Though motioned away by him, I came close. I had attracted some of the most popular Brimmer School boys. For the first time I had gotten favorable attention from several little girls. I came close. I shouted. Was Eric afraid of girls? I imitated his German. *Ein, zwei, drei, BEER.* I imitated Eric's coughing. "He is afraid he will give you whooping cough if he talks or lets you come nearer," the nurse said in her musical Swiss-English voice. I came nearer. Eric flushed, grew white, bent double with coughing. He began to cry, and had to be led away from the Public Garden. For a whole week I routed Eric from the garden daily, and for two or three days I was a center of interest. "Come see the Lake Geneva spider monkey!" I would shout. I don't know why I couldn't stop. Eric never told his father, I think, but when he recovered we no longer spoke. The breach was so unspoken and intense that our classmates were actually horrified. They even devised a solemn ritual for our reconciliation. We crossed our hearts, mixed spit, mixed blood. The reconciliation was hollow.

My parents' confidences and quarrels stopped each night at ten or eleven o'clock, when my father would hang up his tuxedo, put on his commander's uniform, and take a trolley back to the Naval Yard at Charlestown. He had just broken in a new car. Like a chauffeur, he watched this car, a Hudson, with an informed vigilance, always giving its engine hair-trigger little tinkerings of adjustment or friendship, always fearful lest the black body, unbeautiful as his boiled shirts, should lose its outline and gloss. He drove with flawless, almost instrumental, monotony. Mother, nevertheless, was forever encouraging him to walk or take taxis. She would tell him that his legs were growing vestigial from disuse and remind him of the time a jack had slipped and he had broken his leg while shifting a tire. "Alone and at night," she would say, "an amateur driver is unsafe in a car." Father sighed and obeyed—only, putting on a martyred and penny-saving face, he would keep his self-respect by taking the trolley rather than a taxi. Each night he shifted back into his uniform, but his departures from Revere Street were so furtive that several months passed before I realized what was happening —we had *two* houses! Our second house was the residence in the Naval Yard assigned to the third in command. It was large, had its own flagpole, and screen porches on three levels—yet it was something to be ashamed of. Whatever pomp or distinction its possession might have had for us was destroyed by an eccentric humiliation inflicted on Father by his superior, Admiral De Stahl, the commandant at Charlestown. De Stahl had not been consulted about our buying the 91 Revere Street house. He was outraged, stormed about "flaunting private fortunes in the face of naval tradition," and ordered my father to sleep on bounds at the Yard in the house provided for that purpose.

On our first Revere Street Christmas Eve, the telephone rang in the middle of dinner; it was Admiral De Stahl demanding Father's instant return to the Navy Yard. Soon Father was back in his uniform. In taking leave of my mother and grandparents he was, as was usual with him under pressure, a little evasive and magniloquent. "A woman works from sun to sun," he said, "but a sailor's watch is never done." He compared a naval officer's hours with a doctor's, hinted at surprise maneuvers, and explained away the uncommunicative arrogance of Admiral De Stahl: "The Old Man has to be hush-hush." Later that night, I lay in bed and tried to imagine that my father was leading his engineering force on a surprise maneuver through Arctic wastes. A forlorn hope! "Hush-hush, hush-hush," whispered the snowflakes as big as street lamps as they broke on Father—broke and buried. Outside, I heard real people singing carols, shuffling snow off their shoes, opening and shutting doors. I worried at the meaning of a sentence I had heard quoted from the *Boston Evening Transcript:* "On this Christmas Eve, as usual, the whole of Beacon Hill can be expected to become a single old-fashioned open house—the names of mine host, the Hill, and her guests will read like the contents of the Social Register." I imagined Beacon Hill changed to the Snow Queen's palace, as vast as the North Pole. My father pressed a cold finger to his lip: "Hush-hush," and led his surprise squad of sailors around an altar, but the altar was a tremendous cash register, whose roughened nickel surface was cheaply decorated with trowels, pyramids, and Arabic swirls. A great drawer helplessly chopped back and forth, unable to shut because choked with greenbacks. "Hush-hush!" My father's engineers wound about me with their eye patches, orange sashes, and curtain-ring earrings, like the Gilbert and Sullivan pirates' chorus . . . Outside, on the streets of Beacon Hill, it was night, it was dismal, it was raining. Something disturbing had befallen the familiar and honorable Salvation Army band; its big drum and accordion were now accompanied by drunken voices howling: *The Old Gray Mare, she ain't what she used to be, when Mary went to milk the cow.* A sound of a bosun's whistle. Women laughing. Someone repeatedly rang our doorbell. I heard my mother talking on the telephone. "Your inebriated sailors have littered my doorstep with the dregs of Scollay Square." There was a gloating panic in her voice that showed she enjoyed the drama of talking to Admiral De Stahl. "Sir," she shrilled, "you have compelled my husband to leave me alone and defenseless on Christmas Eve!" She ran into my bedroom. She hugged me. She said, "Oh, Bobby, it's such a comfort to have a man in the house." "I am not a man," I said. "I am a boy."

Boy—at that time this word had private associations for me; it meant weakness, outlawry, and yet was a status to be held on to. Boys were a sideline at my Brimmer School. The eight superior grades were limited to girls. In these grades, moreover, scholarship was made subservient to discipline, as if in contempt of the male's two idols: career and earning power. The school's tone, its *ton*, was a blend of the feminine and the military, a bulky reality governed in turn by stridency, smartness, and steadiness. The girls wore white jumpers, black skirts, stockings, and rectangular low-heeled shoes. An ex-West Pointer had been appointed to teach drill; and at the moment of my enrollment in Brimmer, our principal, the hitherto staid Miss Manice, was rumored to be showing signs of age and of undermining her position with the school trustees by girlish, quite out-of-character rhapsodies on the varsity basketball team, winner of two consecutive championships. The lower four grades, peaceful and lackadaisical, were, on the other hand, almost a separate establishment. Miss Manice regarded these "co-educated" classes with amused carelessness, allowed them to wear their ordinary clothes, and . . . carelessness, however, is incorrect—Miss Manice, in her administration of the lower school, showed the inconsistency and euphoria of a dual personality. Here she mysteriously shed all her Prussianism. She quoted Emerson and Mencken, disparaged the English, threatened to break with the past, and boldly coquetted with the nonmilitary American genius by displaying movies illustrating the careers of Edison and Ford. Favored lower-school teachers were permitted to use us as guinea pigs for mildly radical experiments. At Brimmer I *un*learned writing. The script that I had mastered with much agony at my first school was denounced as illegible: I was taught to print according to the Dalton Plan—to this day, as a result, I have to print even my two middle names and can only really *write* two words: "Robert" and "Lowell." Our instruction was subject to bewildering leaps. The usual fall performance by the Venetian glass blowers was followed by a tour of the Riverside Press. We heard Rudy Vallee, then heard spirituals sung by the Hampton Institute choir. We studied grammar from a formidable, un-reconstructed textbook written by Miss Manice's father. There, I battled with figures of speech and Greek terminology: *chiásmus*, the arrangement of corresponding words in opposite order; *brachyology*, the failure to repeat an element that is supplied in more or less modified form. Then all this pedantry was nullified by the introduction of a new textbook which proposed to lift the face of syntax by using game techniques and drawings.

Physical instruction in the lower school was irregular, spon-taneous, and had nothing of that swept and garnished barracks-room camaraderie of the older girls' gymnasium exercises. On the roof of our school building, there was an ugly concrete area that looked as if it had been intended for the top floor of a garage. Here we played tag, drew lines with chalk, and chose up sides for a kind of kids' soccer. On bright spring days, Mr. Newell, a sub-merged young man from Boston University, took us on botanical hikes through the Arboretum. He had an eye for inessentials—read us Martha Washington's poems at the Old State House, pointed out the roof of Brimmer School from the top of the Customs House, made us count the steps of the Bunker Hill Monument, and one rainy afternoon broke all rules by herding us into the South Boston Aquarium in order to give an un-healthy, eager little lecture on the sewage consumption of the conger eel. At last Miss Manice seemed to have gotten wind of Mr. Newell's moods. For an afternoon or two she herself served as his substitute. We were walked briskly past the houses of

Parkman and Dana, and assigned themes on the spunk of great persons who had overcome physical handicaps and risen to the top of the ladder. She talked about Elizabeth Barrett, Helen Keller; her pet theory, however, was that "women simply are not the equals of men." I can hear Miss Manice browbeating my white and sheepish father: "How can we stand up to you? Where are our Archimedeses, our Wagners, our Admiral Simses?" Miss Manice adored "Sir Walter Scott's *big bow-wow*," wished "Boston had banned the tubercular novels of the Brontës," and found nothing in the world "so simpatico" as the "strenuous life" lived by President Roosevelt. Yet the extravagant hysteria of Miss Manice's philanthropy meant nothing; Brimmer was entirely a woman's world—*dumkopf*, perhaps, but not in the least Quixotic, Brimmer was ruled by a woman's obvious aims and by her naïve pragmatism. The quality of this regime, an extension of my mother's, shone out in full glory at general assemblies or when I sat with a handful of other boys on the bleachers of Brimmer's new Manice Hall. In unison our big girls sang "America"; back and forth our Amazons tramped— their brows were wooden, their dress was black-and-white, and their columns followed standard-bearers holding up an American flag, the white flag of the Commonwealth of Massachusetts, and the green flag of Brimmer. At basketball games against Miss Lee's or Miss Winsor's, it was our upper-school champions who rushed onto the floor, as feline and fateful in their pace as lions. This was our own immediate and daily spectacle; in comparison such masculine displays as trips to battle cruisers commanded by comrades of my father seemed eyewash—the Navy moved in a realm as ghost-like and removed from my life as the elfin acrobatics of Douglas Fairbanks or Peter Pan. I wished I were an older girl. I wrote Santa Claus for a field-hockey stick. To be a boy at Brimmer was to be small, denied, and weak.

I was promised an improved future and taken on Sunday afternoon drives through the suburbs to inspect the boys' schools: Rivers, Dexter, Country Day. These expeditions were stratagems designed to give me a chance to know my father; Mother noisily stayed behind and amazed me by pretending that I had forbidden her to embark on "men's work." Father, however, seldom insisted, as he should have, on seeing the headmasters in person, yet he made an astonishing number of friends; his trust begat trust, and something about his silences encouraged junior masters and even school janitors to pour out small talk that was detrimental to rival institutions. At each new school, however, all this gossip was easily refuted; worse still, Mother was always ready to cross-examine Father in a manner that showed that she was asking questions for the purpose of giving, not of receiving, instruction; she expressed astonishment that a wishy-washy desire to be everything to everybody had robbed a naval man of any reliable concern for his son's welfare. Mother regarded the suburban schools as "gerrymandered" and middle-class; after Father had completed his round of inspections, she made her own follow-up visits and told Mr. Dexter and Mr. Rivers to their faces that she was looking for a "respectable stopgap" for her son's "three years between Brimmer and Saint Mark's." Saint Mark's was the boarding school for which I had been enrolled at birth, and was due to enter in 1930. I distrusted change, knew each school since kindergarten had been more constraining and punitive than its predecessor, and believed the suburban country day schools were flimsily disguised fronts for reformatories. With the egotistic, slightly paranoid apprehensions of an only child, I wondered what became of boys graduating from Brimmer's fourth grade, feared the worst—we were darkly imperiled, like some annual bevy of Athenian youths destined for the Minotaur. And to judge from my father, men between the ages of six and sixty did nothing but meet new challenges, take on heavier responsibilities, and lose all freedom to explode. A ray of hope in the far future was my white-haired Grandfather Winslow, whose unchecked commands and demands were always upsetting people for their own good—he was all I could ever want to be: the bad boy, the problem child, the commodore of his household.

When I entered Brimmer I was eight and a half. I was distracted in my studies, assented to whatever I was told, picked my nose whenever no one was watching, and worried our third-grade teacher by organizing creepy little gangs of boys at recess. I was girl-shy. Thick-witted, narcissistic, thuggish, I had the conventional pre-puberty character of my age; whenever a girl came near me, my whole person cringed like a sponge wrung dry by a clenching fist. I was less rather than more bookish than most children, but the girl I dreamed about continually had wheel-spoke black-and-gold eyelashes, double-length page-boy blond hair, a little apron, a bold, blunt face, a saucy, shivery way of talking, and . . . a paper body—she was the girl in John Tenniel's illustrations to *Alice in Wonderland.* The invigorating and symmetrical aplomb of my ideal Alice was soon enriched and nullified by a second face, when my father took me to the movies on the afternoon of one of Mother's headaches. An innocuous child's movie, the bloody, all-male *Beau Geste* had been chosen, but instead my father preferred a nostalgic tour of places he had enjoyed on shore leave. We went to the Majestic Theater, where he had first seen Pola Negri—where we, too, saw Pola Negri, sloppy-haired, slack, yawning, ravaged, unwashed . . . an anti Alice.

Our class belles, the Norton twins, Elie and Lindy, fell far short of the Nordic Alice and the foreign Pola. Their prettiness, rather fluffy, freckled, bashful, might have escaped notice if they had been one instead of two, and if their manners had been less good-humored, entertaining, and reliable. What mattered more than sex, athletics, or studies to us at Brimmer was our popularity; each child had an unwritten class-popularity poll inside his head. Everyone was ranked, and all day each of us mooned profoundly on his place, as it quivered like our blood or a compass needle with a thousand revisions. At nine character is, perhaps, too much *in ovo* for a child to be strongly disliked, but sitting next to Elie Norton, I glanced at her and gulped prestige from her popularity. We were not close at first; then nearness made us closer friends, for Elie had a gracious gift, the gift of gifts, I suppose, in a child: she forgot all about the popularity rank of the classmate she was talking to. No moron could have seemed so uncritical as this airy, chatty, intelligent child, the belle of our grade. She noticed my habit of cocking my head on one side, shutting my eyes, and driving like a bull through opposition at soccer—wishing to amuse without wounding, she called me Buffalo Bull. At General Assembly she would giggle with contented admiration at the upper-school girls in their penal black-and-white. "What bruisers, what beef-eaters! Dear girls," she would sigh, parroting her sophisticated mother, "we shall all become fodder for the governess classes before graduating from Brimmer." I felt that Elie Norton understood me better than anyone except my playful little Grandmother Winslow.

One morning there was a disaster. The boy behind me, no friend, had been tapping at my elbow for over a minute to catch my attention before I consented to look up and see a great golden puddle spreading toward me from under Elie's chair. I dared not speak, smile, or flicker an eyelash in her direction. She ran bawling from the classroom. Trying to catch every eye, yet avoid commitment, I gave sidelong and involuntary smirks at space. I began to feel manic with superiority to Elie Norton and struggled to swallow down a feeling of goaded hollowness—was I deserting her? Our teacher left us on our honor and ran down the hall. The class milled about in a hesitant hush. The girls blushed. The boys smirked. Miss Manice, the principal, appeared. She wore her whitish-brown dress with darker brown spots. Shimmering in the sunlight and chilling us, she stood mothlike in the middle of the classroom. We rushed to our seats. Miss Manice talked about how there was "nothing laughable about a malaise." She broke off. Her face took on an expression of invidious disgust. She was staring at me . . . In the absent-mindedness of my guilt and excitement, I had taken the nearest chair, the chair that Elie Norton had just left. "Lowell," Miss Manice shrieked, "are you going to soak there all morning like a bump on a log?"

When Elie Norton came back, there was really no break in her friendliness toward me, but there was something caved in, something crippled in the way I stood up to her and tried to answer her disengaged chatter. I thought about her all the time; seldom meeting her eyes now, I felt rich and raw in her nearness. I wanted passionately to stay on at Brimmer, and told my mother a fib one afternoon late in May of my last year. "Miss

Manice has begged me to stay on," I said, "and enter the fifth grade." Mother pointed out that there had never been a boy in the fifth grade. Contradicted, I grew excited. "If Miss Manice has begged me to stay," I said, "why can't I stay?" My voice rose, I beat on the floor with my open hands. Bored and bewildered, my mother went upstairs with a headache. "If you won't believe me," I shouted after her, "why don't you telephone Miss Manice or Mrs. Norton?"

Brimmer School was thrown open on sunny March and April afternoons and our teachers took us for strolls on the polite, landscaped walks of the Public Garden. There I'd loiter by the old iron fence and gape longingly across Charles Street at the historic Boston Common, a now largely wrong-side-of-the-tracks park. On the Common there were mossy bronze reliefs of Union soldiers, and a captured German tank filled with smelly wads of newspapers. Everywhere there were grit, litter, gangs of Irish, Negroes, Latins. On Sunday afternoons orators harangued about Sacco and Vanzetti, while others stood about heckling and blocking the sidewalks. Keen young policemen, looking for trouble, lolled on the benches. At nightfall a police lieutenant on horseback inspected the Common. In the Garden, however, there was only Officer Lever, a single white-haired and mustached dignitary, who had once been the doorman at the Union Club. He now looked more like a member of the club. "Lever's a man about town," my Grandfather Winslow would say. "Give him Harris tweeds and a glass of Scotch, and I'd take him for Cousin Herbert." Officer Lever was without thoughts or deeds, but Back Bay and Beacon Hill parents loved him just for being. No one asked this hollow and leonine King Log to be clairvoyant about children.

One day when the saucer magnolias were in bloom, I bloodied Bulldog Binney's nose against the pedestal of George Washington's statue in full view of Commonwealth Avenue; then I bloodied Dopey Dan Parker's nose; then I stood in the center of a sundial tulip bed and pelted a little enemy ring of third-graders with wet fertilizer. Officer Lever was telephoned.

Officer Lever telephoned my mother. In the presence of my mother and some thirty nurses and children, I was expelled from the Public Garden. I was such a bad boy, I was told, "that *even* Officer Lever had been forced to put his foot down."

New England winters are long. Sunday mornings are long. Ours were often made tedious by preparations for dinner guests. Mother would start airing at nine. Whenever the air grew so cold that it hurt, she closed the den windows; then we were attacked by sour kitchen odors winding up a clumsily rebuilt dumbwaiter shaft. The windows were again thrown open. We sat in an atmosphere of glacial purity and sacrifice. Our breath puffed whitely. Father and I wore sleeveless cashmere jerseys Mother had bought at Filene's Basement. A do-it-yourself book containing diagrams for the correct carving of roasts lay on the arm of Father's chair. At hand were Big Bill Tilden on tennis, Capablanca on chess, newspaper clippings from Sidney Lenz's bridge column, and a magnificent tome with photographs and some American's nationalist sketch of Sir Thomas Lipton's errors in the Cup Defender races. Father made little progress in these diversions, and yet one of the authors assured him that mastery demanded only willing readers who understood the meaning of English words. Throughout the winter a gray-whiteness glared through the single den window. In the apoplectic brick alley, a fire escape stood out against our sooty plank fence. Father believed that churchgoing was undignified for a naval man; his Sunday mornings were given to useful acts such as lettering his three new galvanized garbage cans: R.T.S. LOWELL—U.S.N.

Our Sunday dinner guests were often naval officers. Naval officers were not Mother's sort; very few people *were* her sort in those days, and that was her trouble—a very authentic, human, and plausible difficulty, which made Mother's life one of much suffering. She did not have the self-assurance for wide human experience; she needed to feel liked, admired, surrounded by the approved and familiar. Her haughtiness and chilliness came from apprehension. She would start talking like a *grande dame* and then stand back rigid and faltering, as if she feared being crushed by her own massively intimidating offensive.

Father's old Annapolis roommate, Commander Billy "Battleship Bilge" Harkness, was a frequent guest at Revere Street and one that always threw Mother off balance. Billy was a rough diamond. He made jokes about his "all-American family tree," and insisted that his name, pronounced H*a*rkness, should be spelled H*e*rkness. He came from Louisville, Kentucky, drank whiskey to "renew his Bourbon blood," and still spoke with an accent that sounded—so his colleagues said—"like a bran-fed stallion." Like my father, however, Commander Billy had entered the Naval Academy when he was a boy of fourteen; his Southernisms had been thoroughly rubbed away. He was teased for knowing nothing about race horses, mountaineers, folk ballads, hams, sour mash, tobacco . . . Kentucky colonels. Though hardly an officer and a gentleman in the old Virginian style, he was an unusual combination of clashing virtues: he had led his class in the sciences and yet was what his superiors called "a *mathmaddition* with the habit of command." He and my father, the youngest men in their class, had often been shipmates. Bilge's executive genius had given color and direction to Father's submissive tenacity. He drank like a fish at parties, but was a total abstainer on duty. With reason Commander Harkness had been voted the man most likely to make four-star admiral in the class of '07.

Billy called his wife Jimmy or Jeems, and had a rough friendly way of saying, "Oh, Jimmy's bright as a penny." Mrs. Harkness was an unpleasant rarity: she was the only naval officer's wife we knew who was also a college graduate. She had a flat flapper's figure, and hid her intelligence behind a nervous twitter of vulgarity and toadyism. "Charlotte," she would almost scream at Mother, "is this mirAGE, this MIRacle your *own* dining room!"

Then Mother might smile and answer in a distant, though cozy and amused, voice, "I usually manage to make myself pretty comfortable."

Mother's comfort was chic, romantic, impulsive. If her silver service shone, it shone with hectic perfection to rebuke the functional domesticity of naval wives. She had determined to make her ambiance beautiful and luxurious, but wanted neither her beauty nor her luxury unaccompanied. Beauty pursued too exclusively meant artistic fatuity of a kind made farcical by her Aunt Sarah Stark Winslow, a beauty too lofty and original ever to marry, a prima donna on the piano, too high-strung ever to give a public recital. Beauty alone meant the maudlin ignominy of having one's investments managed by interfering relatives. Luxury alone, on the other hand, meant for Mother the "paste and fool's-gold polish" that one met with in the foyer of the new Statler Hotel. She loathed the "undernourishment" of Professor Burckhard's Bauhaus modernism, yet in moments of pique she denounced our pompous Myers mahoganies as "suitable for politicians at the Bellevue Hotel." She kept a middle-of-the-road position, and much admired Italian pottery with its fresh peasant colors and puritanical, clean-cut lines. She was fond of saying, "The French *do* have taste," but spoke with a double-edged irony which implied the French, with no moral standards to support their finish, were really no better than naval yahoos. Mother's beautiful house was dignified by a rich veneer of the useful.

"I have always believed carving to be *the* gentlemanly talent," Mother used to proclaim. Father, faced with this opinion, pored over his book of instructions or read the section on table carving in the Encyclopaedia Britannica. Eventually he discovered among the innumerable small, specialized Boston "colleges" an establishment known as a carving school. Each Sunday from then on, he would sit silent and erudite before his roast. He blinked, grew white, looked winded, and wiped beads of perspiration from his eyebrows. His purpose was to reproduce stroke by stroke his last carving lesson, and he worked with all the formal rightness and particular error of some shaky experiment in remote control. He enjoyed quiet witticisms at the expense of his carving master—"a philosopher who gave himself all the airs of a Mahan!" He liked to pretend that the carving master had stated that "no two cuts are identical"; *ergo*, "each offers original problems for the *executioner*." Guests were appeased by Father's saying, "I am just a plebe at this guillotine. Have a hunk of my roast beef hash."

What angered Father was Mrs. Harkness's voice grown merciless with excitement, as she studied his hewing and hacking. She was sure to say something tactless about how Commander Billy was "a stingy artist at carving who could shave General Washington off the dollar bill."

Nothing could stop Commander Billy, that born carver, from reciting verses:

> *By carving my way*
> *I lived on my pay;*
> *This* reeward, *though small,*
> *Beats none at all . . .*

> *My carving paper-thin*
> *Can make a guinea hin,*
> *All giblets, bones, and skin,*
> *Canteen a party of tin.*

And I, furious for no immediate reason, blurted out, "Mother, how much does Grandfather Winslow have to fork up to pay for Daddy's carving school?"

These Sunday dinners with the Harknesses were always woundingly boisterous affairs. Father, unnaturally outgoing, would lead me forward and say, "Bilge, I want you to meet my first coupon from the bond of matrimony."

Commander Billy would answer, "So this is the range finder you are raising for future wars!" They would make me salute, stand at attention, stand at ease. "Angel-face," Billy would say to me, "you'll skipper a flivver."

"Jimmy" Harkness, of course, knew that Father was anxiously negotiating with Lever Brothers' Soap, and arranging for his resignation from the service, but nothing could prevent her from proposing time and again her "hens' toast to the drakes." Dragging Mother to her feet, Jimmy would scream, "To Bob and Bilgy's next battleship together!"

What Father and Commander Billy enjoyed talking about most was their class of '07. After dinner, the ladies would retire to the upstairs sitting room. As a special privilege I was allowed to remain at the table with the men. Over and over, they would talk about their ensigns' cruise around the world, escaping the "reeport," gunboating on the upper Yangtse during the Chinese Civil War, keeping sane and sanitary at Guantanamo, patrolling the Golfo del Papayo during the two-bit Nicaraguan Revolution, when water to wash in cost a dollar a barrel and was mostly "alkali and wrigglers." There were the class casualties: Holden and Holcomb drowned in a foundered launch off Hampton Roads; "Count" Bowditch, killed by the Moros and famous for his dying words to Commander Harkness: "I'm all right. Get on the job, Bilge."

They would speak about the terrible 1918 influenza epidemic, which had killed more of their classmates than all the skirmishes or even the world war. It was an honor, however, to belong to a class which included "Chips" Carpender, whose destroyer, the *Fanning*, was the only British or American warship to force a German submarine to break water and surrender. It was a feather in their caps that three of their classmates, Bellinger, Reade, and another, should have made the first transatlantic seaplane flight. They put their faith in teamwork, and Lindbergh's solo hop to Paris struck them as unprofessional, a newspaper trick. What made Father and Commander Billy mad as hornets was the mare's-nest made of naval administration by "deserving Democrats." Hadn't Secretary of State Bryan ordered their old battlewagon the *Idaho* to sail on a goodwill mission to Switzerland? "Bryan, Bryan, Bryan," Commander Billy would boom, "the pious swab had been told that Lake Geneva had annexed the Adriatic." Another "guy with false gills," Josephus

Daniels, "ordained by Divine Providence Secretary of the Navy," had refused to send Father and Billy to the war zone. "You are looking," Billy would declaim, "at martyrs in the famous victory of red tape. Our names are rubric." A man they had to take their hats off to was Theodore Roosevelt; Billy had been one of the lucky ensigns who had helped "escort the redoubtable Teddy to Panama." Perhaps because of his viciously inappropriate nickname, "Bilge," Commander Harkness always spoke with brutal facetiousness against the class *bilgers*, officers whose services were no longer required by the service. In more Epicurean moods, Bilge would announce that he "meant to accumulate a lot of dough from complacent, well-meaning, although misguided West Point officers gullible enough to bet their shirts on the Army football team."

"Let's have a squint at your *figger* and waterline, Bob," Billy would say. He'd admire Father's trim girth and smile familiarly at his bald spot. "Bob," he'd say, "you've maintained your displacement and silhouette unmodified, except for somewhat thinner top chafing gear."

Commander Billy's drinking was a "pain in the neck." He would take possession of Father's sacred "rhino" armchair, sprawl legs astraddle, make the tried-and-true framework groan, and crucify Mother by roaring out verbose toasts in what he called "me boozy cockney-h'Irish." He would drink to our cocktail shaker. " 'Ere's to the 'older of the Lowelldom nectar," he would bellow. "Hip, hip, hooray for Señor Martino, h'our h'old hipmate, and hhonorary member of '07—h'always h'able to navigate and never says dry." We never got through a visit without one of Billy's "Bottoms up to the 'ead of the Nation. "Ere's to herbgarden 'Erb." This was a swaggering dig at Herbert Hoover's notoriously correct, but insular, refusal to "imbibe anything more potent than Bromo-Seltzer" at a war-relief banquet in Brussels. Commander Billy's bulbous, water-on-the-brain forehead would glow and trickle with fury. Thinking of Herbert Hoover and Prohibition, he was unable to contain himself. "What a hick! We haven't been steered by a gentleman of parts since the redoubtable Teddy." He recited *wet* verses, such as the following inserted in Father's class book:

> *I tread the bridge with measured pace;*
> *Proud, yet anguish marks my face—*
> *What worries me like crushing sin*
> *Is where on the sea can I buy dry gin?*

In his cups, Commander Bilge acted as though he owned us. He looked like a human ash-heap. Cigar ashes buried the heraldic hedgehog on the ashtray beside him; cigar ashes spilled over and tarnished the golden stork embroidered on the table cover; cigar ashes littered his own shiny blue-black uniform. Greedily Mother's eyes would brighten, drop and brighten. She would say darkly, "I was brought up by Papá to be like a naval officer, to be ruthlessly neat."

Once Commander Billy sprawled back so recklessly that the armchair began to come apart. "You see, Charlotte," he said to Mother, "at the height of my *climacteric* I am breaking Bob's chair."

Harkness went in for tiresome, tasteless harangues against Amy Lowell, which he seemed to believe necessary for the enjoyment of his after-dinner cigar. He would point a stinking baby stogie at Mother. "'Ave a peteeto cigareeto, Charlotte," he would crow. "Puff on this whacking black cheroot, and you'll be a match for any reeking senorita *femme fatale* in the spiggotty republics, where blindness from Bob's bathtub hooch is still unknown. When you go up in smoke, Charlotte, remember the *Maine*. Remember Amy Lowell, that cigar-chawing, guffawing, senseless and meterless, multimillionheiress, heavyweight mascot on a floating fortress. Damn the *Patterns!* Full speed ahead on a cigareeto!"

Amy Lowell was never a welcome subject in our household. Of course, no one spoke disrespectfully of Miss Lowell. She had been so plucky, so *formidable, so beautifully and unblushingly immense*, as Henry James might have said. And yet, though irreproachably decent herself apparently, like Mae West she seemed to provoke indecorum in others. There was an anecdote which I was too young to understand: it was about Amy's getting her migraine headaches from being kept awake by the exercises of honeymooners in an adjacent New York hotel room. Amy's relatives would have liked to have honored her as a *personage*, a personage a little *outrée* perhaps, but perfectly within the natural order, like Amy's girlhood idol, the Duse. Or at least she might have been unambiguously tragic, short-lived, and a classic, like her last idol, John Keats. My parents piously made out a case for Miss Lowell's *Life of Keats*, which had killed its author and was so much more manly and intelligible than her poetry. Her poetry! But was *poetry* what one could call Amy's loud, bossy, unladylike *chinoiserie*—her free verse! For those that could understand it, her matter was, no doubt, blameless, but the effrontery of her manner made my parents relish Robert Frost's remark that "writing free verse was like playing tennis without a net."

Whenever Amy Lowell was mentioned, Mother bridled. Not distinguishing, not caring whether her relative was praised or criticized, she would say, "Amy had the courage of her convictions. She worked like a horse." Mother would conclude characteristically, "Amy did insist on doing everything the *hard* way. I think, perhaps, that her brother, the president of Harvard, did more for *other* people."

Often Father seemed to pay little attention to the conversation of his guests. He would smack his lips, and beam absentmindedly and sensuously, as if he were anticipating the comforts of civilian life—a perpetual shore leave in Hawaii. The Harknesses, however, cowed him. He would begin to feel out the subject of his resignation and observe in a wheedle obscurely loaded with significance that "certain *cits*, no brighter than you or I, pay income taxes as large as a captain's yearly salary."

Commander Harkness, unfortunately, was inclined to draw improper conclusions from such remarks. Disregarding the "romance of commerce," he would break out into ungentlemanly tirades against capital. "Yiss, old Bob," he would splutter, "when I consider the ungodly hoards garnered in by the insurance and broking gangs, it breaks my heart. Riches, reaches, overreaches! If Bob and I had half the swag that Harkness of Yale has just given Lowell of Harvard to build Georgian houses for Boston quee-eers with British accents!" He rumbled on morosely about retired naval officers "forced to live like coolies on their half pay. Hurrah for the Bull Moose Party!" he'd shout. "Hurrah for Boss Curley! Hurrah for the Bolshies!"

Nothing prevented Commander Billy from telling about his diplomatic mission in 1918, when "his eyes had seen the Bolshie on his native heath." He had been in Budapest "during the brief sway of Béla Kun-Whon. Béla was giving those Hunkyland moneybags and educators the boot into the arms of American philanthropy!"

Then Mother would say, hopefully, "Mamá always said that the *old* Hungarians *did* have taste. Billy, your reference to Budapest makes me heartsick for Europe. I am dying for Bob and Bobby's permission to spend next summer at Etretat."

Commander Billy Harkness specialized in verses like "The Croix de Guerre":

> *I toast the guy who, crossing over,*
> *   Abode in London for a year,*
> *The guy who to his wife and lover*
> *   Returned with conscience clean and clear,*
> *Who nightly prowling Piccadilly*
> *   Gave icy stares to floozies wild,*
> *And when approached said, "Bilgy Billy*
> *   Is mama's darling angel child—"*
> *Now he's the guy who rates the croy dee geer!*

Mother, however, smiled mildly. "Billy," she would say, "my cousin Admiral Ledyard Atkinson always has a twinkle in his eye when he asks after your *vers de société*."

"'Tommy' Atkins!" snorted Commander Billy. "I know Tommy better than my own mother. He's the first chapter in a book I'm secretly writing and leaving to the archives called *Wild Admirals I Have Known*. And now my bodily presence may no longer grace the inner sanctum of the Somerset Club, for fear Admiral Tommy'll assault me with five new chapters of his *Who Won the Battle of Jutland?*"

After the heat and push of Commander Billy, it was pleasant to sit in the shade of the Atkinsons. Cousin Ledyard wasn't exactly an admiral: he had been promoted to this rank during the world war and had soon reverted back to his old rank of captain. In 1926 he was approaching the retiring age and was still a captain. He was in charge of a big, stately, comfortable, but anomalous warship, which seldom sailed farther than hailing distance from its Charlestown drydock. He was himself stately and anomalous. Serene, silver-maned, and Spanish-looking, Cousin Ledyard liked full-dress receptions and crowed like a rooster in his cabin crowded with liveried Filipinos, Cuban trophies, and racks of experimental firearms, such as pepperbox pistols and a machine gun worked by electric batteries. He rattled off Spanish phrases, told firsthand adventure stories about service with Admiral Schley, and reminded one of some lands-man and diplomat commanding a galleon in Philip II's Armada. With his wife's money he had bought a motor launch which had a teak deck and a newfangled diesel engine. While his war-ship perpetually rode at anchor, Cousin Ledyard was forever hurrying about the harbor in his launch. "Oh, Led Atkinson has dash and his own speedboat!" This was about the best my father could bring himself to say for his relative. Commander Billy, himself a man of action, was more sympathetic: "Tommy's about a hundred horse-and-buggy power." Such a dinosaur, however, had little to offer an '07 Annapolis graduate. Billy's final judg-ment was that Cousin Ledyard knew less *trig* than a schoolgirl, had been promoted through mistaken identity or merely as "window dressing," and "was really plotting to put airplane carriers in square sails to stem the tide of our declining Yankee seamanship." Mother lost her enthusiasm for Captain Atkinson's stately chatter—he was "unable to tell one woman from another."

Cousin Ledyard's wife, a Schenectady Hoes distantly related to my still living Great-grandmother Myers, was twenty years younger than her husband. This made her a trying companion; with the energy of youth she demanded the homage due to age. Once, while playing in the Mattapoisett tennis tournament, she had said to her opponent, a woman her own age but married to a young husband, "I believe I'll call you Ruth; you can call me Mrs. Atkinson." She was a radiant Christian Scientist, darted about in smart serge suits and blouses frothing with lace. She filled her purse with Science literature and boasted without irony of "Boston's greatest grand organ" in the Christian Science mother temple on Huntington Avenue. As a girl, she had grown up with our Myers furniture. We dreaded Mrs. Atkinson's descents on Revere Street. She pooh-poohed Mother's taste, snorted at our ignorance of Myers family history, treated us as mere custodians of the Myers furniture, resented alterations, and had the memory of a mastodon for Cousin Cassie's associations with each piece. She wouldn't hear of my mother's distress from neuralgia, dismissed my asthma as "growing pains," and sought to rally us by gossiping about healers. She talked a prim, sprightly babble. Like many Christian Scientists, she had a bloodless, euphoric, inexhaustible interest in her own body. In a discourse which lasted from her first helping of roast beef through her second demitasse, Mrs. Atkinson held us spellbound by telling how her healer had "surprised and evaporated a cyst inside a sac" inside her "major intestine."

I can hear my father trying to explain his resignation from the Navy to Cousin Ledyard or Commander Billy. Talking with an unnatural and importunate jocularity, he would say, "Billy Boy, it's a darned shame, but this State of Massachusetts doesn't approve of the service using its franchise and voting by mail. I haven't had a chance to establish residence since our graduation in '07. I think I'll put my blues in mothballs and become a *cit* just to prove I still belong to the country. The directors of Lever Brothers' Soap in Cambridge . . . I guess for *cits*, Billy, they've really got something on the ball, because they tell me they want me on their team."

Or Father, Cousin Ledyard, Commander Billy, and I would

be sitting on after dinner at the dining-room table and talking man-to-man. Father would say, "I'm afraid I'll grow dull and drab with all this goldbricking ashore. I am too old for tennis singles, but too young for that confirmed state of senility known as golf."

Cousin Ledyard and Commander Billy would puff silently on their cigars. Then Father would try again and say pitifully, "I don't think a naval man can ever on the *outside* replace the friends he made during his years of wearing the blue."

Then Cousin Ledyard would give Father a polite, funereal look and say, "Speaking of golf, Bob, you've hit me below the belt. I've been flubbing away at the game for thirty years without breaking ninety."

Commander Billy was blunter. He would chaff Father about becoming a "beachcomber" or "purser for the Republican junior chamber of commerce." He would pretend that Father was in danger of being jailed for evading taxes to support "Uncle Sam's circus." *Circus* was Commander Billy's slang for the Navy. The word reminded him of a comparison, and once he stood up from the table and bellowed solemnly: "Oyez, oyez! Bob Lowell, our bright boy, our class baby, is now on a par with 'Rattle-Ass Rats' Richardson, who resigned from us to become press agent for Sells-Floto Circus, and who writes me: 'Bilgy dear—Beating the drum ahead of the elephants and the spangled folk, I often wonder why I run into so few of my classmates.' "

Those dinners, those apologies! Perhaps I exaggerate their embarrassment because they hover so grayly in recollection and seem to anticipate ominously my father's downhill progress as a civilian and Bostonian. It was to be expected, I suppose, that Father should be in irons for a year or two, while becoming detached from his old comrades and interests, while waiting for the new life.

I used to sit through the Sunday dinners absorbing cold and anxiety from the table. I imagined myself hemmed in by our new, inherited Victorian Myers furniture. In the bleak Revere Street dining room, none of these pieces had at all that air of unhurried condescension that had been theirs behind the summery veils of tissue paper in Cousin Cassie Julian-James's memorial volume. Here, table, highboy, chairs, and screen—mahogany, cherry, teak—looked nervous and disproportioned. They seemed to wince, touch elbows, shift from foot to foot. High above the highboy, our gold National Eagle stooped forward, plastery and doddering. The Sheffield silver-plate urns, more precious than solid sterling, peeled; the bodies of the heraldic mermaids on the Mason-Myers crest blushed a metallic copper tan. In the harsh New England light, the bronze sphinxes supporting our sideboard looked as though manufactured in Grand Rapids. All too clearly, no one had worried about synchronizing the grandfather clock's minutes, days, and months with its mellow old Dutch seascape-painted discs for showing the phases of the moon. The stricken but still striking gong made sounds like steam banging through pipes. Colonel Myers's monumental Tibetan screen had been impiously shortened to fit it for a low Yankee ceiling. And now, rough and gawky, like some Hindu water buffalo killed in mid-rush but still alive with mad momentum, the screen hulked over us . . . and hid the pantry sink.

Our real blue-ribbon-winning *bête noir* was of course the portrait of Cousin Cassie's father, Mordecai Myers's fourth and most illustrious son: Colonel Theodorus Bailey Myers. The Colonel, like half of our new portraits, was merely a collateral relation; though he was really as close to us as James Russell Lowell, no one called the Colonel "great-grand-uncle," and Mother playfully pretended that her mind was overstrained by having to remember his full name, rank, and connection. In the portrait, Colonel Theodorus wore a black coat and gray trousers, an obsequiously conservative costume which one associated with undertakers and the musicians at Symphony Hall. His spats were pearl-gray plush with pearl buttons. His mustache might have been modeled on the mustache of a bartender in a Western. The majestic Tibetan screen enclosed him as though he were an ancestor-god from Lhasa, a blasphemous yet bogus attitude. Mr. Myers's colonel's tabs were crudely stitched to a civilian coat; his

New York Yacht Club button glowed like a carnation; his vainglorious picture frame was a foot and a half wide. Forever, his right hand hovered over a glass dome that covered a model locomotive. He was vaguely Middle Eastern and waiting. A lady in Mother's sewing circle had pertly interpreted this portrait as "King Solomon about to receive the Queen of Sheba's shares in the Boston and Albany Railroad." Gone now was the Colonel's place of honor at Cousin Cassie's Washington mansion; gone was his charming satire on the belles of 1850, entitled *Nothing to Wear*, which had once been quoted "throughout the length and breadth of the land as generally as was Bret Harte's *Heathen Chinee*"; gone was his priceless collection of autographed letters of *all* the Signers of the Declaration of Independence—he had said once, "My letters will be my tombstone." Colonel Theodorus Bailey Myers had never been a New Englander. His family tree reached to no obscure Somersetshire yeoman named Winslowe or Lowle. He had never even, like his father, Mordecai, gloried in a scarlet War of 1812 waistcoat. His portrait was an indifferent example from a dull, bad period. The Colonel's only son had sheepishly changed his name from Mason-Myers to Myers-Mason.

Waiting for dinner to end and for the guests to leave, I used to lean forward on my elbows, support each cheekbone with a thumb, and make my fingers meet in a clumsy Gothic arch across my forehead. I would stare through this arch and try to make life stop. Out in the alley the sun shone irreverently on our three garbage cans lettered: R.T.S. LOWELL—U.S.N. When I shut my eyes to stop the sun, I saw first an orange disc, then a red disc, then the portrait of Major Myers apotheosized, as it were, by the sunlight lighting the blood smear of his scarlet waistcoat. Still, there was no *coup de théatre* about the Major as he looked down on us with his portly young man's face of a comfortable upper New York State patroon and the friend of Robert Livingston and Martin Van Buren. Great-great-grandfather Myers had never frowned down in judgment on a Salem witch. There was no allegory in his eyes, no *Mayflower*. Instead, he looked peacefully at his sideboard, his cut-glass decanters, his cellaret—the worldly bosom of the Mason-Myers mermaid engraved on a silver-plated urn. If he could have spoken, Mordecai would have said, "My children, my blood, accept graciously the loot of your inheritance. We are all dealers in used furniture."

The man who seems in my memory to sit under old Mordecai's portrait is not my father but Commander Billy— *the* commander after Father had thrown in his commission. There Billy would sit glowing, perspiring, bragging. Despite his rowdiness, he even then breathed the power that would make him a vice-admiral and hero in World War II. I can hear him boasting in lofty language of how he had stood up for democracy in the day of Lenin and Béla Kun; of how he "practiced the sport of kings" (i.e., commanded a destroyer) and combed the Mediterranean, Adriatic, and Black Seas like a gypsy—seldom knowing what admiral he served under or where his next meal or load of fuel oil was coming from.

It always vexed the Commander, however, to think of the strings that had been pulled to have Father transferred from Washington to Boston. He would ask Mother, "Why in God's name should a man with Bob's brilliant cerebellum go and mess up his record by actually *begging* for that impotent field nigger's job of second-in-command at the defunct Boston Yard!"

I would squirm. I dared not look up because I knew that the Commander abhorred Mother's dominion over my father, thought my asthma, supposedly brought on by the miasmal damp of Washington, a myth, and considered our final flight to Boston a scandal.

My mother, on the other hand, would talk back sharply and explain to Billy that there was nothing second-string about the Boston Yard except its commandant, Admiral De Stahl, who had gone into a frenzy when he learned that my parents, supposed to live at the Naval Yard, had set themselves up without his permission at 91 Revere Street. The Admiral had *commanded* Father to reside at the Yard, but Mother had bravely and stubbornly held on at Revere Street.

"A really great person," she would say, "knows how to be courteous to his superiors."

Then Commander Harkness would throw up his hands in despair and make a long buffoonish speech. "Would you believe it?" he'd say. "De Stahl, the anile slob, would make Bob Lowell sleep seven nights a week and twice on Sundays in that venerable twenty-room pile provided for his third-in-command at the Yard. 'Bobby, me boy,' the Man says, 'henceforth I will that you sleep wifeless. You're to push your beauteous mug into me boudoir each night at ten-thirty and each morn at six. And don't mind me laying to alongside the Missus De Stahl,' the old boy squeaks; 'we're just two oldsters as weak as babies. But Robbie boy,' he says, 'don't let me hear of you hanging on your telephone wire and bending off the ear of that forsaken Frau of yours sojourning on Revere Street. I might have to phone you in a hurry, if I should happen to have me stroke.' "

Taking hold of the table with both hands, the Commander tilted his chair backward and gaped down at me with sorrowing Gargantuan wonder: "I know why Young Bob is an only child."

[1956]

Near the Unbalanced Aquarium

One morning in July 1954 I sat in my bedroom on the third floor of the Payne-Whitney Clinic of New York Hospital, trying as usual to get my picture of myself straight. I was recovering from a violent manic seizure, an attack of pathological enthusiasm. What I saw were the blind white bricks of other parts of the hospital rising in my window. Down the corridor, almost a city block away, I heard the elevator jar shut and hum like a kettle as it soared to the top floor with its second and last allotment of sixteen of my fellow patients going to Occupational Therapy. My mind, somewhat literary and somewhat muscle-bound, hunted for the clue to the right picture of itself. In my distraction, the walls of the hospital seemed to change shape like limp white clouds. I thought I saw a hard enameled wedding cake, and beside it, holding the blunt silver knife of the ritual, stood the tall white stone bride—my mother. Her wedding appeared now less as a day in the real past than as a photograph.

The hospital was a blending of the latest and laciest Gothic-and-skyscraper styles of the twenties and thirties—arch, groin, coign, and stainless steel. I thought for a moment of that island in the Seine, a little Manhattan with river water on both sides, the island of King Louis's Sainte-Chapelle, all heraldry and color and all innocent, built to house a thorn! Under its veneer of fragile white bricks, how merely geometrical this New York hospital was, how securely skeletonized with indestructible steel, how purely and puritanically confined to its office of cures. Counting the tiers of metal-framed windows, I myself was as if building this hospital like a child, brick by brick or block by block.

The mornings were long because, after breakfast and bed-making and an informal lounging and television-news period, we were all expected to walk for some forty minutes in the court-yard. It was a formal, flowerless place covered with bright gray octagonal paving stones, like some unaccountably secluded and clean French *place*. Two by two, we walked round and round, and without any props or screens or diverting games, we tried to make conversation. It was thought uncooperative and morbid if we walked with another man. The women were terrible to me. Some were concave and depressed, some worried endlessly about their doctors' feelings and remarks, some flattered, some flirted, some made fierce well-expressed sarcastic thrusts—they all talked. Distant, thorny, horny, absentminded, ineptly polite, vacantly rude, I walked with the ladies. They were hurt, and I was hurt. The men were almost as bad. I had my cronies, but I had soon exhausted their novelty, which mattered little to me. What hurt me was that in a matter of minutes I used up any strength I had to be new or fresh or even there. Then there were the student nurses, crisp-fronted, pageboy bobbed, pale-blue-denim bloused, reading new *Herald Tribunes* and eyeing watchfully the strategic angles of the courtyard. They were ready to engage me gently and bring me back, if ever I dawdled into single file or sat down by myself on a bench. The unflowering shrubbery was healthily a full green, the leaves were all there, and in spite of the dusty dreariness of midsummer New York all about us, it all seemed cool, spontaneous, and adequate. That's how all the other patients seemed. And a great iron gate, some twenty feet high, protected us from the city and living. The gate was just a little bit prettier and more ornate than use demanded. It was really locked, and a patient would have had to be an athlete or a thief to scale it. Beyond it we could see the blinding blue sparkle of the East River. Often, an orange tugboat was moored a few feet away from us. It had a swollen fleece-and-rawhide buffer on its prow. As if begging admission to our asylum, the boat kept moving with chafing sounds toward the concrete embankment.

My mind moved through the pictures of conscience and remained in its recollections, weightless, floating. On a sallow sheet of onionskin paper, whose semitransparency half revealed and half concealed the pink pads of my fingers, I tried to write some lines of verse:

> *In Boston the Hancock Life Insurance Building's beacon*
> *   flared*
> *Foul weather, Father, as far as the Charlestown Naval Yard.*
> *And almost warmed . . .*

On the nights when Mother was dying all alone at that little private hospital in Rapallo, the needle of the Hancock Life Insurance Building was flashing storm warnings. As I took the taxi to the Boston airport, I watched the angry discouraging red lights go on and off. Far to my left, men were working with blowtorches on the blistered gray of old battleships scrapped at the Charlestown Naval Yard, Father's old hunting ground. This was the last place he had found employment worthy of his optimistic esprit de corps and his solid grounding in higher mathematics. In New Hampshire, the White Mountains would have been freezing. And at our family cemetery in Dunbarton the black brook, the pruned fir trunks, the iron spear fence, and the memorial slates would have been turning blacker. The motto on Father's family crest would still say *Occasionem Cognosce*, as he lay buried under his ostentatiously recent unacclimatized tombstone, the single Lowell among some twenty-five Starks and Winslows. And as the moonlight and the burning cold illuminated the carved names of Father's in-laws, one might have thought they were protesting Father's right to hold a single precious inch of the overcrowded soil, unless he produced a dead wife, a Winslow.

I arrived at Rapallo half an hour after Mother's death.* On the next morning, the hospital where she died was a firm and tropical scene from Cézanne: sunlight rustled through the watery plucked pines, and streaked the verticals of a Riviera villa above the Mare Ligure. Mother lay looking through the blacks and greens and tans and flashings from her window. Her face was too formed and fresh to seem asleep. There was a bruise the size of an earlobe over her right eye. The nurse who had tended Mother during her ten days' dying stood at the bed's head. She was a great gray woman and wore glasses whose diaphanous blue frames were held together by a hairpin. With a flourish, she had just pulled aside the sheet that covered Mother's face, and now she looked daggers at the body as if death were some sulky animal or child who only needed to be frightened. We stood with tears running down our faces, and the nurse talked to me for an hour and a half in a patois that even Italians would have had difficulty in understanding. She was telling me everything she could remember about Mother. For ten minures she might just as well have been imitating water breaking on the beach, but Mother was alive in the Italian words. I heard how Mother thought she was still at her hotel and wanted to go walking, and said she was only suffering from a little indigestion, and wanted to open both French windows and thoroughly air her bedroom each morning while the bed was still unmade, and how she kept trying to heal the hemorrhage in her brain by calling for her twenty little jars and bottles with their pink plastic covers, and kept dabbing her temples with creams and washes, and felt guilty because she wasn't allowed to take her quick cold bath in the morning and her hot aromatic bath before dinner. She kept asking about Bob and Bobby. "I have never been sick in my life. *Nulla malettia mai! Nulla malettia mai!*" And the nurse went out. "*Qua insieme per sempre.*" She closed the door, and left me in the room.

* Charlotte Lowell died on February 14, 1954; her husband had died in 1950.

That afternoon I sat drinking a Cinzano with Mother's doctor. He showed me a copy of Ezra Pound's *Jefferson and/or Mussolini*, which the author had personally signed with an ideogram and the quotation *"Non . . . como bruti."*

At the Italian funeral, I did everything that Father could have desired. I met the Rapallo English colony, Mother's brief acquaintances. I made arrangements at the simple red-brick English chapel, and engaged a sober Church of England clergyman. Then I went to Genoa and bought Mother a black-and-gold baroque casket that would have been suitable for burying her hero Napoleon at Les Invalides. It wasn't disrespect or even impatience that allowed me to permit the undertakers to take advantage of my faulty knowledge of Italian and Italian values and to overcharge me and to make an ugly and tasteless error. They misspelled Mother's name on her coffin as *Lovel*. While alive, Mother had made a point of spelling out her name letter by letter for identification. I could almost hear her voice correcting the workmen: "I am Mrs. Robert Lowell of One Seventy Marlborough Street, Boston, L, O, W, E, *double* L."

On the Sunday morning when we sailed, the whole shoreline of the Golfo di Genova was breaking into fiery flower. A crazy Piedmontese raced about us in a particolored sea sled, whose outboard motor was of course unmuffled. Our little liner was already doing twenty knots an hour, but the sea sled cut figure-eights across our bow. Mother, permanently sealed in her coffin, lay in the hold. She was solitary, just as formerly when she took her long walks by the Atlantic at Mattapoisett in September, "the best season of the year," after the summer people had gone. She shone in her bridal tinfoil and hurried homeward with open arms to her husband lying under the White Mountains.

When Mother died, I began to feel tireless, madly sanguine, menaced, and menacing. I entered the Payne-Whitney Clinic for "all those afflicted in mind." One night I sat in the mixed lounge, and enjoyed the new calm which I had been acquiring with much cunning during the few days since my entrance. I remember coining and pondering for several minutes such phrases as "the Art of Detachment," "Off-handed Involvement," and "Urbanity: Key to the Tactics of Self-Control." But the old menacing hilarity was growing in me. I saw Anna and her nurse walk into our lounge. Anna, a patient from a floor for more extreme cases, was visiting our floor for the evening. I knew that the evening would soon be over, that the visitor would probably not return to us, and that I had but a short time to make my impression on her. Anna towered over the piano, and pounded snatches of Mozart sonatas which she half remembered and murdered. Her figure, a Russian ballerina's or Anna Karenina's, was emphasized and *illuminated,* as it were, by an embroidered Middle European blouse that fitted her with the creaseless, burnished, curved tightness of a medieval breastplate. I throbbed to the music and the musician. I began to talk aimlessly and loudly to the room at large. I discussed the solution to a problem that had been bothering me about the unmanly smallness of the suits of armor that I had seen "tilting" at the Metropolitan Museum. "Don't you see?" I said, and pointed to Anna. "The armor was made for *Amazons!*" But no one took up my lead. I began to extol my tone deafness; it was, I insisted, a providential flaw, an auditory fish weir that screened out irrelevant sonority. I made defiant adulatory remarks on Anna's touch. Nobody paid any attention to me.

Roger, an Oberlin undergraduate and fellow patient, sat beside Anna on the piano bench. He was small. His dark hair matched his black-flannel Brooks Brothers suit; his blue-black eyes matched his blue-black necktie. He wore a light cashmere sweater that had been knitted for him by his mother, and his yellow woolen socks had been imported from the Shetlands. Roger talked to Anna with a persuasive shyness. Occasionally, he would stand up and play little beginner's pieces for her. He explained that these pieces were taken from an exercise book composed by Béla Bartók in protest against the usual, unintelligibly tasteless examples used by teachers. Anna giggled with incredulous admiration as Roger insisted that the clinic's music instructor could easily teach her to read more skillfully. Suddenly I felt compelled to make a derisive joke, and I announced

cryptically and untruly that Rubinstein had declared the eye
was of course the source of all evil for a virtuoso. "If the eye
offends thee, pluck it out." No one understood my humor. I
grew red and confused. The air in the room began to tighten
around me. I felt as if I were squatting on the bottom of a huge
laboratory bottle and trying to push out the black rubber stopper
before I stifled. Roger sat like a rubber stopper in his black suit.
Suddenly I felt I could clear the air by taking hold of Roger's
ankles and pulling him off his chair. By some crisscross of logic,
I reasoned that my cruel boorishness would be an act of self-
sacrifice. I would be bowing out of the picture, and throwing
Roger into the arms of Anna. Without warning, but without
lowering my eyes from Anna's splendid breastplate blouse, I
seized Roger's yellow ankles and pulled. Roger sat on the floor
with tears in his eyes. A sigh of surprised revulsion went round
the room. I assumed a hurt, fatherly expression, but all at once
I felt eased and sympathetic with everyone.

When the head nurse came gliding into the lounge, I pretended that I was a white-gloved policeman who was directing
traffic. I held up my open hands and said, "No roughage,
Madam; just innocent merriment!" Roger was getting to his
feet; I made a stop signal in his direction. In a purring, pompous
James Michael Curley voice, I said, "Later, he will thank me."
The head nurse, looking bored and tolerant, led me away to
watch the Liberace program in the men's television parlor. I was
left unpunished. But next morning, while I was weighing in and
"purifying" myself in the cold shower, I sang

> *Rex tremendae majestatis*
> *qui salvandos salvas gratis*

at the top of my lungs and to a melody of my own devising. Like
the catbird, who will sometimes "interrupt its sweetest song by
a perfect imitation of some harsh cry such as that of the great
crested flycatcher, the squawk of a hen, the cry of a lost chicken,
or the spitting of a cat," I blended the lonely tenor of some
fourteenth-century Flemish monk to bars of "Yankee Doodle,"

and the *mmm-mmm* of the padlocked Papageno. I was then transferred to a new floor, where the patients were deprived of their belts, pajama cords, and shoestrings. We were not allowed to carry matches, and had to request the attendants to light our cigarettes. For holding up my trousers, I invented an inefficient, stringless method which I considered picturesque and called Malayan. Each morning before breakfast, I lay naked to the waist in my knotted Malayan pajamas and received the first of my round-the-clock injections of chloropromazine: left shoulder, right shoulder, right buttock, left buttock. My blood became like melted lead. I could hardly swallow my breakfast, because I so dreaded the weighted bending down that would be necessary for making my bed. And the rational exigencies of bedmaking were more upsetting than the physical. I wallowed through badminton doubles, as though I were a diver in the full billowings of his equipment on the bottom of the sea. I sat gaping through Scrabble games, unable to form the simplest word; I had to be prompted by a nurse, and even then couldn't make any sense of the words the nurse had formed for me. I watched the Giants play the Brooklyn Dodgers on television.

Prince Scharnhorst, the only other patient watching the game, was a pundit and could have written an article for the encyclopedia on each batter's technique and the type of pitching that had some chance of outwitting him. The Prince understood catcher Roy Campanella's signals to the Dodger pitchers, and criticized Campanella's strategy sympathetically but with the authority of an equal. My head ached and I couldn't keep count of the balls and strikes for longer than a single flash on the screen. I went back to my bedroom and wound the window open to its maximum six inches. Below me, patients circled in twos over the paving stones of the courtyard. I let my glasses drop. How freely they glittered through the air for almost a minute! They shattered on the stones. Then everyone in the courtyard came crowding and thrusting their heads forward over my glasses, as though I had been scattering corn for pigeons. I felt my languor lift and then descend again.

I already seemed to weigh a thousand pounds because of my

drug, and now I blundered about, nearly blind from myopia. But my nervous system vibrated joyfully when I felt the cool air brushing directly on my eyeballs. And I was reborn each time I saw my blurred, now unspectacled, now unprofessorial face in the mirror. Yet all this time I would catch myself asking whining questions. "Why don't I die, die?" I quizzed my face of suicide in the mirror; but the body's warm, unawed breath befogged the face with a dilatory inertia. I said, "My dreams at night are so intoxicating to me that I am willing to put on the nothingness of sleep. My dreams in the morning are so intoxicating to me that I am willing to go on living." Even now I can sometimes hear those two sentences repeating themselves over and over and over. I say them with a chant-like yawn, and feel vague, shining, girlish, like Perdita, or one of the many willowy allegoric voices in Blake's *Prophetic Books.*

"For my dreams, I will endure the day; I will suffer the refreshment of sleep." In one's teens these words, perhaps, would have sealed a Faustian compact. Waking, I suspected that my whole soul and its thousands of spiritual fibers, immaterial ganglia, apprehensive antennae, psychic radar, and so on, had been bruised by a rubber hose. In the presence of persons, I was ajar. But in my dreams I was like one of Michelangelo's burly ideal statues that can be rolled downhill without injury.

Three days after Father's death, the Beverly Farms house almost gave the impression of having once been lived in. Its rooms, open, eviscerated, empty, and intimate, were rooms restored to "period." Perhaps this vacancy, this on-tiptoe air, came from my knowing that everything about me had waited three days for Father's return to us from the undertaker. But it was obvious that my parents had lived at Beverly Farms less than eighteen months. Mother had bought the Beverly Farms house as a compensation for Father, whose ten years' dream of moving from Boston to Puget Sound had been destroyed by a second heart attack. Fearfully, she had looked out of her windows at Beverly Farms, as though she were looking from the windows of a train that was drawing into one station beyond her destination.

From the beginning, she had lived with an eye cocked toward Boston. She wanted to be in Boston, and dreaded Boston's mockery of this new house, which was so transparently a sheepish toy house for Father.

The third day after Father's death was an overcast day. His little ship's-cabin-sized bedroom, the blue bedroom, lay overlooking the sloping garden, the huge, smooth boulder, the gunmetal railroad tracks showing through scarlet sumac. Whitecaps on a patch of black Atlantic appeared through the lopped tops of garden trees, chalk writing on a blackboard. The blueness of the bedroom had been achieved by Mother through an accumulation of inconspicuous touches: blue lines on the top of the bedspread, blue fringe on the curtains, blue velvet straps on the Chinese sandals, a blue kimono. Blue symbolized baths twice a day, a platonic virility, the sea—*Thalassa!* But the bedroom was ninety-nine one-hundredths white of course. Elbow grease, an explosive simplicity—the floor's old broad softwood boards seemed sandblasted into cleanliness. On a white enamel bedside table, and besides a glass lamp with a lace lampshade, lay Volume I of Lafcadio Hearn's *Glimpses of Unfamiliar Japan.* The cover, olive green ornamented with silver bamboo stalks in leaf, was as wrinkled and punished and discolored as an old schoolbook. On the flyleaf my Grandmother Lowell had written: "Rob, from Mother. September 1908." The book had originally been given her by someone named Alice on January 23, 1908. This, too, was noted down. On another page, she had written: "This book had hard usage on the Yangtse River, China, when R.T.S.L. was on the gunboat *Villalobos*. It was left under an open porthole in a storm." This inscription was unlike the ones written by Mother's family the Winslows: it was correctly spelled, and made no attempt to amuse or improve.

Mother's bedroom was a better place. It was four times as large as Father's. Sensibly, world-acceptingly, it overlooked a driveway and faced away from the ocean. Here were objects which proclaimed admirable pleasures: an adjacent, pavilion-like bathroom, a window seat, a boudoir table, lending-library whodunits with plastic covers, an electric blanket; and, perhaps crowning all in its idyllic symbolism, a hot-water bottle, silver, engraved like an old-fashioned hip flask with a family crest and covered by a loosely woven pink woolen slip which Mother had knitted herself. Mother's double bed, her tall bureau, her short bureau, her boudoir table bench, her telephone stand and stool, her rocker, her hearth broom, and her breakfast tray with folding legs all matched, were painted a mustard yellow ornamented with wheels and ripplings of green and gold. Alas, her innocent breakfasts in bed—*ubi sunt!*

On the third day, one room, as though it were a person, seemed to experience Father's absence. This was the "den." All its soft, easeful, chilly leather surfaces glistened and mourned: the brown oak-and-iron escritoire brought back from Palermo by Grandfather Winslow; the brown rug, lampshades, and curtains; the brown wood of paper knife, chairs, and ship's-clock base; the helmsman's-wheel frame of the ship's clock, a hollow brass rod that was a combination poker and bellows. His ivory slide rule protruded from a pigeonhole of the desk, where it rested in its leather case, as handy as some more warlike householder's holstered revolver.

Also on the desk was a red-and-gold portfolio which held pitilessly complete and clear records of Father's interests since 1945. Here was the twenty-page booklet of scaled diagrams executed in inks of five colors, a page to each room at Beverly Farms. The position and measurements of each sofa, bed, table, chair, etc., were given. Father had spent a cheerful month devising and correcting this booklet; it had proved a godsend to the movers. Here was a similar booklet filled with hypothetical alternative plans for a rearrangement of the Salem Museum's display cases. These furniture-position booklets were derivative art; Father had learned how to make them from his cousin A. Lawrence Lowell. When Lawrence Lowell was elected president of Harvard in 1908, he packed up the furniture in his Marlborough Street house and moved to the Yard. He was a man who always landed on his feet, and who looked with modest foresight into the sands of time, and before moving he had accordingly drawn up a furniture-position plan of his old house. In 1936 he had returned to Marlborough Street—an ex-president, a widower, an octogenarian, and an automobilist who had just been deprived of his license for reckless driving. But not a piece of the old furniture had been lost; the position plans were consulted and each piece unalterably reoccupied its old position. Here finally were Father's estimates and drawings for the installation of the new Sears, Roebuck furnace, which by its low fuel consumption was to pay for itself in ten years. Missing only were the innumerable graphs on which Father had plotted out catastrophic systems for his private investments in those years before the war when he had been an investment counsel and his own chief customer.

I was the only person Mother permitted to lift the lid of the casket. Father was there. He wore his best sport coat—pink, at ease, obedient! Not a twist or a grimace recalled those unprecedented last words spoken to Mother as he died: "I feel awful." And it was right that he should have the slight over-ruddiness so characteristic of his last summer. He looked entirely alive, or as he used to say, *W & H*: Well and Happy. Impossible to believe that if I had pressed a hand to his brow to see if it were hectic, I would have touched the *cold thing!* There were flowers; not too many. To one side of the casket, someone had accidentally left Admiral K—'s framed photograph. In the Navy, officers are listed according to rank and age; Father and K— had once been the only officers in their class who were not outranked by younger men. And now in the photograph Admiral K—, who had risen from glory to glory, stood on his Mediterranean flagship holding his binoculars half-raised to his eyes, and seemed to squint through the sun's dazzling, difficult glare into what were either folds of an awning or thirty uniforms on hangers. The picture was inscribed: "To my old friend, classmate + shipmate 'Bob' Lowell."

Occupational Therapy, or O.T., was held in a suite of rooms on the top floor. It was a sunny, improving world; and here, unable to "think" with my hands, I spent a daily hour of embarrassed anguish. Here for weeks I saw my abandoned pine-cone basket lying on the pile for waste materials. And as it sank under sawdust and shavings, it seemed to protest the pains Mr. Kemper, our instructor, had once taken to warp, to soak, to reweave, to rescue it. And there in an old cigar box I saw my materially expensive, massively hideous silver ring, which Mr. Kemper had mostly forged and then capped off with an intaglio of an Iroquis corn shock ripening under the arrowy rays of a crescent moon. And as I stood there, obsequious, scornful, fearful, and fierce, Mr. Kemper would come to me in his mild, beach-colored smock. He was a shy, precise man who, blushing as if at his own presumption, would tell gentle, instructive anecdotes so as to avoid crude, outright answers to my haphazard questions on techniques. He was used to the impatience of patients; but he seemed stunned when he discovered that my polite, hesitant, often erratically detailed questions seldom implied even an appearance of attending to his answers. I would interrupt in midsentence with new questions, or drive deafly, blindly, marringly into my work.

At Occupational Therapy there was the room of the loom and the room of the potter's wheels. I spent several mornings in each, inquiring. But when the loom or the wheel was put in my hands, I excused myself by explaining Charles Collingwood's theory that art could never be merely craft, "despite all the attacks made on inspiration by our friends the anti-romantic critics." I pretended that my doctor had given me permission to read *Kim*.

But in the end, of course, I gravitated to young Ms. Rodgers's painting class, which was held in a long light room whose windows surveyed the East River and its shipping. For a few mornings, I asked questions about method, drew cones, and tried to memorize the complementary colors; then, wearying, I began to shout against representation, the laws of perspective, and the Hollywoodization of America. I declaimed paragraphs from a brochure of Cézanne written by Meyer Schapiro. I praised that "plodding dispositional ferocity" which had ruined Cézanne's *White Monk* but later made possible the serene and triumphant *Madame Cézanne Tête Bassé*. Prince Scharnhorst was finishing a delicate and architecturally correct nocturne of the U.N. building. I enraged him by calling his picture an "impromptu Whistler," and sneered pityingly at his "deployment of mass." I began my life-size copy of *Madame Cézanne dans la Serre*; obscenely tried to add the nude male bodies of *Les Bagneurs* as background, and then, prompted by Ms. Rodgers, consented to content myself with *Les Grandes Bagneuses*. Ms. Rodgers mixed my paints, measured my proportions, steered my brush. Halfway through, I began to experiment with late van Gogh and Jackson Pollock palate-knife techniques. My picture was finally almost a likeness, almost attractive, but in a moment of vandalistic *Freiheit*, I plastered a Dali mustache on Madame Cézanne and made my picture hideous. Then I discovered Paul Klee. Prince Scharnhorst had meanwhile abandoned painting in disgust, and now sat putting the finishing touches on an exact replica of a new Swedish plywood sloop. I showed him a Klee reproduction, *Die Hoehe*—a girl with triangle body and pumpkin head on a tightrope over a pink and purplish glare. The Prince said this was work that would disgrace a child or a criminal psychopath, so I began a Klee. I used a formula that my Grandmother Winslow, Gaga, had taught me as a child. By making O's of different sizes and adding rectangles and a few dots, I could draw a picture which began as a farmhouse, a yard, a path, and a pond; and then presto! a man's face.

After six or seven weeks at the Payne-Whitney Clinic, my bluster and manic antics died away. Images of my spoiled childhood echoed inside me. I would lean with my chin in my hand, and count the rustling poplars, so many leagues below me, which lined the hospital driveway and led out to the avenues of Manhattan, to life. "Rock" was my name for Grandfather Winslow's country place at Rock, Massachusetts. An avenue of poplars led from the stable to the pine grove. The leaves on these trees were always crisp, brilliant, dusty, athirst. "But I don't want to go anywhere. I want to go to *Rock*!" That's how I would stop conversation when my father and mother talked about trips to

Paris, Puget Sound, Mattapoisett, anywhere. The letter paper at Rock bore the name "Chardesa," taken from the names of my grandfather's three children—Charlotte, Devereux, and Sarah.

On an August afternoon in 1922, I sat squatting on the screened porch. The porch was ranch-style. Like everything Grandfather built, it was a well of comfort. Comfortable, yes; but stern, disproportioned, overbearing. The maids, Sadie and Nellie, came in bearing frosted pitchers of iced tea, made with lemons, oranges, mint. Or it was a pitcher of shandygaff, which Grandfather made by blending yeasty, wheezing, exploding homemade beer with homemade root beer. Chardesa had been our family property and hobby for fifteen years. No one, except a silly gun-shy setter, had ever died there. I sat on the tiles, all of three and a half. My new formal gray shorts had been worn for all of three minutes. Obsequious little drops of water pin-pricked my face reflected in the basin. I felt like a stuffed toucan with a bibulous, multi-colored beak. Up in the air, on the glass porch, my Great-aunt Sarah played the overture to *The Flying Dutchman*. She thundered on the keyboard of her dummy piano, a little soundless box bought to spare the nerves of her sister-in-law, my Grandmother Winslow, who despaired of all music except the pastoral symphony from Handel's *Messiah*. But once in a vexed mood, my grandmother had said, "I don't see why Sally must thump all day on that thing she can't hear." Great-aunt Sarah lifted a hand dramatically to the mute keys of the dummy piano. "Barbarism lies behind me," she declaimed grandly. "Mannerism is ahead." It was teatime in New England.

I scratched destructively at the blue anchors on my sailor blouse, which was like a balloon jib. What in the world could I be in want of? Nothing, except perhaps a wishes-are-white-horses horse; or a fluff of west wind to ruffle the waters, to stretch my canvas sail, to carry me kiting over the seven chimneys of Chardesa, the white farmhouse, and on over the bunched steel-blue barrels of the shotguns fortifying my Uncle Devereux's duck blind, and on over the three ample, unislanded miles of Assa-wamsett, the great lake. I was going far, farther than was useful.

I had always loved my Uncle Devereux's hunting cabin at Chardesa on the island between the lakes Pochsha and Assawamsett. And now I entered. Uncle Devereux had already shut up shop for the winter almost. He was heaving a huge Stillson wrench to fasten down the bars on the last window blind. I cowered in a corner behind a pyramid of Friends Baked Beans cans. Sunlight from the open doorway struck the loud period posters nailed everywhere on the cabin's raw, splintery wood. On the boards I saw Mr. Punch, watermelon-bellied in crimson Harvard hockey tights, tippling a bottle of Mr. Pimm's stirrup cup; the remnants of a British battalion formed in hollow square on the terrible veldt, and dying to a man before the enfilading fire of the cowardly, nigger-hating unseen Boer; flocks of pre-war opera stars with their goose necks, their beauty spots, their hair like rooster tails, and their glorious signatures; and finally, the patron of all good girls, Entente Cordiale himself, the porcine, proper, majestic Edward VII, who raised a model of a city, *gai Paree*, above Big Ben. "What an eye for the girls," someone had scribbled tentatively in pencil.

I wasn't a child at all. Unseen and all-seeing, I was Agrippina at the palace of Nero. I would beg my Uncle Devereux to read me more stories about that Emperor, who built a death barge for his mother, one that collapsed like a bombarded duck blind! And now I sat in my sailor blouse, as clean as Bayard, our carriage horse. And Uncle Devereux stood behind me. His face was putty. His blue coat and white-flannel trousers grew straighter and straighter, as though he were in a clothes press. His trousers were like solid cream from the top of the bottle. His coat was like a blue jay's tail feather. His face was animated, hieratic. His glasses were like Harold Lloyd's glasses. He was dying of the incurable Hodgkin's disease.

One morning toward the end of my stay at the hospital, I told my psychiatrist about an experience I had had during the war, when I was serving a five months' sentence in jail as a conscientious objector. I belonged to a gang that walked outside the prison gates each morning and worked on building a barn. The work was mild: the workers were slow and absentminded. There were long pauses, and we would sit around barrels filled with burning coke and roast wheat seeds. All the prisoners were sentenced for a cause, all liked nothing better than talking the world to rights.

Among the many eccentrics, one group took the prize. They were Negroes who called themselves Israelites. Their ritual compelled them to shave their heads and let their beards grow. But the prison regulations forced them to shave their beards. So, with unnaturally smooth and shining faces and naked heads wrapped in Turkish towels, they shivered around the coke barrels, and talked wisdom and non-sense. Their non-sense was that they were the chosen people. They had found a text in the Bible which said, "But I am black though my brother is white." This convinced them that the people of the Old Testament were Negroes. The Israelites believed that modern Jews were impostors. Their wisdom was a deep ancestral knowledge of herbs and nature. They were always curing themselves with queer herbal remedies that they gathered from the fields.

Once, as we sat by the coke, the most venerable and mild of the Israelites stretched out his hand. Below him lay the town of Danbury, which consisted of what might be called filling-station architecture; the country was the fine, small rolling land of Connecticut. One expected to see the flash of a deer's white scut as it jumped a boulder wall by a patch of unmelted snow. My friend stretched out his arm, and said, "Only man is miserable." I told my doctor that this summed up my morals and my aesthetics.

I am writing my autobiography literally to "pass the time." I almost doubt if the time would pass at all otherwise. However, I also hope the result will supply me with swaddling clothes, with a sort of immense bandage of grace and ambergris for my hurt nerves. Therefore, this book will stop with the summer of 1934. A few months after the end of this book, I *found* myself.

As I try to write my own autobiography, other autobiographies naturally come to mind. The last autobiography I looked into was a movie about a bullterrier from Brooklyn. The dog's name was, I think, House on Fire. The district he came from was so tough that smoking had to be permitted in the last three pews at High Mass. House on Fire's mother had been deserted by his father. House knows that his father is a great dog in the great world, either as a champion fighter or as a champion in exhibitions. House on Fire keeps saying with his Brooklyn accent, "I want to be a champ so that I can kill my father." In the end, there is peace.

My own father was a gentle, faithful, and dim man. I don't know why I was agin him. I hope there will be peace.

[1957]

Appendix

Public Letters
to Two Presidents

To President Roosevelt

[*On October 13, 1943, after sending the following letter and declaration to President Roosevelt, Lowell was arraigned before the U.S. District Court in New York and sentenced to prison for one year and one day. Before his transfer to the Federal Correctional Center in Danbury, Connecticut, he spent a few days in the West Street jail in New York.*]

September 7, 1943

Dear Mr. President:

I very much regret that I must refuse the opportunity you offer me in your communication of August 6, 1943, for service in the Armed Forces.

I am enclosing with this letter a copy of the declaration which, in accordance with military regulations, I am presenting on September 7 to Federal District Attorney in New York, Mr. Matthias F. Correa. Of this declaration I am sending copies also to my parents, to a select number of friends and relatives, to the heads of the Washington press bureaus, and to a few responsible citizens who, no more than yourself, can be suspected of subversive activities.

You will understand how painful such a decision is for an American whose family traditions, like your own, have always found their fulfillment in maintaining, through responsible participation in both the civil and the military services, our country's freedom and honor.

> I have the honor, Sir, to inscribe myself,
> with sincerest loyalty and respect,
> your fellow-citizen,

> Robert Traill Spence Lowell, Jr.

DECLARATION OF
PERSONAL RESPONSIBILITY

Orders for my induction into the armed forces on September eighth 1943 have just arrived. Because we glory in the conviction that our wars are won not by irrational valor but through the exercise of moral responsibility, it is fitting for me to make the following declaration which is also a decision.

Like the majority of our people I watched the approach of this war with foreboding. Modern wars had proved subversive to the Democracies and history had shown them to be the iron gates to totalitarian slavery. On the other hand, members of my family had served in all our wars since the Declaration of Independence: I thought—our tradition of service is sensible and noble; if its occasional exploitation by Money, Politics and Imperialism is allowed to seriously discredit it, we are doomed.

When Pearl Harbor was attacked, I imagined that my country was in intense peril and come what might, unprecedented sacrifices were necessary for our national survival. In March and August of 1942 I volunteered, first for the Navy and then for the Army. And when I heard reports of what would formerly have been termed atrocities, I was not disturbed: for I judged that savagery was unavoidable in our nation's struggle for its life against diabolic adversaries.

Today these adversaries are being rolled back on all fronts and the crisis of war is past. But there are no indications of peace. In June we heard rumors of the staggering civilian casualties that had resulted from the mining of the Ruhr Dams. Three weeks ago we read of the razing of Hamburg, where 200,000 non-combatants are reported dead, after an almost apocalyptic series of all-out air-raids.

This, in a world still nominally Christian, is *news*. And now the Quebec Conference confirms our growing suspicions that the bombings of the Dams and of Hamburg were not mere isolated acts of military expediency, but marked the inauguration of a new long-term strategy, indorsed and co-ordinated by our Chief Executive.

The war has entered on an unforeseen phase: one that can by no possible extension of the meaning of the words be called defensive. By demanding unconditional surrender we reveal our complete confidence in the outcome, and declare that we are prepared to wage a war without quarter or principles, to the permanent destruction of Germany and Japan.

Americans cannot plead ignorance of the lasting consequences of a war carried through to unconditional surrender— our Southern states, three-quarters of a century after their terrible battering down and occupation, are still far from having recovered even their material prosperity.

It is a fundamental principle of our American Democracy, one that distinguishes it from the demagoguery and herd hypnosis of the totalitarian tyrannies, that with us each individual citizen is called upon to make voluntary and responsible decisions on issues which concern the national welfare. I therefore realize that I am under the heavy obligation of assenting to the prudence and justice of our present objectives before I have the right to accept service in our armed forces. No matter how expedient I might find it to entrust my moral responsibility to the State, I realize that it is not permissible under a form of government which derives its sanctions from the rational assent of the governed.

Our rulers have promised us unlimited bombings of Germany and Japan. Let us be honest: we intend the permanent destruction of Germany and Japan. If this program is carried out, it will demonstrate to the world our Machiavellian contempt for the laws of justice and charity between nations; it will destroy any possibility of a European or Asiatic national autonomy; it will leave China and Europe, the two natural power centers of the future, to the mercy of the USSR, a totalitarian tyranny committed to world revolution and total global domination through propaganda and violence.

In 1941 we undertook a patriotic war to preserve *our lives, our fortunes, and our sacred honor* against the lawless aggressions of a totalitarian league: in 1943 we are collaborating with the most unscrupulous and powerful of totalitarian dictators to destroy law, freedom, democracy, and above all, our continued national sovereignty.

With the greatest reluctance, with every wish that I may be proved in error, and after long deliberation on my responsibilities to myself, my country, and my ancestors who played responsible parts in its making, I have come to the conclusion that I cannot honorably participate in a war whose prosecution, as far as I can judge, constitutes a betrayal of my country.

To President Lyndon Johnson

[*After accepting an invitation to the White House Festival of the Arts for June 14, 1965, Lowell reconsidered his decision because of his concern over the Vietnam War and other aspects of "our present foreign policy," and sent the following letter to the President.*]

June 3, 1965

Dear President Johnson:

When I was telephoned last week and asked to read at the White House Festival of the Arts on June fourteenth, I am afraid I accepted somewhat rapidly and greedily. I thought of such an occasion as a purely artistic flourish, even though every serious artist knows that he cannot enjoy public celebration without making subtle public commitments. After a week's wondering, I have decided that I am conscience-bound to refuse your courteous invitation. I do so now in a public letter because my acceptance has been announced in the newspapers and because of the strangeness of the Administration's recent actions.

Although I am very enthusiastic about most of your domestic legislation and intentions, I nevertheless can only follow our present foreign policy with the greatest dismay and distrust. What we will do and what we ought to do as a sovereign nation facing other sovereign nations seem now to hang in the balance between the better and the worse possibilities. We are in danger of imperceptibly becoming an explosive and suddenly chauvinistic nation, and may even be drifting on our way to the last nuclear ruin. I know it is hard for the responsible man to act; it is also painful for the private and irresolute man to dare criticism. At this anguished, delicate and perhaps determining moment, I feel I am serving you and our country best by not taking part in the White House Festival of the Arts.

Respectfully yours,

Robert Lowell

Notes and Sources

FORD MADOX FORD / *New York Review of Books*, May 12, 1966. Published as a preface to *Buckshee* by Ford Madox Ford (Cambridge, Mass.: Pym-Randall Press, 1966).

ROBERT FROST / *New York Review of Books*, August 29, 1963.

WALLACE STEVENS / *The Nation* CLXIV (April 5, 1947), 400–2.

JOHN CROWE RANSOM / "Mr. Ransom's Conversation," *Sewanee Review* LVI (Summer 1948), 374–7. "John Crowe Ransom: 1888–1974," *The New Review* (London) I, 5 (August 1974), 3–5.

WILLIAM CARLOS WILLIAMS / "Paterson I," *Sewanee Review* LV (Summer 1947), 493–503. "Paterson II," *The Nation* CLXVI (June 19, 1948), 693–4. "Dr. Williams," *Hudson Review* XIV (Winter 1961–2), 530–6.

T. S. ELIOT / "Four Quartets," *Sewanee Review* LI (Summer 1943), 432–5. "Two Controversial Questions," written in 1965; published here for the first time.

I. A. RICHARDS / Review of *Goodbye Earth and Other Poems* (London: Routledge, 1960), in *Encounter* XIV (February 1960), 77–8.

VISITING THE TATES / *Sewanee Review* LXVII (Autumn 1959), 557–9. Reprinted in *Allen Tate and His Work*, ed. Radcliffe Squires (University of Minnesota Press, 1972).

YVOR WINTERS / "Yvor Winters, a Tribute," *Poetry* XCVIII (April 1961), 40–3.

ROBERT PENN WARREN'S "BROTHER TO DRAGONS" / *Kenyon Review* XV (Autumn 1953), 619–23.

AUDEN AT SIXTY / *Shenandoah*, Winter 1967, 45.

ELIZABETH BISHOP'S "NORTH & SOUTH" / *Sewanee Review* LV (Summer 1947), 493–503.

STANLEY KUNITZ'S "FATHER AND SON" / *The Poet and His Critics II*, ed. Anthony Ostroff, *New World Writing* 21, 1962, 155–9.

RANDALL JARRELL / Review of "The Seven-League Crutches," *The New York Times Book Review*, October 7, 1951, 7. "Randall Jarrell: 1914–1965," *New York Review of Books*, November 25, 1965. Both essays reprinted in *Randall Jarrell 1914–1965*, eds. Robert Lowell, Peter Taylor, and Robert Penn Warren (New York: Farrar, Straus & Giroux, 1967).

DYLAN THOMAS / *Sewanee Review* LV (Summer 1947), 493–503.

JOHN BERRYMAN / Review of "77 Dream Songs," *New York Review of Books*, May 28, 1964, 3. Correction in issue of June 11, 1964. "For John Berryman: 1914–1972," *New York Review of Books*, March 30, 1972.

ANDREI VOZNESENSKY / Lowell's introduction of the poet at a reading on May 17, 1967; published here for the first time.

SYLVIA PLATH'S "ARIEL" / *New York Review of Books*, May 12, 1966. Published as a foreword to *Ariel* by Sylvia Plath (New York: Harper & Row, 1966).

ART AND EVIL / A lecture written in 1956; published here for the first time.

THE ILIAD / *The Vindex*, St. Mark's School, June 1935, 205–10.

OVID'S "METAMORPHOSES" / Review of "The Metamorphoses of Ovid," tr. A. E. Watts, *Kenyon Review* XVII (Spring 1955), 317–24.

HAWTHORNE'S PEGASUS / Introduction to *Pegasus, the Winged Horse*, retold by Nathaniel Hawthorne (New York: Macmillan, 1963).

ON THE GETTYSBURG ADDRESS / Read at the Library of Congress on January 3, 1964. Published in *Lincoln and the Gettysburg Address*, Commemorative Papers, edited by Allan Nevins (Urbana: University of Illinois Press, 1964). President Kennedy's undelivered address at Dallas ended with the hope "that we may exercise our strength with wisdom and restraint, and that we may achieve in our time and for all time the ancient vision of 'peace on earth, good will toward men.' That must always be our goal, and the righteousness of our cause must always underlie our strength. For as was written long ago: 'Except the Lord keep the city, the watchman waketh but in vain.' "

HOPKINS'S SANCTITY / "A Note (on Gerard Manley Hopkins)," *Kenyon Review* VI (Autumn 1944), 583–6. Reprinted in *Gerard Manley Hopkins*, by the Kenyon Critics (The Makers of Modern Literature Series) (New York: New Directions, 1945), 89–93, under the title "Hopkins' Sanctity."

ENGLISH METRICS / *Hudson Review* XV (Summer 1962), 317–20.

POETS AND THE THEATER / Written in 1964; published here for the first time.

NEW ENGLAND AND FURTHER / Published here for the first time, except for "The New England Spirit," a short excerpt in *The New York Times Book Review*, October 16, 1977, 34.

EPICS / *New York Review of Books*, February 21, 1980, 3.

ON "SKUNK HOUR" / From *The Poet and His Critics III*, a symposium edited by Anthony Ostroff, *New World Writing* 21, 1962, 155–9.

ON TRANSLATING "PHÈDRE" / Preface to *Phaedra, a Verse Translation of Racine's Phèdre* (New York: Farrar, Straus and Giroux, 1961).

ON "IMITATIONS" / Preface to Robert Lowell's *Imitations* (New York: Farrar, Straus and Giroux, 1961).

AN INTERVIEW WITH FREDERICK SEIDEL / *Paris Review* XXV (Winter–Spring 1961), 57–95.

A CONVERSATION WITH IAN HAMILTON / *The Review* (London), Summer 1971, 10–29. Reprinted in *Modern Occasions* 2 (Winter 1972), 28–48.

ANTEBELLUM BOSTON / Probably written in 1957; published here for the first time.

91 REVERE STREET / First published in *Partisan Review* XXIII (Fall 1956), 445–77. Reprinted as the middle section of *Life Studies* (New York: Farrar, Straus and Giroux, 1959).

NEAR THE UNBALANCED AQUARIUM / Probably written in 1957; scheduled for publication in *New York Review of Books* early in 1987.